A Handbook to Literary Research

edited by Simon Eliot and W.R. Owens

ROUTLEDGE

in association with

The Open
University

Published by Routledge, written and produced by The Open University
11 New Fetter Lane
London EC4P 4EE

Simultaneously published in the USA and Canada
by Routledge
29 West 35th Street
New York, NY 10001

Edited, designed and typeset by The Open University
Printed and bound in the United Kingdom by TJ International, Padstow, Cornwall

A catalogue record for this book is available from the British Library

Library of Congress Cataloging-in-Publication Data

A handbook to literary research/edited by Simon Eliot and W.R. Owens
p. cm.
includes bibliographical references and index.

1. Literature–Research–Methodology. 2. Criticism–Authorship
I. Eliot, Simon. II. Owens, W.R.
PN73.H36 1999
807′.2–dc21   98–41735

ISBN 0 415 198593 hardback
ISBN 0 415 198607 paperback

This book forms part of the Open University course AA810, *The Postgraduate Foundation Module in Literature*. Details of this and other Open University courses can be obtained from the Course Reservations and Sales Office, PO Box 724, The Open University, Milton Keynes MK7 6ZS, United Kingdom; tel. + 44 (0)1908 653231.

For availability of this and other course components, contact Open University Worldwide Ltd, The Berrill Building, Walton Hall, Milton Keynes MK7 6AA, United Kingdom; tel. + 44 (0)1908 858585, fax + 44 (0)1908 858787.
email ouwenq@open.ac.uk

Alternatively, much useful course information can be obtained from The Open University's website: http://www.open.ac.uk

19142B/aa810hblri1.1

CONTENTS

CONTRIBUTORS

Simon Eliot is Staff Tutor and Senior Lecturer in Literature at The Open University. He has published extensively on biographical, bibliographical and book history topics from the period 1800–1919. He is currently joint editor of Volume 6 of Cambridge University Press's *History of the Book in Britain,* an associate editor on the new *Dictionary of National Biography,* and general editor of *The Oxford Companion to the Book.*

W.R. Owens is Staff Tutor and Senior Lecturer in Literature at The Open University. He has published a number of scholarly editions, notably two volumes in the Clarendon edition of *The Miscellaneous Works of John Bunyan,* and is co-author (with P.N. Furbank) of: *The Canonisation of Daniel Defoe* (Yale University Press, 1988); *Defoe De-Attributions* (Hambledon Press, 1994); and *A Critical Bibliography of Daniel Defoe* (Pickering and Chatto, 1998).

Richard Allen is Staff Tutor and Senior Lecturer in Literature, and Sub-dean of the Faculty of Arts, at The Open University. He has published articles on E.M. Forster and on post-colonial British culture. He is a contributing author to The Open University's series of textbooks, *Approaching Literature,* copublished with Routledge (4 vols, 1996).

Anthony Coulson is Learning Resources Manager of the Arts Faculty at The Open University. He is the author of *A Bibliography of Design in Britain 1851–1970* (Design Council, 1979), and co-editor (with W.R. Owens and P.N. Furbank) of Daniel Defoe, *A Tour Through the Whole Island of Great Britain* (Yale University Press, 1991).

Graham Martin is a former Professor of Literature at The Open University. Among his many publications he has edited the *Open Guides to Literature* series (twenty-five titles, Open University Press), *Eliot in Perspective* (Macmillan, 1970) and *Great Expectations* (Open University Press, 1986).

Stephen Regan is Lecturer in Literature at The Open University. He is editor of *The Eagleton Reader* (Blackwell, 1998) and *The Politics of Pleasure* (Open University Press, 1992), and founding editor of *The Year's Work in Critical and Cultural Theory* (Blackwell). He has written extensively on the poetry of Philip Larkin, including *Philip Larkin* (Macmillan, 1992) and the *New Casebook* on Larkin (Macmillan, 1997).

Stuart Sim is Professor of English Studies at The University of Sunderland. He is the author of *The A–Z Guide to Modern Literary and Cultural Theorists* (Harvester Wheatsheaf, 1995), *Georg Lukács* (1994) and *Jean François Lyotard* (1996) in the Harvester Modern Cultural Theorists series.

Dennis Walder is Senior Lecturer and Head of Literature at The Open University. He has written five books, including *Dickens and Religion* (Allen and Unwin, 1981), and edited five others, including the best-selling *Literature in the Modern World* (Oxford University Press, 1990). His most recent publication is *Post-Colonial Literatures in English* (Blackwell, 1998).

1 INTRODUCTION TO THE HANDBOOK

by Simon Eliot and W.R. Owens

Undertaking any programme of postgraduate study or piece of independent research work in literature is both an exciting and a daunting prospect. The aim of this Handbook is to make the whole process of research more exciting and less daunting – and, we might add, more productive and more rewarding.

How are we to do this?

- firstly, by introducing you to the range of research skills and methods needed by anyone who wants to do the job effectively and productively

- secondly, by offering you a broad survey of the wide variety of intellectual endeavour that now characterizes the study of literature at postgraduate level

- thirdly, by providing advice and guidance on what is frequently the most tricky (and most postponed) part of research – writing up the dissertation or thesis

- fourthly, by giving you a substantial quantity of useful and usable information in the form of a glossary and a large bibliographical Checklist.

Although you could certainly gain something by dipping into the book, you may well find it better to start by reading Parts 1–4 in sequence as they build steadily from learning about using libraries and IT, to writing the final dissertation. Once you are familiar with its contents, you could keep this Handbook by you for frequent reference.

All the contributors are, or have been, full-time academics at The Open University, and so they share the tradition of skilful at-a-distance university teaching for which the OU is famous. The chapters have certain characteristics in common, therefore: they all include the identification of key ideas and texts within their subject; they all involve discussion of the significant developments in their field; they all discuss the specific nature of research within their subject; and they all include a set of 'Questions and exercises' designed to get you to practise the knowledge and skills that you learnt as you worked your way through the given chapter. At the same time the Handbook has a variety of voices because of the wide range of experts who have contributed to it, and we hope that the reader will find this stimulating and refreshing.

Although much of the material in this Handbook was originally written for The Open University's MA in Literature programme, it is more widely applicable: in practice the basic skills and knowledge required to complete an MA successfully are the same as those needed by students beginning a research degree (an M.Phil. or Ph.D) and, indeed, by anyone in or outside higher education wishing to pursue independent research in literature. For this reason the Handbook is best thought of as a general guide to basic techniques for anyone wishing to undertake literary research.

Structure and content of the Handbook

Part 1: Tools of the trade

Every postgraduate student needs, like any apprentice, to understand and to be able to use effectively the tools of his or her trade. Part 1 is an introduction to the basic research methodologies of literature; for convenience we have divided it into two chapters:

Chapter 2 deals with the traditional range of skills associated with the effective use of a research library and its contents (by 'research library' we mean a university library, or a major city library, or one of the great national libraries). The chapter includes a list of practical questions and exercises which will help you test your growing competence in this set of key skills.

Chapter 3 introduces you to the use of information technology (IT) in literary research, and in particular looks at the ways in which the Internet is becoming an increasingly important scholarly tool. Although the chapter applies to the Internet generally, we also take the opportunity to introduce the reader to The Open University's MA home page (on the Internet) as a way of illustrating the points made. The MA home page contains links to most of the scholarly research resources mentioned in the chapter, and anyone with access to the Internet is welcome to use it.

Parts 2 and 3:
Textual scholarship and book history
Literary research and literary theory

Thirty years ago it was reasonably easy to define literary research: it was either a critical analysis of a text or group of texts ('literary criticism'), or it was an attempt to put a text or group of texts into some form of historical context (usually thought of as 'literary history'). Since the 1960s, however, the subject has been expanded, enriched and complicated by a whole set of new influences – literary theory in all its rich variety, of course, but also developments in the history of the book as a material object. A further enriching influence has been the arrival of IT in a form that is powerful and cheap enough to be applied extensively in literary studies; it can be used for anything from the linguistic analysis of a complete novel, to the retrieval – from the Internet – of the latest information on post-colonial studies.

Literary studies has proved to be a broad church, and the arrival of new approaches has tended to modify rather than exclude the more traditional forms of study; this has resulted in a rich but potentially confusing range of approaches from which to choose. Thus one of the aims of this Handbook is to provide a brief guide to what a student might choose in terms of approach. This guide is divided into two parts. The first – Part 2, 'Textual scholarship and book history' – is concerned with the more his-

torical and empirical aspects of literature and deals with classic bibliography in all its variety (Chapter 4), with the new subject of book history
(Chapter 5), and with the disciplines of scholarly editing (Chapter 6).
Although these subjects are discussed in discrete chapters, their inter-
connectedness is made clear.

Part 3 moves you on to a different set of approaches of a more theoretical
kind. Chapter 7 is a broad study of the developments in literary criticism in,
roughly, the first half of the century – from 'New Criticism' to structuralism.
Having set the context, we then have a series of chapters (8–12) covering the
main contemporary theoretical positions from gender studies through to
post-colonial theory. As with Part 2, there are some clear intellectual links
between these theoretical positions, and the reader will find that there are
possibilities for creatively combining two or more.

Part 4: The dissertation

When the area of study has been selected, the approach understood and the
tools of the trade sharpened, the job itself is still to be done. The ultimate
aim of most literary research is to produce some critical, theoretical or
historical writing that either is a piece of original research or proves the
candidate's ability to produce such research. In most cases such work takes
the form of a thesis or dissertation. All of the contributors to this Handbook
are aware that, ultimately, the student has to sit down in front of a blank
sheet of paper or screen and write a formal piece of scholarly prose. But in
addition we offer a sizeable chapter on 'planning, writing and presenting a
dissertation', and this includes down-to-earth advice on choosing a topic,
preparing a research proposal, writing the dissertation and ensuring that it
is properly presented. We also include advice on scholarly conventions of
presentation and give you practical examples of how these work.

In part, learning to write in a scholarly way is about acquiring good writing
habits early. For example, you should train yourself – whenever in a piece of
writing you refer to the origin of your information – to provide the necessary evidence in terms of a properly referenced source. When making notes,
you should always record the exact location of your information – including
page numbers so that, if you or anyone else wanted to check that information, it could be done quickly and accurately. None of this is very
complicated, but it does require you to understand and use the 'scholarly
conventions'. These are discussed in this part, and you should make sure
that you get the hang of them as soon as possible and practise them as much
as you can.

Part 5: Reference

Any subject, even one that should pride itself on the clarity and exactness of
its language, will need occasionally to use jargon and abbreviations, and
literature is no exception. In order to ensure you are not slowed down by
this, we have provided a 'jargon survival kit' in the form of a short Glossary.

This is by no means exhaustive, but we have provided explanations of the most common terms that you are likely to meet in your research. As with most other sections in the Handbook, we round off the Glossary with a short list of reference books to which you can turn if necessary.

The Checklist is perhaps that part of the book to which you will return most frequently throughout your period of research. It lists, describes and occasionally discusses the huge variety of catalogues, bibliographies, dictionaries and multifarious other reference works – in printed, microform and electronic versions – without which literature as a scholarly discipline would hardly be possible. As with every other chapter of this book, the Checklist cannot hope to be comprehensive. But it should provide you with a good introduction to the most important material, and will give you plenty of leads that you can follow up in your own research library or via the Internet.

The Handbook and how to use it

This Handbook is not designed merely to be read once, as an introduction: it is meant to accompany you from start to finish. For this reason we don't just tell you how to go about literary research, we also *show* you how to do it and provide you with much of the initial material that you will need.

Postgraduate work in literature, as in any subject, is about becoming more intellectually independent. This means that you spend much less time in a seminar room with a prescribed and restricted range of texts, and much more time in research libraries working through an extended list of texts that you yourself, to a large extent, have compiled.

Selected and suggested reading

One of the Handbook's functions, then, is to send you off to read extensively and critically. For this reason there is a strong emphasis on what we have described as 'Selected reading'. This consists of lists of books, articles and other material relevant to the topic under discussion, at least some of which you ought to consult. Lists of 'Selected reading' occur throughout the book, and sometimes a chapter will include a number of them. They are often quite long because we are acutely aware that even the best research libraries are nowadays struggling to maintain and update their stocks. This means that the research library you choose will not necessarily have all the works we would like you to consult, so we offer a broad range out of which you should be able to construct a list of works accessible to you.

Sometimes the link between the Handbook and the scholarly books it recommends is even closer, with the writer constructing a dialogue between a specified book and his chapter. In these cases, precise page or chapter references are given, and the books may be listed in a separate category called 'Suggested reading'. In these cases it will be necessary for you to get hold of these suggested titles if you are fully to understand the subject under discussion. These cases are few and far between and the books involved are very widely available.

Questions and exercises

Another recurrent feature of this Handbook are the sections entitled 'Questions and exercises'. These usually occur at the end of a chapter or at the end of a section within a chapter, and are designed to give you practice in using the knowledge and skills that you will have just acquired. As with the reading-lists, we have tried to offer a wide range of choices so that, whatever your intellectual interests and library resources, you should be able to find one question that interests you or, at least, is do-able. At the lowest level these 'Questions and exercises' illustrate the sorts of scholarly problem with which specialists in the field are preoccupied.

However, such questions will be much more beneficial if you actually try to answer one or two of them. This is not a trivial point: it is very easy to believe, having read something, that you understand it. But the acid test is whether you are then able to put that understanding and knowledge into your own words. If you *are* able to do so, then you can move on in the comforting knowledge that you really have grasped the key points of what you have been reading and have made the information your own.

Writing an answer does not necessarily mean producing a full, formal essay: your answer could be in the form of notes or of an essay plan. Nevertheless, given that you may well be moving towards preparing a dissertation, the more practice you can get in writing scholarly prose the better, so answering one or two of the questions in the Handbook by means of a formal essay would be a very good idea indeed. If you can't do that very often, at least put pen to paper or finger to keyboard whenever you can in response to 'Questions and exercises'. As you will learn again and again as you work through the Handbook, the early and frequent practice of good scholarly writing is the key to producing a successful (and possibly impressive) dissertation or thesis.

Themes

Although this Handbook covers the wide variety of approaches and disciplines now to be found under the banner of 'English literature', you will find that many of the authors will, while dealing with the most esoteric subjects, nevertheless mention basic reference works or techniques of study that also feature in other chapters. However diverse the disciplines of English literature appear to be, they are linked by common concerns, approaches and texts that will be relevant to you whatever the subject of your dissertation. These common strands may be as simple as the effective use of, for instance, *The Cambridge Bibliography of English Literature* in all its editions, as technical as an awareness of the ways in which a text can be corrupted in printing, or as broad as the need to understand that the nature of literary language (indeed, all language) is problematical, but these strands will, and do, crop up in different guises again and again.

Textual examples

The final feature that binds the whole Handbook together is the focus on the textual examples. One of the worst features of many books on research methods is that they frequently talk in abstractions: they discuss technique without giving a sufficient number of examples rooted in reality. Because this Handbook has its origins in the taught MA in Literature programme offered by The Open University, and because that MA was originally run with options entitled 'The Eighteenth-century Novel' and 'Poetry and Criticism, 1830–90', we decided to focus on two texts, one from each option:

> Daniel Defoe's *Moll Flanders*, ed. G.A. Starr (Oxford: Oxford University Press, 1981)

> Alfred Lord Tennyson, *Selected Poems*, ed. Aidan Day (Harmondsworth: Penguin Books, 1991).

We asked all the authors to include examples from one or both of these texts, or from the periods in which they were written, in order to illustrate the points made. We have not stuck to this slavishly, but it does mean that you would probably gain even more from this Handbook if you were to get hold of these two texts and read them before working through the Handbook. However, don't worry if you can't: the examples are sufficiently broad that you are likely to find useful and relevant material even if you haven't read Defoe or Tennyson.

Providing explanations, presenting information and offering practice is what this Handbook is all about. Used properly, it should provide you at the outset with a quick and clear introduction to literary research and, later on, offer you support and guidance as your scholarly confidence grows and your work matures.

Acknowledgements

As editors, we would like to record here our warmest thanks to a number of people at The Open University who have helped enormously in the production of this book: Pam Berry, Text Processing Services; Jonathan Davies, graphic designer; Robert Doubleday, course manager; Jonathan Hunt, Copublishing Department; Kiki Ioannides, Project Control; and Erleen Pilkington, secretary. We particularly wish to thank our editor, John Pettit, whose contribution has immeasurably improved the book. We are also grateful to Dr Dinah Birch, Trinity College, Oxford, who in her role as external assessor commented on earlier versions of much of the material here; and to Dr David Goldthorpe for his help, in particular with the library exercises.

Simon Eliot and W.R. Owens

Part 1

TOOLS OF THE TRADE

an introduction to research libraries

practical questions and exercises

the Internet and literary research

2 RESEARCH TECHNIQUES AND THE USE OF LIBRARIES

by W.R. Owens

One of the essential skills to be learned by anyone undertaking research is the ability to make the best use of libraries; researchers often waste a great deal of time by working in ignorance of quite basic reference sources or techniques for finding information and materials in libraries. However, the use of libraries is something that can only be learned *in practice* – that is to say, in the course of pursuing specific enquiries. It is when you have put to yourself some particular query and then found a reference book or other source (printed or electronic) which answers it – or which at least takes you a step forward in answering it – that the reference work and its nature and function will imprint themselves on your memory. Consequently, this chapter ends with a series of practical exercises which you might try out in a library. Each one requires you to search for some specific piece of information, or to answer some specific query or problem. The point, however, is not simply that you find the answer. It is also (and this is the heart of the matter) to encourage you *to record the route you take*, and the books or other sources you use, even if the route proves to be a very roundabout one or, in fact, leads nowhere. In Chapter 15 below, you will find 'model answers' to the exercises, against which you can check your own results.

Obviously, if you have not used a particular library before, you will have to spend some time just finding out where things are and learning how to use the cataloguing system. Most UK libraries classify their stock according to the Dewey Decimal Classification, devised by the US librarian Melvil Dewey, and introduced in 1876. Although there are hundreds of sub-divisions, these flow from Dewey's initial division of all knowledge into ten classes:

000	General works (including bibliographies, encyclopaedias, etc.)
100	Philosophy and related disciplines
200	Religion
300	Social sciences
400	Languages
500	Pure sciences
600	Technology (applied sciences)
700	The arts
800	Literature
900	General geography and history (including biography and genealogy)

Within '800 Literature', English and Old English (Anglo-Saxon) literatures will be found at 820, immediately following American literature at 810, and before literatures of the Germanic languages at 830. The main 820 sequence is divided into three categories, each arranged chronologically:

821: English poetry
822: English drama
823: English fiction.

This is really all you need to remember if you want to browse purposefully among the shelves of a large library: by scanning along the 800s you will soon find your way to the literature section you are interested in. In what follows, however, I am going to be concentrating on works of reference, which will mainly be found under '000: General works'.

Printed sources

At the end of this Handbook you will find a fairly extensive Checklist of libraries, reference books and other sources. This is intended to help you with a range of possible scholarly enquiries and you should look through it carefully, noting particularly how it is arranged under *headings* which point you to reference works on various *topics*. But before you launch into the Checklist, it may be helpful here just to pick out a small number of the absolutely key reference works, to highlight their importance and say a few introductory words about them. When you go to the library, search for these books on the reference shelves and have a good look at them, to begin to get to know them for yourself.

1 General guides

There are two main guides for students of literature. The longer established is *The Oxford Companion to English Literature*, currently in its sixth edition, revised by Margaret Drabble (Oxford: Oxford University Press, 1995). This provides short factual accounts of authors and summaries of works, and also much useful information on allusions. There are helpful appendices on censorship, on the history of English copyright, and on the various reforms that led to the establishment of the modern calendar.

The main competition to the *Oxford Companion* is *The Cambridge Guide to Literature in English*, ed. Ian Ousby (Cambridge: Cambridge University Press, 1988; rev. edn, 1994). As its title indicates, this takes a wider approach by including literature in English from many other countries. As well as brief accounts of authors and works, there are also useful essays on broader literary topics, such as the rise of the English newspaper, the development of libraries, Romanticism, structuralism, tragedy, and such like.

2 Bibliographical guides

The quickest way to get some basic information about the works of almost any given English author is by consulting the relevant volume of *The New Cambridge Bibliography of English Literature*, ed. George Watson *et al.*, 5 vols (Cambridge: Cambridge University Press, 1969–77). This absolutely indispensable work covers the period from 600 up to about 1950 in a remarkably comprehensive way. Each author entry includes a checklist of works in chronological order, together with the main bibliographical and critical studies up to about 1970. In addition to the author bibliographies, there are also extremely useful subject bibliographies in each volume – covering, for example, travel writing, book publishing, education and political thought. Though not without errors, omissions and sundry weaknesses (it is currently undergoing revision, planned for publication in the next few years), the *NCBEL*, as it is referred to, is a work you should become thoroughly acquainted with as soon as possible.

Another work you should get to know is the *British Library General Catalogue of Printed Books*. The copy in the famous (and now closed) Round Reading Room in the British Museum extended to over two thousand large volumes, incorporating details of all works acquired up to 1975, when the library began cataloguing its accessions on computer. This unique catalogue has been published as *The British Library General Catalogue of Printed Books to 1975*, 360 vols (London, Munich, New York, Paris: Clive Bingley and K.G. Saur, 1979–87), with a further *Supplement*, in six volumes (London, Munich, New York, Paris: K.G. Saur, 1987–8). It has subsequently been extended by nearly 200 volumes, to include works acquired between 1976 and 1994. Most decent-sized libraries hold a copy of this published edition, now known as *BLC*, and it is also accessible through the World Wide Web and available on cd-rom. What makes the *General Catalogue* invaluable is, quite simply, its massive size. The British Library has the richest collection in the world of English literature, and so its catalogue represents the most exhaustive author bibliography available. Under each author's name you will find their own works, followed by works about them. Anonymous works are entered under their titles.

3 Articles in learned journals

Once you have tracked down information about *primary* sources (details of works published by the author you are studying, etc.), you will obviously want to find what has been written about your author (i.e. the *secondary* source material). It's fairly easy to trace books using bibliographies and library catalogues (see above), but more difficult to get hold of references to articles in learned journals. For these, perhaps the best place to start is the MLA *International Bibliography of Books and Articles on the Modern Languages and Literatures* (New York: Modern Language Association of America, 1922–). Each large volume of this series covers one year, and entries are arranged under period and author. It is therefore very simple to look up the entry on, say, Hardy and find both general articles and articles on specific works. Trawling through the printed volumes is fairly laborious, but it will produce a tolerably comprehensive list of articles; these can then be read if the library you are working in holds copies of the relevant journals, or copies can be ordered using inter-library loan. Since 1981 the MLA *Bibliography* has also been published on cd-rom, and your library may have a copy: it obviously offers a much quicker way of locating the information you want.

The *MLA Bibliography* is the most comprehensive source, but also very useful is the *Annual Bibliography of English Language and Literature*, published since 1920 by the Modern Humanities Research Association (Cambridge: Bowes and Bowes, 1921–). *The Year's Work in English Studies* (London: English Association, 1919–; published annually), though more selective, offers informed comment on works listed.

4 Biographical dictionaries

The *Oxford Companion* and *Cambridge Guide* (see 1 above) give thumbnail sketches of the biographies of authors, but for more information you should turn first to *The Dictionary of National Biography*, ed. Leslie Stephen and Sidney Lee, 63 vols (London: Smith, Elder, 1885–1900); reprinted in 21 vols (London: Oxford University Press, 1917); and with various supplements thereafter, including, most recently, a volume sub-titled *Missing Persons*, ed. C.S. Nicholls (Oxford and New York: Oxford University Press, 1993). Obviously much new information on authors may have come to light since the *DNB* was written, so information should whenever possible be checked against more up-to-date biographies. Plans are afoot for a major revision and expansion of the *DNB*, but in the meantime it remains the most convenient starting place for information of this kind, particularly since most entries conclude with a bibliography.

5 General encyclopaedias

Finally, mention should be made of works such as the *Encyclopaedia Britannica* and *Chambers Encyclopaedia*. It hardly needs saying what an amazing source of information these are – except that some students take a long time to discover this and waste much time in the interim!

Computerized information

As you will no doubt be aware, when you go into a library nowadays you may well find that the only available catalogue of its collections is in computer (i.e. online) form. The computer offers a simple and efficient way of searching for a particular author by name, or for a particular book by its title.

Where more experience and thought are needed is in making the best use of the computer as a *subject* catalogue. This entails thinking about which 'key words' will be most likely to lead you to works on the subject of your enquiry. What must always be remembered is that each library classifies books in its collection according to its own selection of key words. Thus, to give an example:

> **if you were doing research on the representation of orphans in nineteenth-century literature**, you might search not simply under *orphans*, but also under synonyms and related or similar words such as *foundling, charity, fostering* and the like. But these may not yield much, so you might also need to think of larger terms used to describe books

that might include material relevant to your subject. So, for example, you might try *children* AND *nineteenth century*, or *children* AND *literature*, or *children* AND *hospitals*, etc.

As you will see, the possibilities in a case like this are very extensive and require a good deal of thought, imagination and hit-or-miss experimentation. (For a more detailed explanation of how to construct effective search strategies, see Chapter 3 below, 'Using the Internet for literary research'.)

Although computerized subject catalogues and bibliographical databases are extremely useful, it should never be forgotten that they are no more infallible than printed sources.

Using libraries: practical exercises

To conclude this introduction to research techniques and the use of libraries, I have provided a series of questions for you to follow up. In doing these practical exercises in the library, you should make notes on any of the works in the Checklist that you use in your quest. These notes could be of all sorts: they might do no more than record the library classification number of the work, or they might be a reminder to yourself of the way in which the work is arranged, and of its individual quirks. You should also *add* the titles of works that you have found useful, with suitable annotations. Remember that most sources contain inaccuracies and uncertainties, but some have many more than others, and part of the value of your search will be to form an idea of which are the most reliable.

Some of the questions that follow can be answered by using computer searches, but others can only be tackled through printed sources. In each case it is important to record the route that you took. After you have attempted a question, you should turn to the relevant discussion in Chapter 15, 'Library exercises – model answers'.

1   When did Tennyson go to live on the Isle of Wight?

2   Say you live in Preston, and that you want to consult the volume for 1864 of the periodical *Blackwood's Magazine*: where is the nearest library in which you would find it?

3   What was the earliest, and which is the most recent, book-length critical study of the novelist Henry Fielding?

4   List all the critical studies of the novelist Laurence Sterne in print at the present moment in the UK, with their publishers and prices.

5   Name a history of publishing which covers publishing in Britain in the eighteenth and nineteenth centuries.

6   What famous works of English literature were published in 1862?

7   What major world events took place in 1862?

8   What authors wrote under the following pseudonyms: (a) Andrew Moreton, (b) Michael Field?

9   What is 'sprung rhythm'?

10 Prepare a reading-list of at least eight books on the 'chivalric revival' in Victorian Britain.

11 Name two forthcoming books concerned with nineteenth-century poetry or poets (i.e. books that have been announced but have not yet been published).

12 When was Matthew Arnold's essay 'The study of poetry' first published, and how did it acquire its title?

13 When was the first collection of the poems of G.M. Hopkins published? Who edited it, and was it a *complete* edition of his extant poems?

14 How did the term 'Gothic' come to be applied to certain eighteenth-century novels, and what would it have meant to a reader of that century?

15 Dr Johnson wrote an essay about Fielding's novels, and also spoke about him on a number of occasions. How would you proceed to track down his comments?

16 You are exploring the rise of the circulating library in England. How would you track down sources of information in this subject?

17 'The year 1830 is an important date in the history of English poetry, but largely owing to biographical accident. Several of the great Romantic poets had died in the previous decade; those who survived produced no important work after 1830. The way was open for fresh poetic talent to make its mark, and the evidence of such talent appeared almost at once.' How would you check up on: (a) the factual items in that paragraph, and (b) its statements of opinion?

18 'At the beginning of the year 1740, the English novel was in its infancy. Fifteen years later it was a fully grown literary genre.' How would you set about testing the truth of this statement, taking into account both its factual and evaluative aspects?

Selected reading

Ann Hoffmann, *Research for Writers*, 5th edn (London: A. and C. Black, 1996). Aimed at general writers and journalists, this is an extremely helpful handbook for anyone undertaking research; available in paperback.

Richard D. Altick and John J. Fenstermaker, *The Art of Literary Research*, 4th edn (New York and London: Norton, 1993). A comprehensive, up-to-date and attractively written book, aimed primarily at North American students. The first half outlines some of the main areas of scholarly endeavour – biographical study; determination of authorship; establishment of texts; tracing of sources, influence and reputation; the placing of works in appropriate and illuminating historical context. The second half covers practical matters – how to find materials and use libraries; methods of note-taking; how to write up research effectively.

3 USING THE INTERNET FOR LITERARY RESEARCH

by Simon Eliot

I suggest that, at one go, you read the whole of this brief introduction to using information technology in literary research. You can then reread individual sections as you need them. No attempt is made to cover the whole subject: what follows is a crash course aimed at getting the Internet to work for you as quickly and painlessly as possible. Should you wish to learn more, you can find references below to books and electronic sources that will take you further.

Note: this introduction assumes that you have the minimum system required. This is normally a PC or a Mac or any other computer that can run a modern Internet browser (such as Netscape Navigator or Microsoft Internet Explorer), a modem that connects your computer via a telephone line to a network, and an account with an Internet Service Provider (ISP) who, for a monthly rental fee, will give you a connection to the Internet.

The only rule: don't panic

This introduction is all about how you can get access to huge quantities of bibliographical and other scholarly information relevant to your research by searching world-wide electronic resources from home. This is an astonishing capability, and one that was unavailable only a few years ago. Things happen fast in the world of information technology, and most of what happens is to our advantage. However, because of the speed of developments, and because all computer systems are designed and run by highly fallible human beings, things do not always work first time (sometimes they don't work at all!). As you search through the Internet, you will frequently find references to parts of it being 'under construction', and that's a good image: it is like a building site with finished dwellings, half-constructed houses and marked-out building plots. Nevertheless, the buildings one can visit are already sufficiently numerous to make the whole enterprise very rewarding.

Having said that, there will be pieces of information that you expect to get from the Internet but discover that you cannot – or not immediately. There will be library catalogues that you will hope to search, and yet will apparently not be able to access. The use of IT is so seductive, the possibilities are so great, that there is danger of a revolution of rising expectations. A student searches the Library of Congress catalogue, finds the reference he or she has been looking for unsuccessfully for ages, and immediately – for that person – the Internet becomes a panacea for all ills, a completely trustworthy system that will always deliver the goods. Of course, the next time it doesn't work so well: hopes are dashed, expectations betrayed and the system denounced as useless.

Those who use IT most successfully have a more measured view: in many ways the Internet for a scholar is rather like any other research resource writ large. Think of it as just another research library: if you went to your library and found that the book you wanted was out, or mis-shelved, or that a reference in the catalogue was misleading or inaccurate, you wouldn't leave in a huff, denouncing the librarian and all his works. You might curse and fume, but you'd be back the next week to have another go, or to find an alternative source of information. If you adopt the same flexible, tolerant and resilient attitude to the Internet as you do to any other imperfect scholarly resource, then you will find that it is just as rewarding (possibly more so) as any of the other information sources that researchers use.

A few points to remember

- **The Internet is designed and run by human beings.** It will therefore be as rewarding and as irritating as any other human institution.

- **Do not give up too easily.** If something doesn't work, try again. If it still doesn't work, go away and make yourself a cup of coffee, drink it (not near the keyboard!) and then try again. If it still doesn't work, try again in a few days. If it still doesn't work, try something else.

- **You can always switch off**. If you get really cross with your computer, remember that – if necessary – you can always show it who's boss: pull the plug (but save your work first).

- **Remember that computers are just tools**. They are there to help you do the job of scholarship more efficiently and more thoroughly. They can't solve the intellectual problems of sorting out data and making sense of it. That's up to you.

- **Computers should not be used as a distraction**. It is too easy to get so excited by what computers can do that you spend too much time playing around with them. It is seductive – but a mistake. By all means use the computer for 'creative browsing' (as you might use a research library) but remember, contrary to popular opinion, information in itself does not empower or liberate: ultimately it is those who know how to filter, interpret and use information who will gain the greatest benefit from the IT revolution.

- **Do not abandon scholarly scepticism**. Information from the Internet is no more reliable than information from other sources. In some circumstances it can be less reliable. Electronic texts, for instance, may not be corrected, many are from old out-of-copyright editions that are themselves flawed. The very copying of a text from a printed to an electronic medium may introduce new errors. As much of the Internet is set up by numerate but not very literate enthusiasts, you will find that spelling, punctuation and grammar are not always of a high standard.

The Internet

Much, perhaps too much, has been written about the Internet. If you want to know something of its history and its organization, please consult the works listed below. In essence, and put crudely, the Internet is the result of linking up hundreds of thousands of computers world-wide. In practice it means that, via your computer and a modem, you can make contact with a huge range of research resources from around the world.

There are two problems facing anyone writing even the simplest description of the Internet: first, no one is in overall control of it and, second, it is changing literally from day to day. More and more computer systems are being added to it each day so we can never be certain how many computers are linked, or how many additional services have become available. These few pages can be nothing more than an approximate and partial guide to a few of the sources on the Internet that we feel might be useful. It is quite likely during your use of the Internet for your research work that you will discover useful sources that we know nothing about, or that have come online since this description was written.

It is very difficult to recommend books about the Internet because they tend to go out of date as soon as they have been published. You might be well advised to check guides to the Internet which are on the Internet itself. A number of these are available via links on The Open University's MA home page, the address of which is:

    http://www.open.ac.uk/StudentWeb/artsma/

If you would rather go to a book, and I wouldn't blame you, then try the ones below. Most are frequently updated, so the dates should only be taken as a guide. Although most books on the Internet are currently published in the USA, almost all of them are readily available in the UK.

P. Gilster, *Finding It on the Internet* (New York: John Wiley and Sons, 1996)

Ed Kroll, *The Whole Internet User's Guide and Catalogue* (Sebastopol, California: O'Reilly and Associates, 1994); more recent editions are available. This is a useful introduction, though it probably spends too much time discussing arcane procedures which, because of the new Internet browsers (see overleaf), you shouldn't need to know about; useful for dipping into

J.R. Levine and C. Baroudi, *The Internet for Dummies* (Foster City, California: IDG Books, 1997)

Davey Winder, *All You Need to Know About the World Wide Web* (Bath: Future Publishing, 1995); short and relatively cheap.

You will find that many of the broadsheet newspapers now have pages or even sections devoted to IT and the Internet.

Internet browsers

If you read any of the books listed above, you will stumble across a host of ways in which, in the past, users might have contacted other computers over the Internet – Telnet, File Transfer Protocol (FTP), Gopher, World Wide Web (WWW), etc. In the last few years a new sort of software called an Internet browser has been developed which provides the user with a friendly, consistent front-end. At the time of writing the two best-known browsers are Netscape Navigator and Microsoft Internet Explorer. It really doesn't matter which you use because all browsers work in roughly the same way. The browser will know what sort of connection to make and will make it without your needing to know anything about it. However, you will be aware of the different sorts of connection because the screen will look slightly different according to the type of connection made (see Figures 3.1–3.3).

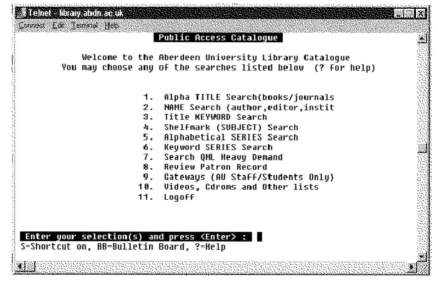

Figure 3.1   A Telnet screen (from the Aberdeen University Library Catalogue, via Hytelnet)

Because the Internet has been developing over a number of years, it includes a range of ways of displaying the information to you. The simplest you are likely to meet is the Telnet-based screen. This is the standard screen you will use when making a connection with many university library catalogues. Telnet screens look like rather old-fashioned computer screens, with lines of text and nothing more. In a Telnet screen you are usually offered a menu of choices which are numbered (or lettered), and you choose an option by typing its number or letter and then pressing the key marked **Return**. As Telnet screens are the least 'friendly' of the screens you are likely to encounter on the Internet, some general advice on how to use them is given below.

Using Telnet screens

1   When using a Telnet screen, it is important to remember to read the information on the introductory screens. For instance, before you click on the Uniform Resource Locator that will connect you to the library you have chosen, make sure you know whether a password is required; if it is, the screen will tell you what to type. (The Uniform Resource Locator – URL – is the equivalent of an address on the Web.)

    Also the library catalogue may require you to tell it what sort of screen display you have got (if you are not told, the safe answer is usually VT100). Usually all this 'log-on' information will be provided on the screen, so make sure that you read it before clicking on the library's URL.

2   Once you are in a library catalogue, make sure that you read its introductory screen; again, this will tell you what you need to know in order to search for author, title, subject etc.

3   Once you have finished using that library catalogue and have exited from it (another reason to read the introductory information: you will know how to get out!), you will usually have to go to the **File** menu in the top left-hand corner of the screen and select **Exit**, which should bring you back to the start screen with the library's URL on it. You can then click the **Back** button on your browser to go back to the list of libraries.

4   If you get stuck and cannot find your way out of a Telnet screen, use the emergency keys: hold down the control key (usually marked **Ctrl**) and at the same time tap the key with the closing angle bracket **]**; in instructions, this procedure is normally indicated by the cryptic command **Ctrl–]**. This should clear the screen and allow you to choose **Exit** from the **File** menu.

Gopher screens

A slightly more sophisticated presentation can be found in Gopher-based screens. (If you want to know the origin of this rather whimsical term, please refer to one of the works on the Internet listed above.) Gopher screens consist of text and symbols; significant words or phrases are highlighted (in your screen they may well appear in blue) to make them stand out. You will notice that when the mouse-cursor (or pointer) is placed over these words, it changes from an arrow to a pointing finger symbol. These words or phrases are 'hot'. Essentially this means that they have a link to some other source of information. If you click on your mouse button when the mouse pointer is over such a hot word, it will activate that link and take you to the new source.

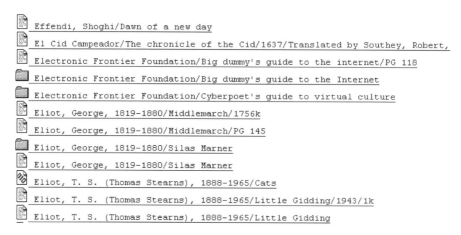

```
Effendi, Shoghi/Dawn of a new day
El Cid Campeador/The chronicle of the Cid/1637/Translated by Southey, Robert,
Electronic Frontier Foundation/Big dummy's guide to the internet/PG 118
Electronic Frontier Foundation/Big dummy's guide to the Internet
Electronic Frontier Foundation/Cyberpoet's guide to virtual culture
Eliot, George, 1819-1880/Middlemarch/1756k
Eliot, George, 1819-1880/Middlemarch/PG 145
Eliot, George, 1819-1880/Silas Marner
Eliot, George, 1819-1880/Silas Marner
Eliot, T. S. (Thomas Stearns), 1888-1965/Cats
Eliot, T. S. (Thomas Stearns), 1888-1965/Little Gidding/1943/1k
Eliot, T. S. (Thomas Stearns), 1888-1965/Little Gidding
```

Figure 3.2   A Gopher screen (from Alex, a database of electronic texts)

World Wide Web screens

The most sophisticated screen of all so far available on the Internet is generated by the World Wide Web (www, or 'The Web': see p.198). This not only has text and hot words, but also includes colour images and – if you have the right software and hardware – links to audio and video. WWW pages also have the ability to offer you forms that you can fill in (this is very useful when you are searching a catalogue or database for a particular word) and buttons you can click on. In fact, a WWW screen is remarkably similar to the screen of a modern personal computer of the sort that you run when you are word-processing, etc. More and more sources on the Internet are moving towards WWW screens, so these are rapidly becoming the norm. However, for some time yet you may also have to be familiar with Telnet and Gopher screens.

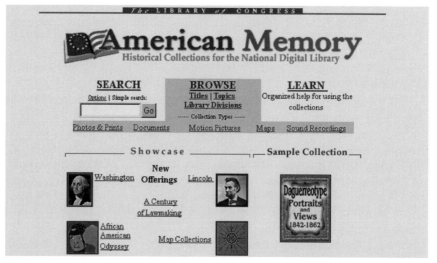

Figure 3.3   A WWW screen (from the Library of Congress Web site; courtesy of the Library of Congress, USA: http://lcweb2.loc.gov/ammem/ammemhome.html)

Getting started: pages and their URLs

The Web works on a basic unit of a 'page'. Any institution, interest group or company you wish to contact is likely to have a *home page*. This acts as a sort of 'introduction and contents page' and from it you can move to all sorts of subordinate pages. Each page on the Web has its own URL.

Suppose you want to go directly to a particular page. Say it's The Open University's MA home page, and you know its URL; at the time of writing, this is:

> http://www.open.ac.uk/StudentWeb/artsma/

Then if you type it in the right place and click on **OK** or **Open**, you will go directly to that page. The 'right' place will vary from browser to browser, but usually it can be found in the **File** menu as **Open Location** or **Open Page** or just **Open**.

Clicking on a hot word is another way of going off to a new address. This is because lurking under each hot word is a URL. The URL of the current page you are on is shown on your browser screen in the line labelled **Address**, **Location** or **Netsite**.

A very quick guide to using Internet browsers

Given that different browsers work in different ways, we can talk here only in general terms. However, what follows should be enough to equip you to do basic but worthwhile searches for academic material on the Internet without getting too confused or completely lost.

1   How to use a browser so you don't get lost

1.1 As you move from page to page on the Web, and as you click on hot link after hot link, it is very easy to get lost and to forget how you got to a certain place. Don't worry, there are various ways in which you can get back either to home or to a place that you recognize.

1.2 Firstly, make sure that you have correctly set up your start page – the page that automatically appears when you start. The **Help** menu should allow you to search for terms such as 'Start' or 'Home', and the information under those headings should tell you how to alter the page in which you start. For the time being you may want to start in The Open University's MA home page because we shall be referring to it quite frequently. However, where you start from is entirely a matter of personal choice.

1.3 Once you have defined your home page, you can always get back to it by simply pressing the **Home** button on your browser screen.

1.4 If that's a bit drastic, then simply click the **Back** arrow on your browser screen. This will take you back to the page you were on before the current page. You can click on the **Back** key repeatedly until you get to where you want to be or, at least, to a place that you recognize.

1.5 If you want to go back a few pages but can't quite remember how far back, then click on the **Go** drop-down menu in your browser: that should list the last few pages that you have visited. Then just click on the page you want to go to.

1.6 Finally, if you are lost, you can always call up your bookmarks and select one of these (see 2.2).

2 *How to find and save information*

2.1 Despite the name, some 'pages' are quite long and consist of many screens of information. If you know what you are looking for, there is a short cut: you can search the whole page for a particular, significant word. Usually in the **Edit** menu there will be listed a **Find** or **Find in page** option; click on this and then type the word you want to find, and then click on **Find Next**. This should work whether the page being searched is a Web page or a piece of text you've just called up.

2.2 When you discover a page that will be very useful to you and to which you will want to return, you can store its URL as a bookmark. You should be able to add bookmarks by going either to a menu or a button labelled **Bookmarks**, or to a menu item labelled **Favourites** – depending on which browser you are using. Once you have added a bookmark, all you need to do – to get back to the chosen page – is go to the listed bookmarks and click on the one you want.

2.3 One of the labour-saving features of IT is that you don't have to spend time noting things down: if you want to record things, you can normally send them to a printer or save them to your hard or floppy disk.

Printing: in most cases you can do this by going to the **File** menu and selecting **Print**. If this doesn't work, try selecting the on-screen text by pressing the left mouse button and dragging the mouse pointer down the text that you want to print, thus 'highlighting' it. Then select from the **Edit** menu **Copy**. Then open up a word-processing file and, while you are in it, go to the **Edit** menu and choose **Paste**. This should dump the text from your Web page into the word-processor and you can then print or save the file as you choose.

Saving to disk: you can usually save a Web page to either a hard or a floppy disk. Go to the **File** menu and select **Save As**. This will give you the option of saving the file as an '.htm' file or as a '.txt' file. Save as '.htm' if you want to keep all the formatting and some of the images. If you then want to see these files properly, you have to call them up within your browser. You can usually launch your browser without going online but, if you do so, you then have to tell it what file to read. You do this by going to the **File** menu and selecting **Open** and then searching for wherever you saved your file. If you just want the text, then save as a '.txt' file: you will be able to read it in your ordinary word-processing package.

Some words of warning: if you copy something, beware of copyright implications. Only use the material for your own personal study and, if you do incorporate any substantial amount of Internet-derived material into a dissertation or article, do make sure that you check with the originator of that material first. To avoid any accusations of plagiarism, make sure that you acknowledge in a footnote the origin of any material you use from the Internet. (There are Web sites that will tell you how to reference an Internet site. You will find some of these on The Open University's MA home page, under 'General Research Resources', 'Study Tools, Information etc.'.) Because it is so technically easy to copy material, you are advised to make a note of its source *at the time* that you copy it, even if you are not certain that you will use it in your final dissertation or publication. If you don't make a note at the time, you may have great difficulty at some later date in recalling which material came from where. You can easily record the source by highlighting the address under **Location**, copying it, and pasting it into your document.

3   *Saving yourself time*

3.1 Some pages take a long time to load; this may be because they are large, it may be because the browser is having some difficulty in making contact, or it may because the page in question has one or more pictures (graphics) in it. Graphics take up much more memory than text, so they take longer to download. If you need those graphics, then you will simply have to wait. If all you want is the text, then you can tell your browser to switch off the graphics and thus speed up loading. This is usually done by going to the **Options** or **View** menu and switching off the images but, if in doubt, call up **Help** and search for information on 'images' or 'graphics'.

3.2 There are times when the Internet is busy and times when it is less busy. For instance, the USA is a great user of the Internet, so when various parts of the USA wake up, users in the UK often find that things slow down. Mornings, therefore, can be a good time to work on the Internet if you are in the UK. However, even if your call to an Internet Service Provider is a local one (and it is very likely to be), weekday mornings will be more expensive. Weekends are much cheaper, so it might be a good idea to save up your long searches for a Saturday or Sunday morning. The only trouble with this is that certain pages or catalogues, for instance, may not be available owing to maintenance or up-grading. To an extent, sorting out the best and most efficient time to search is a very individual matter, so the best advice is: experiment.

3.3 The final way of saving time and money is to make sure that your searches are as precise as possible: using 'search engines' to generate thousands of hits which you will never have the time to sort out is a great way of wasting time. Do make sure that when you download data from the Internet you really will find it useful: there are data junkies out there who download megabytes of material in the fond belief that just collecting information is somehow virtuous and beneficial. If you can't cope with it, if you can't sort it out and make sense of it, then data is nothing more than electronic kapok.

What is on the Web for a literary researcher?

The simplest answer is: too much to describe here. Another answer might be: it all depends on what you are researching. Subjects such as gender studies and post-colonial literatures are so popular that it is almost impossible to keep up with the number of sites offering information on – or opinions about – them. More arcane or newer subjects, such as bibliography or book history, have fewer sites; but, even so, they are pretty well served. What follows is a very select range of types of Internet site that you might be interested in exploring. They are based on the selection we have made available to Open University MA students on their home page. We shall concentrate here on sites listed on two of the linked Open University pages:

> **General Research Resources** (this lists a range of useful links for anyone studying a humanities-based subject); and

> **Literature Line Research Resources** (which, as you might have guessed, concentrates on material specifically linked to literature and, within that, to areas that we currently study in The Open University's MA: the eighteenth-century novel; poetry and criticism, 1830–90; and the novel in English, 1880–1930).

One point more before we begin our brief survey. One of the great strengths of the Internet is that there are many ways of getting to the same information. Sites are linked in a multitude of ways so, if you miss one link, you are likely to find a score of alternative ways of getting through to the information you want. For instance, the British Library has a splendid exhibition concerning the manuscript of the Old English poem *Beowulf*. You can get to this, of course, by going to the BL's home page (called 'Portico'), but you can also find a link to it in various lists of museums, in lists of electronic texts, and on home pages dealing with resources for medievalists on the Web. When we come to describing some of the most useful resources on the Web, you will find that, although we list a resource under one heading, it will frequently be accessible through other home pages listed under other headings. For instance, electronic texts can be accessed through sources that we list on the MA home page under 'Libraries', 'Other bibliographical and scholarly resources' and 'Reference works' – as well as under the obvious heading 'Electronic texts and text tools'.

What is available on The Open University's MA pages

The following section tells you about what, at the time of writing, is available at:

http://www.open.ac.uk/StudentWeb/artsma/

General research resources

This is divided into a number of headings. Under each heading, one or two examples are given to illustrate the resources available.

1 Libraries

Although one of the simplest research tools (and often visually the dullest: many libraries are still using Telnet screens), a library catalogue is one of the most useful tools you will find on the Internet. Under this heading you will find not only the catalogues of the British Library and the Library of Congress, but also a list of almost all the university libraries in the UK. If you are within travelling distance of two or three universities, use this list to search their libraries and to find out which has the most useful collection of books for your research topic.

2 Other bibliographical and scholarly resources

A mixed bag here, which includes links to large collections of humanities-based information systems such as HUMBUL (Humanities Bulletin Board), which has a considerable number of useful links out to History sites, to a whole selection of dictionaries and to a wide variety of sources for electronic texts. Also here is the rather unpromising sounding AHDS (the Arts and Humanities Data Service) which is, in fact, a marvellously rich source of electronic data produced as a by-product of teaching and research in the humanities. There is also a link to the Royal Commission on Historical Manuscripts which allows a student to search the National Register of Archives (extremely useful if you are trying to track down the diaries, letters and other personal documents of writers).

3 Reference works

Material available here at the time of writing includes a thesaurus, a range of dictionaries, dictionaries of quotations, links to census information, and that most remarkable, yearly-updated source – the CIA's *World Factbook*. This provides a wealth of information on each and every country (including fascinating data on literacy rates and size of the telephone system – very revealing information if your work is in any way related to the history or theory of communications).

4 Electronic texts and text tools

One of the really impressive features of the Internet, particularly for those researching in literature and related fields, is the number of full electronic texts already available through it; even more impressive is the rate at which texts are being added. There are a number of national and international projects aimed at increasing the number of electronic texts in a systematic way, and there are many private individuals who, as a by-product of their own research or just out of sheer love of an author, put up a text or two. Most of these texts can be downloaded onto the hard disk of your own computer.

Listed under 'Electronic texts and text tools' is a variety of sources of electronic texts and also information, as and when available, about 'text analysis' tools. These are programs which allow you to identify keywords, create concordances, map out word frequencies in a given text, etc. You can, of course, use an ordinary word-processing program to search for individual words (using the **Find** option in the **Edit** menu) but the process is laborious and limited. The text-analysis programs usually cost money, but most will allow you to download a trial version for free. This trial version is often restricted in some way (in functions, in the amount of text it will handle, or in the amount of time you can use it) but it will give you some idea of how these programs work and whether it would be worth buying the full version.

A word of warning about copyright: any official e-text project will ensure that it understands the copyright position of each text before it makes that text available. An individual text may be out of copyright, or the copyright owner may have given permission, or there may be restrictions on how you can use the text (exclusively for your own private study, for instance). Sometimes a description of the copyright status of a particular text will be attached to it. Private individuals putting up texts on the Internet may not be so scrupulous, or may simply be ignorant of copyright law. It is up to you, if you use one of these texts, to be cautious about copyright.

5 Newspapers, journals and articles

Quite a few newspapers and magazines now have sites on the Internet. Some are wholly free, some give limited free access; most will allow you to search at least some of their back files for useful articles. Some learned journals are now on the Web (and some are published only, or mainly, on the Web). There are also some services which will allow you to search thousands of scholarly journals and then order offprints of relevant articles via the Web.

A note of advice and caution: it is very useful to have a widely recognized credit card if you want to buy things (for example, offprints or books) via the Web. However, there is always the danger that your credit card number might be 'hacked' (in other words, some unauthorized person might get access to it). Many sites now have a 'secure' system which allows you to send them your card details in relative safety. If they do not (many smaller book-dealers do not), then you can decrease your chances of being hacked by sending your credit card details in two parts in two separate email messages.

6 Museums and visual resources

There is now a wide variety of museums with a presence on the Web; there are also extensive lists of museums organized under national headings. Although perhaps not the first resource you might go to if you were doing some form of literature-related research, many museums nevertheless have some highly relevant materials – particularly for those interested in the physical aspects of literature (in particular, bibliography and book history).

7 Publishers, bookshops etc.

Each successive technical revolution in communications prompts another version of the cry, 'print culture is dead'. Nevertheless print continues to survive and, in certain circumstances, to flourish. Print seems highly adaptable, whether in the form of books tied in to TV soap operas, or the innumerable handbooks and magazines devoted to PCs and/or the Internet. Part of this adaptability is displayed by the way in which the book industry, in the form of publishers and booksellers, has taken to the Web. Under this heading the MA home page includes a list of publishers' Web sites (most of them having searchable catalogues attached), and a number of bookshops on the Web – including one which, at the time of writing, allows you to search the equivalent of *Books in Print* for either the UK or USA or both and order anything you find there.

Even more impressive for the researcher in literature is the way in which second-hand and antiquarian bookdealers have taken to the Web. There are now search engines which allow you to search through hundreds of second-hand bookdealers' catalogues simultaneously. Many of these engines will search for any string of characters, so searches for keywords in titles, specific publishers, places of publication or publication dates are as possible as searches for named authors. If you wish to buy anything on your credit card from bookdealers on the Web, please refer to the advice given in 5 above.

8 Study tools, information etc.

In this rather miscellaneous category you will find useful information about international standards governing the presentation of electronic documentation and advice from such scholarly organizations as the Modern Humanities Research Association (MHRA) on how to refer in a scholarly thesis to electronic sources.

Literature Line research resources

This is divided into four sections, the last three being specific to courses studied on The Open University's MA in Literature:

1 General literature resources

There are on the Web many lists of useful links for researchers in literature; this section of the MA home page merely provides a small selection of them – from a site explaining the process of interpreting ancient manuscripts, through a link to the Bibliographical Society of the University of Virginia, to a site that lists pages dealing with a variety of modern literary theories.

2 The eighteenth-century novel

This has links to lists of scholarly projects on the eighteenth century, a route out to a major project in the University of Chicago (American and French Research on the Treasury of the French language – ARTFL), and access to an electronic version of the Brabourne edition (1884) of Jane Austen's letters.

3 Poetry and criticism, 1830–90

Among other things, there are hot links to two sites located at the University of Virginia ('British Poetry 1780–1910' and 'The Dante Gabriel Rossetti Research Index') and to a remarkable site on '19th Century British and Irish Authors' which lists useful links to pages dealing with the majority of the canonical writers of the period and quite a few of the non-canonical figures as well.

4 The novel in English, 1880–1930

This consists of a number of links to Web pages relevant to the six novels studied, namely: George Gissing's *New Grub Street*, Olive Schreiner's *The Story of an African Farm*, Thomas Hardy's *Jude the Obscure*, D.H. Lawrence's *Sons and Lovers*, James Joyce's *A Portrait of the Artist as a Young Man* and Virginia Woolf's *The Waves*. A particularly strong feature of this page is that it provides links to full electronic text versions of most of the novels, and to some other contemporary writings that help to provide a context for the study. These texts can usually be downloaded onto an individual's computer for private study; this might well include textual analysis, a process for which the computer is an ideal tool.

Taking things a little further

It may well be that straightforward searches of the sources provided by The Open University's resource pages will provide you with all the bibliographical and other material that you need. However, if you need to go further, or need to try more complicated searches, the following points might help.

Search strategies

In most cases, certainly when you are searching a single electronic library catalogue, you will need to type in no more than an author's name or a title; this alone will narrow down to a manageable number the 'hits' (the number of references the catalogue finds that satisfy your search criterion/criteria). However, when you are dealing with very large catalogues or other sorts of database, you are likely to need to narrow down your criteria (otherwise you will be overwhelmed by the quantity of only vaguely relevant or totally irrelevant material). This is where search strategies come into their own.

These strategies are most useful when you are searching for 'keywords' or 'subject words' – words that crucially define your topic. If, for instance, you were working on the novels of Dickens, clearly one such keyword would be 'Dickens' itself, for you might want to search for occurrences of that word under author (thus finding the works that Dickens wrote himself) and title (thus finding books and articles about Dickens that mentioned him in the title). Many catalogues now have entries which include 'descriptors' for each work. These descriptors are the cataloguer's summary of what the work is about. Thus a book or article that is about Dickens (or includes him among other authors), but that does not mention his name in its title, may still be found by a keyword search if 'Dickens' is one of its descriptors.

The most common search strategies consist of using two or more keywords at the same time, the keywords being joined by one of three 'operators' which control the way in which those keywords are searched for. The three operators are: AND, OR, NOT (sometimes called 'Boolean operators'). The best way to explain how these operators work is to take an example and go through AND, OR, NOT, showing how the use of each changes the results of your search. Let's assume that you are researching the representation of law in Dickens's novels. Inescapably two of your most important keywords will be 'dickens' and 'law'.

The operators

1   If we link our two words by AND, what we are saying to the electronic catalogue we are searching is: please get all those records that mention both 'dickens' and 'law'; records that mention 'dickens' but not 'law' are no good, nor are those that mention 'law' but not 'dickens'; both terms must be present in the record if you are to select it.

2   If we link our two words by OR, what we are saying to the electronic catalogue is: please get all records that mention either 'dickens' or 'law'; in other words, records that mention just 'dickens' will be collected, records that mention just 'law' will be collected, and so will those that mention both 'dickens' and 'law' (the ones that would have been selected by AND).

3   If we link our two words with NOT (for example, 'dickens NOT law'),
     what we are saying to the electronic catalogue is: please get all records
     that mention 'dickens' but do not mention 'law'; in other words, no
     record that mentions just 'law' will be selected, and no record that
     mentions 'dickens' and 'law' will be selected. If we put it the other way
     around ('law NOT dickens'), the opposite would happen: everything
     that mentioned law would be selected, but nothing that mentioned
     'dickens' and nothing that mentioned both 'dickens' and 'law'.

     This use of 'NOT' is a way of filtering out unwanted information. For
     example, if you were interested in Dickens on the theme of imprison-
     ment, but you knew that critics had nearly exhausted *Little Dorrit* as an
     exemplary text, you could search a list of critical works on Dickens's
     novels with the phrase 'prison NOT dorrit'.

Figure 3.4 should make this clear.

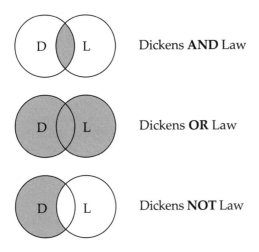

Dickens **AND** Law

Dickens **OR** Law

Dickens **NOT** Law

Figure 3.4   The shaded areas indicate the records that would be selected
by the given operator

Wild cards
Some search systems will allow you to use what is often called a 'wild card'.
Wild cards usually take one of two forms:

1   A symbol (sometimes a $ sign) which represents any single letter. If, for
     instance, you typed in:

     c$t

     the system would find 'cat', 'cot' and 'cut'.

2   A symbol (sometimes a * sign) which stands for any number of letters
     (and is therefore most likely to be used at the end of a word when you

are searching for related words from one stem). If, for instance, you typed in

law*

the system would find 'law', 'laws', 'lawyer', 'lawyers', 'lawcourt', 'lawcourts', etc.

If the search system you are using allows wild cards, the introductory or 'Help' information associated with it will tell you, and will give you the correct symbols to use.

Search engines

These sound rather industrial, but search engines have proved extremely useful to students trying to cope with the huge but amorphous research resource represented by the ever-growing Internet. What search engines attempt to do is create large indexes of subjects covered by the Internet. Most of them do this by using what are frequently called 'crawlers' (the analogy is that of a spider tending its web); these are programs that spend their time 'crawling' over the Web to find newly-added sources which they then catalogue or index in a variety of ways according to the particular search engine they serve. These indexes can be searched, usually by means of a form in which you type your search strategy and by a **Search** or **Submit** button on which you then click your mouse pointer to begin the search. The results of the search are normally a set of URLs which you can then explore. Many search engines allow you to specify the maximum number of references that you want to receive back (if you get too many, you won't be able to deal with them all).

Some search engines allow you to search for a word, some allow you to search in more sophisticated ways using Boolean operators (see 'Search strategies' above). As search engines classify information in different ways, it is usually worth using two or three of them in order to maximize the number of useful references you have at your disposal – as long as you keep in mind the fact that too many references can be a curse rather than a blessing in terms of workload and time.

You will find a number of very useful search engines if you click on a button in your browser which will be labelled **Search**, **Net Search** or something similar. The best advice is to try a number of such engines by searching on a subject you know a reasonable amount about. In this way you will be able to judge the quality and usefulness of the information that a particular search engine returns to you.

Accessing electronic information not freely available on the Internet

So far we have concentrated on how to use the Internet to get hold of useful scholarly information. However, there are many valuable sources of information which are not currently on the Internet or, at least, are not accessible through the Internet for free. Some of these databases can be accessed online but only on a payment to a system provider. Such is the case with BLAISE-LINE, which is run by the British Library and includes the *Eighteenth Century Short Title Catalogue* (ESTC).

However, if they are not freely available on the Internet, it is more common nowadays for databases to be published on cd-roms. (For instance, currently *Palmer's Index to the Times*, the ESTC and the *Nineteenth Century Short Title Catalogue* (NSTC) are all available on cd-rom.) On the whole these are more likely to be bought by university libraries than private individuals, as most of them are very expensive. The libraries will then make these cd-roms available to their readers directly on PCs in the library or via a local network. (In the latter case the library will have bought an associated licence which will allow a certain number of researchers to consult the cd-rom at any given time.) These local networks, which often look and function very like the Internet, are called *Intranets* – a term usually implying that they are local networks with access limited to an identified group. You may well find that when you arrive at a university library home page, there will be things that everyone can use, and resources that only members of that university library or institution can use. As a researcher you will need to identify the research library you will use most frequently, and then see if you can negotiate rights of access to its cd-roms.

Choosing a real library electronically

If you are a student in the UK, one service that should help you to approach conventional libraries, and thus move you back from electronic to solid, real books, can be found under 'Libraries' in the MA's 'General Research Resources' page. This is an index of all university libraries in the UK and it is maintained by The Open University's library. For each library on this index, you will be able to find useful details – including how easy it is to get access to it, and what sort of fee will be charged for such access. If you

1   identify the university libraries you could travel to reasonably easily and frequently,

2   use the Internet to search their catalogues to see if they have the sort of book stock you need,

3   check likely costs against The Open University's library index,

then you should be able to make a sensible choice of research library from the comfort of your own home.

Part 2

TEXTUAL SCHOLARSHIP AND BOOK HISTORY

bibliography: enumerative, analytical, descriptive, historical

history of the book

editing literary texts

4 BIBLIOGRAPHY

by Simon Eliot

One of the founding principles of this Handbook is that scholars cannot regard themselves as adequately educated unless they have some understanding of both the intellectual and the material history of literature. It is this history that provides the rich soil out of which even the most recent and radical piece of literature grows. If you do research in literature, it is likely that most of your time will be spent studying the 'meaning' or 'significance' of texts. In order to do this you will have to make assumptions about the integrity of that text, assumptions about the way in which the author wrote (or 'produced') it, and assumptions about the way in which the author's contemporaries read (or 'consumed') it. Even if you are not worried about the historical context, you will need to know something about how your texts are produced and consumed today.

For instance, the fact that *Tristram Shandy* was published in a number of discrete volumes over a number of years (1759–67) must have had an effect on how Sterne's contemporaries responded to the work as a whole. (How, for instance, would they know when it was complete?) The fact that it is now available as a single volume in the Oxford World's Classics series, with a critical introduction – a volume that can be read in a few days or weeks (as a whole, as a 'classic') – is bound to give the modern reader a different attitude to it.

To take another example: the fact that Tennyson's 'Charge of the Light Brigade' was first published in the pages of a magazine (*The Examiner* on 9 December 1854) only a week after Tennyson had read an account of the charge in *The Times*, must have coloured contemporaries' attitudes to it. (Even the famous line 'Some one had blundered' was based on a phrase used in *The Times*'s article.) Surrounded by ephemeral political and social comment, the poem must have seemed to some readers like an editorial in verse.

It is not just the physical form of the publication that affects meaning. The very way in which literature gets put into print can change the meaning of a text. For instance, when a compositor's hand misses the correct section of his type tray (or 'case'), or when his assistant puts the type in the wrong section of the case, or when he misreads the manuscript copy from which he is setting the book, then Hamlet's 'too, too solid flesh' becomes 'sullied' or 'sallied', and Falstaff's 'a' babbled o' green fields' becomes a 'table of green fields'. (For other examples of this, see Bruce Harkness, 'Bibliography and the Novelistic Fallacy' in *Bibliography and Textual Criticism*, ed. O.M. Brack, Jnr and Warner Barnes, Chicago and London: University of Chicago Press, 1969.) Never forget that texts are material objects – written, printed, advertised, sold (or borrowed or stolen) and used by fallible human beings, many of whom would not have had a particularly reverential attitude towards the material they were dealing in.

We could summarize all this by saying simply that the meaning and nature of a literary work (indeed, of any text) can be significantly affected by the various processes that enable its transmission from the author's original manuscript to a reader. Even if we cannot agree with Marshall McLuhan that the medium is all of the message, nevertheless we have to accept that it constitutes a significant part of it. It is therefore important to study the text as a physical object, as a product of the material world and as a result of a series of manufacturing processes, most of which can, intentionally or unintentionally, alter the nature of the text being transmitted. The study of the book as a material object is called 'bibliography'. Various types of bibliography are used by other scholarly disciplines for their own purposes, and two such disciplines are examined in later chapters – the history of the book (Chapter 5) and scholarly editing (Chapter 6).

The book we suggest you read in conjunction with the present chapter is

> D.C. Greetham, *Textual Scholarship: An Introduction* (New York and London: Garland, 1994).

It's a book to be dipped into rather than read from cover to cover, and at points in this chapter I will give page references to it – so that you can look up specific subjects in greater detail if you want to.

Good though Greetham is, he suffers from a rather narrow view of bibliography: he believes that enumerative, analytical and descriptive bibliography act essentially as handmaidens to the production of a critical edition. It is certainly true that no modern scholarly editor could do without them, but they can and do exist independently of critical editing – both in their own right and as contributors to other types of scholarship such as media studies, the sociology of literature and, most obvious of all, book history. In order to redress the balance, we have included a chapter on book history immediately after this one.

Selected reading

> O.M. Brack, Jnr and Warner Barnes (eds), *Bibliography and Textual Criticism* (Chicago and London: University of Chicago Press, 1969). An interesting collection of essays by various hands; this is mostly, as the title implies, about textual bibliography.

> John Carter, *ABC for Book Collectors* (London: Granada, 1980); first published in 1952, this is a useful and entertaining handbook which describes and illustrates (using itself) the constituent parts of a book and other relevant bibliographical matters.

> Martin Coyle, Peter Garside, Malcolm Kelsall and John Peck (eds), *The Encyclopaedia of Literature and Criticism* (London: Routledge, 1990). This has a very useful section consisting of ten essays on bibliography and book history, each with its own list of further reading (Section VII, 'Production and Reception', pp.809–940).

> Peter Davison (ed.), *The Book Encompassed* (Cambridge: Cambridge University Press, 1992); a collection of entertaining and informative essays celebrating

the centenary of the most prestigious of all scholarly bibliographical societies, the Bibliographical Society of London.

Philip Gaskell, *A New Introduction to Bibliography* (Oxford: Oxford University Press, 1972). The standard introduction to the subject; it is also invaluable for additional details on the production of the printed (rather than the manuscript) book.

R.B. McKerrow, *An Introduction to Bibliography for Literary Students* (Oxford: Oxford University Press, 1927); now partly replaced by Gaskell but still perfectly usable.

E.W. Padwick, *Bibliographical Method* (Cambridge and London: James Clark, 1969). This has a useful introduction (Chapters 1–2) and information on eighteenth-century books (Chapter 14) and nineteenth-century books (Chapters 15–17).

Roy Stokes, *The Function of Bibliography* (Aldershot: Gower, 1982); 1st edn, 1969; a short and clear introduction to the subject.

Hugh Williamson, *Methods of Book Design* (London: Oxford University Press, 1966). This is very sound on all the processes of book production from paper-making to book-binding; some very helpful illustrations.

For other titles consult the bibliography in Greetham.

What is bibliography?

Books are the material means by which literature is transmitted; therefore bibliography, the study of books, is essentially the science of the transmission of literary documents.

(W.W. Greg, *The Library*, 4th series, XIII (1932–3), 115)

To most students, a 'bibliography' is probably just a 'list of books consulted' which is usually given at the end of a scholarly work. This is certainly the most common meaning of the word, but it is not the only one, nor is it the most important. In many ways, using 'bibliography' to mean a selected list of books is a partial contradiction of its other meanings. The discipline of bibliography, in treating books and other printed matter as physical objects, is *much less evaluative* than most other forms of literary study. In essence, bibliographers are not at all concerned with the contents of a book: the volume before them could be the works of Shakespeare, an atlas, a book of recipes or a collection of the most tedious sermons imaginable. As products of the scribe or printing press, these would all be of equal interest and value to a bibliographer.

Most authorities distinguish a number of types of bibliography, as does Greetham. In some ways these distinctions are rather spurious, because in practice one type merges into another. Nevertheless, for the purpose of this introduction, we shall respect the divisions.

If you have a copy, now would be the time to read Greetham's 'Introduction' (pp.1–12).

Enumerative bibliography

This is, like all other forms of the discipline, not at all interested in literary value-judgements. It is concerned with books as material things, and will find as much to say about the worst piece of published doggerel as it will about *In Memoriam*. Essentially, enumerative bibliography enumerates – it lists and counts all books produced over a given period or in a given country, or defined by some other large and, as far as possible, value-free category. The information offered is much less detailed than that presented in descriptive bibliographies: typically, each entry will contain details of the author, the title, the printer, the year of publication, and a list of libraries in which copies can be found. What is lost in detail, however, is made up for in quantity. Most major enumerative bibliographies draw on the collections of some, and sometimes many, of the great library collections of the world, so their listings can be very comprehensive.

Perhaps the clearest examples of the enumerative bibliographer's art are the sequence of short-title catalogues:

> *The Incunable Short Title Catalogue* (London: The British Library); usually known as *ISTC*, this lists books printed before 1501 (an 'incunable' is a book printed before 1500–1: from the Latin *cunae* meaning 'cradle', as in 'the printed book in its cradle').

> A.W. Pollard and G.R. Redgrave, *A Short Title Catalogue of Books Printed in England, Scotland, and Ireland, and of English Books Printed Abroad, 1475–1640* (London: Bibliographical Society, 1926; rev. 1976–89); this is usually known as *STC*.

The *STC* was continued by

> Donald G. Wing, *Short Title Catalogue of Books Printed in England, Scotland, Ireland, Wales, and British America and of English Books Printed in Other Countries, 1641–1700* (New York: MLA, 1945–1951); this is usually known as Wing.

Both these works are now being revised, but they set a standard which is now being followed by

> *The Eighteenth Century Short Title Catalogue* (London: British Library, 1983–); this is usually known as *ESTC*. It exists in printed form, online and on cd-rom.

From a rather different tradition comes:

> *The Nineteenth Century Short Title Catalogue* (Newcastle upon Tyne: Avero, 1984–); this is usually known as *NSTC*. The *NSTC* is divided into three series (Series I: 1801–15; Series II: 1816–70; Series III: 1871–1919). Series I and II are available in printed form and on cd-rom; at the time of writing, Series III is still in progress.

For the period 1473–1800, there is a project under way to unite the catalogues covering books printed in England (and its dependencies) and books in English wherever printed. This is called the *English Short Title Catalogue* (also confusingly shortened to ESTC).

The chance to search an entire enumerative bibliography quickly and cheaply will allow the scholar, for the first time, to answer very broad questions about book production in earlier centuries. How many books were printed in Oxford in 1759? How many books of poetry did Moxon publish in the 1840s? How many books which refer to 'magistrates' in their titles were published between 1730 and 1750? How many volumes of poetry which made reference to 'Christianity' or 'Christian' in their titles were published during the main period of the Oxford Movement? These questions are not, of course, exclusively bibliographical; but we have bibliography to thank for providing the means to answer them.

Suggested reading

Greetham, Chapter 1, 'Finding the Text' (pp.13–46).

Selected reading

Roy Stokes, *The Function of Bibliography*, Chapter 2 (pp.17–44).

The Encyclopaedia of Literature and Criticism, 'The Bibliographical Record' (pp.915–925).

Questions and exercises

1   What is the link between the earliest libraries (particularly the museum and library at Alexandria) and the creation of the canon of Greek writers? How important are libraries in the creation of a canon?

2   Identify Fredson Bowers's four 'systems' that can be used for organizing a systematic bibliography (see 'Selected reading' under 'Descriptive bibliography', p.47). Using your research library, find your own examples of each of these systems.

3   What is the ISTC, and what is its present stage of development?

4   Using your local reference library, find a subject bibliography that covers your own locale or, alternatively, an author or a subject in which you are interested. Write a brief critique of it: comment on its coverage, on its organizing principles, and on its possible usefulness (or otherwise) as a research tool.

5   Using the National Library of Scotland catalogue and the *Bibliography of Scotland Online Catalogue* in the list of UK libraries (available via the MA's home page on the World Wide Web), compile a bibliography of European translations of Sir Walter Scott's *Ivanhoe*. Each entry should, whenever possible, include the place of publication, publisher, date of publication, translator and any notes about format, number of pages, number of volumes, etc.

Analytical bibliography (and codicology)

Although it is unlikely that you will be dealing with manuscript books, for the sake of completeness (and your broader knowledge) we suggest that you do read the relevant chapters in Greetham on codicology (which is the study of the manufacturing processes that are involved in producing a manuscript book, and is most concerned with ancient and medieval books) and palaeography (the study of the handwriting in which these books were written). We will concentrate here, however, on analytical bibliography, which concerns itself mostly with the manufacture of the printed book.

It would be the job of the analytical bibliographer, in approaching a text, to discuss and describe the ways in which the author's original manuscript might have been put into type, how many compositors might have been used, and which compositors were responsible for which sheets, and what sort of mistakes they might have made in setting the manuscript into type. The bibliographer would then be obliged to go on to consider how the type, once set, would have been used to print the pages of the book, and how corrections to the text might have been introduced during printing (thus leaving, for instance, half of the copies of a given book with a number of pages in an uncorrected state, and the other half of the copies with some or all of the corrected pages).

The bibliographer would then describe how the printed sheets of paper were folded, cut and bound together to produce the final copy, how some of those printed sheets had, perhaps, been kept back as surplus to current requirements, and how those sheets might then have been used in a second edition – thus creating a hybrid in which some of the pages were from a new edition, and some were from the old.

All this knowledge would be derived from two sources. First, information comes from the close physical investigation of the book itself – its physical dimensions; the nature of its paper (colour, texture, watermarks, etc.); the typeface(s) and ornaments used; the way in which the signatures were arranged; page-layout and design; and so on. Secondly, bibliographers can call on the knowledge derived from historical investigations into how printing was and is carried out. (For example, our knowledge of the sort of subdivided trays used by type compositors – and thus which letters were next to which other letters – allows us to detect errors in printing created when a compositor picked up a letter adjacent to the one he actually wanted.)

This close, physical analysis of a given book or books, in the light of known printing practices, is called analytical bibliography, and is of fundamental importance in both bibliography in general and in textual editing.

Suggested reading

Greetham, Chapter 3, 'Making the Text: Bibliography of Printed Books' (pp.77–151) and Chapter 6, 'Reading the Text: Typography' (pp.225–70).

Selected reading

Greetham, Chapter 2, 'Making the Text: Bibliography of Manuscript Books' (pp.47–75) and Chapter 5, 'Reading the Text: Palaeography' (pp.169–224).

If you want to know more about the ancient and medieval book, consult:

David Diringer, *The Book Before Printing* (New York: Dover Publications, 1982). Originally published as *The Hand-Produced Book* (1953), this is a very comprehensive survey of text production – from clay tablets in Sumeria, through papyrus rolls in Egypt, Greece and Rome, the emergence of the parchment codex (book-form), through to medieval books up to *c.*1450 – and it includes a study of text production in the Orient and in Pre-Columbian America. It is to be dipped into rather than read in one go. (If you read nothing else in Diringer, do try the fascinating chapter on book production in Greece and Rome.)

Questions and exercises

1   Distinguish between the three main methods of printing – relief (for example, letterpress), intaglio (for example, engraving) and planographic (for example, lithography) – and suggest a rough date when each process was first used in Western Europe. Describe one of the processes in detail.

2   Define 'broadsheet', 'folio', 'quarto', 'octavo', 'duodecimo' and 'sixteenmo'. What does 'imposition' mean? Describe the imposition and folding of a single printed folio sheet.

3   How was paper made in Europe before 1800? What is the significance of chain lines and watermarks? How can you use them to work out the format of a given book?

4   Describe the job of a hand compositor; discuss the ways in which turning an author's manuscript into set type might lead to errors in the final printed text.

5   Take one change in book production technology that occurred in the period 1780–1900 (for example, the use of powered printing machines, or paper-making machines, or stereotyping or mechanical composition), describe the changes involved and evaluate the impact these changes had on the production of books.

6   Find and identify three forms of script written between the second and fifteenth centuries. Identify one or two characteristic letter forms for each. Give the period during which each script was commonly used. Consider the manuscripts from which the scripts came; for each, decide who was the most likely producer (slave, monk, etc.) and who was the most likely consumer (i.e. what was the manuscript used for, and who would have used it?).

7   Using the resources offered on the home page of the Koninklijke Bibliotheek (see The Open University's MA 'General Research Resources' page, 'Museums and visual resources'), look at three ways of illustrating books – by woodcuts, by engravings and by lithography. Explain

the different technologies involved in each. Can you find an edition of a Defoe novel or a Tennyson poem illustrated by one of these processes? Which process did it use, and how effective was that process in illuminating the text?

Descriptive bibliography

Analytical bibliography, as we have just seen, is concerned with the close analysis of individual copies of books in the light of our knowledge of how books were produced. However, for many reasons we should not assume that one copy of a book from a given edition is going to be identical to another copy from the same edition. This is particularly true of books published in the earlier centuries of printing when there were many more variations and inconsistencies in printing practices. For instance, when in 1968 Charlton Hinman published a facsimile 'ideal copy' of Shakespeare's First Folio, he had to photograph pages from no fewer than thirty copies of that work.

You meet a potential problem if you analyse just one copy of a book: not only may it be unlike the other copies from the same edition, it may also be incomplete. Until you have analysed a number of copies, you will not know whether your first copy was complete. From these doubts – as to whether single copies provide a sound basis for generalization about a particular edition – came the idea of the 'ideal copy'. Now the 'ideal copy' of a given edition does not mean a 'perfect copy' (few if any editions have ever come out of any printing works without a single error, misprinting or blemish). To use Roy Stokes's definition:

> Ideal copy is not concerned with matters governing the correctness of the text, or freedom from misprints, but simply with an assessment of the physical details of the book and their exact relationship to the state in which the book was planned to appear at the time of its initial publication.

This need to pursue and record the 'ideal copy' has given rise to a third type of bibliography – descriptive bibliography.

Descriptive bibliography is concerned with taking the information derived from analysis of a number of copies of the same work, creating out of these a description of an ideal copy, and then recording the bibliographical details of this ideal copy as precisely and as consistently as possible. The final product of an exercise in descriptive bibliography is commonly a comprehensive and exhaustive, not to say exhausting, account of all the editions in a particular area. The three most common areas are:

(a) the works of a single author (for example, *A Bibliography of Elizabeth Barrett Browning*; see Gaskell, pp.376–80).

(b) all the works within a particular genre (for example, *A Bibliography of the English Printed Drama to the Restoration*; see Gaskell, pp.368–70).

(c) all the works produced by a single press or, if the publisher was a large one and long-flourishing, the production of that press over a particular period (for example, *The Cambridge University Press, 1696–1712*; see Gaskell, pp.370–73).

As you will appreciate, such descriptive bibliographies are products of very slow and painstaking work. It would be impossible to record more than a fraction of the books produced by printing presses since the 1450s if all bibliographers were expected to be so thoroughly analytical and so comprehensively descriptive.

Suggested reading

Greetham, Chapter 4, 'Describing the Text: Descriptive Bibliography' (pp.153–68).

Gaskell, *A New Introduction to Bibliography*, 'Bibliographical Description' (pp.321–35).

Selected reading

Padwick, Chapters 12, 13 and 17; these provide a useful summary of the techniques of bibliographical description.

Fredson Bowers, *Principles of Bibliographical Description* (Winchester: St Paul's Bibliographies, 1986); first published by University of Princeton Press in 1949. This is one of the major works on the subject – comprehensive, thorough and somewhat daunting. But, if you are serious about descriptive bibliography, this is the book to have!

Questions and exercises

1 Select a book printed either in the eighteenth century or in the nineteenth, and write out a quasi-facsimile transcription of its title page.

2 Select a book printed either in the eighteenth century or in the nineteenth, and produce a collation formula for it.

3 Discuss the concept of an 'ideal copy'. What is the importance of this concept in descriptive bibliography?

4 What is the difference between an 'edition', an 'impression', an 'issue' and a 'state' (or 'variant')?

5 Before the nineteenth century, most reprints were separate editions; during and after the nineteenth century, most reprints were probably impressions. Why? And what significance has this fact for the bibliographer, the editor and the literary critic?

Historical bibliography

Greetham says that historical bibliography is sometimes described as 'the biology of books' (see p.7); but his second epithet, 'Darwinian', is in fact more accurate. Historical bibliography is strongly 'developmental': it is concerned with the way in which the various processes and materials involved in the construction of a book (themselves subjects of analytical bibliography) developed over time, and the way in which those developments affected the form and contents of the book. For example:

(a) the gradual introduction of paper; the spread of paper mills; the evolution of watermarks (as a means of dating undated or wrongly dated books); the development of paper-making machinery; the introduction of different paper-making materials in the nineteenth century (esparto grass, wood pulp, etc.). (See Greetham, pp.63–4, 138–9; Gaskell, pp.57–77, 214–30.)

(b) the evolution of typecasting; the development of the three main forms of typeface (gothic, roman, italic). (Greetham, pp.225–70; Gaskell, pp.9–39, 207–13, 283–8.)

(c) the development of the techniques of composing and imposing type; the evolution of work practices governing composition and printing; the evolution in the nineteenth century of type-composing machinery. (Greetham, pp.112–43; Gaskell, pp.40–46, 274–82.)

(d) the technical development of printing machinery; the change from wood to metal construction; the change from human-powered to steam-powered presses. (Greetham, pp.143–7; Gaskell, pp.143–5.)

(e) the development of the techniques of gathering, folding and sewing of the printed sheets. (Greetham, pp.119–35; Gaskell, pp.143–5.)

(f) the development of the different techniques of book illustration. (Greetham, pp.136–8, 147–51; Gaskell, pp.154–9, 266–73.)

(g) the evolution of different binding techniques and styles; the emergence of the publisher's standard casing in the nineteenth century. (Greetham, pp.135–8; Gaskell, pp.146–53, 231–50.)

All the above are merely examples of the sorts of study that historical bibliographers have to undertake if they are to understand the structure of the book and the changes it underwent through time. These historical studies, as you can imagine, feed back into all other forms of bibliography, particularly into analytical bibliography. Indeed, it would be daft to assert that any of the types of bibliography described above is an independent study: all of them are inextricably intermixed and interdependent. One sort of bibliographer will put a greater emphasis on one type of bibliography than on another, but that does not mean that he or she can ignore the others.

If you are interested in bibliography and its related disciplines, you should think of joining the Bibliographical Society whose journal, *The Library*, is one of the foremost publications in the field. There are also local bibliographical societies, such as those in Edinburgh, Oxford, Cambridge and Liverpool.

5 HISTORY OF THE BOOK

by Simon Eliot

This relatively new discipline extends some of the techniques of bibliography, which were discussed in Chapter 4, into a very large and challenging subject indeed. This is the historical study of the book in its economic, social and cultural contexts. In many ways this subject is so all-inclusive that it can, when practised well, absorb many aspects of bibliography and turn them to the service of what is, essentially, a new and distinct discipline.

The questions asked by this discipline are commonly much broader than those posed by conventional bibliography: how did the economic, technical and social context in which the book was produced affect its development, its content, its appearance and its reception? How did the book as a communicator of ideas, values and experience affect the society in which it emerged? Such questions highlight a fundamental distinction between books and almost any other artefact produced by society, a distinction which makes the historical study of books such a pressing and important subject. Unlike tables, chairs, bread, wine, guns, shoes, carpets or cars, books are intended to have *specific* intellectual and emotional effects on those who use (read) them. Books therefore consciously aim to influence, and sometimes to change, the economic, social or cultural circumstances in which they were produced. There is a feedback loop built into the relationship between society and its books which ensures that one generation of books will have an influence on the context in which the next generation of books appears, and so on.

The 'history of the book' is, perhaps, something of a misnomer, for the discipline could not, and does not, restrict itself to the study of books alone. Any printed text – whether it be a book, pamphlet, newspaper, magazine, handbill, broadsheet, printed form or raffle-ticket – can come within the notice of the book historian. Some of these examples may sound trivial until one begins to realize, for instance, how much of a local printer's time in the eighteenth century would have been taken up with the printing of legal forms for the local magistrate, or how much of a nineteenth-century jobbing printer's output would be in the form of raffle-tickets and advertising posters. The study of these printed ephemera, themselves an important aspect of the 'history of the book', has much to tell us of the way in which print intruded into the daily life of people who wouldn't even have thought of picking up a novel or reading a poem.

But even with that expansion of the discipline, the historian of the book still runs the risk of being parochial. What about the many centuries before printing? What about the slaves in ancient Rome, or Benedictine monks in the early medieval period, both quite capable of multiplying copies of books without the aid of any sort of mechanical press? To cut a long story short, the historian of the book is interested in any sort of text once it gets disseminated in whatever way society and technology allow – by writing, by printing, by photocopying, by cd-rom or by computer network.

At present the history of the book consists of a number of different but closely related areas of research. Among these are:

> *The history of printing.* This is concerned with all aspects of type-making and design, as well as with the history of the evolution of printing presses, and therefore shares many of its preoccupations with analytical and historical bibliography. Related to this area are the studies of the history of book-illustration, of paper-making and of book-binding.

> *Publishing and general book trade history.* This involves the study of the relationships between publishers (or 'booksellers' as they were known before about 1820), printers and authors, i.e. the way in which contracts were negotiated, copyrights (if any) were sold, profits divided. It is also concerned with the marketing of books (advertising and distribution), the development of the publisher's reader, and (in the nineteenth century) the role of the literary agent. It also includes all those other related activities such as bookselling, stationery-selling, jobbing-printing, advertising – and has much to say about the way in which these trades operated in the provinces.

> *The history of libraries.* This includes: the history of the great national and research collections (for example, the British Library or the Bodleian); the history of the great private collections (such as those created by cultured aristocrats in the eighteenth century); the history of the commercial libraries (for example, the 'circulating libraries' of the eighteenth and nineteenth centuries); and the development of the public library system (particularly after 1850, though there are eighteenth-century examples).

> *The history of reading.* This is a very tricky subject; what is meant here is not the history of literacy (although that is, of course, a relevant study), but rather the history of what people actually read in the past. (The distinction between buying or borrowing a book, and *reading* it, is important here.)

The history of the book is a subject that has evolved very rapidly in the last few decades. It first came to wide public notice in France with the publication of *L'Apparition du livre* in 1958 (translated in 1976 as *The Coming of the Book*) by Lucien Febvre and Henri-Jean Martin. France continued to take the lead, and was the first country to plan and publish a multi-volume book history (*Histoire de l'édition française*). However, in the last fifteen years the subject has begun to spread, and there are now major academic projects in a number of countries: in Great Britain a seven-volume *Cambridge History of the Book in Britain*, which is being published by Cambridge University Press (see Greetham, p.338), and a four-volume *History of the Book in the USA* is in preparation (also to be published by Cambridge University Press); in

Australia a *History of the Book in Australia* is being planned; and in Germany there are discussions on the proposal to publish a history of the book in Germany from 1870.

If you are interested in taking the subject of book history further, there are two societies (apart from the Bibliographical Society mentioned on p.48) that might be of interest to you:

- The Book Trade History Group (BTHG), which produces a newsletter three times a year. This concentrates on British book history and has sub-groups that study book history archives, and work on oral book history (by, for example, interviewing printers and publishers on conditions in the trade in the 1950s and 1960s). Membership secretary: Dr Elizabeth James, BTHG, British Library, 96 Euston Road, London NW1 2DB.

- The Society for the History of Authorship, Reading and Publishing (SHARP), which issues a quarterly newsletter. This is an international learned society which, however, tends to concentrate on Anglophone countries. It holds annual conferences, alternating (usually) between the UK and North America. For more information look at SHARP's Web page at:

  http://www.indiana.edu:80/~sharp/

As book history is a relative new interdisciplinary subject, there is much exciting new work to be done; some of this work, and not the least important, will be small-scale studies of individual local printers, publishers, booksellers in the eighteenth and nineteenth centuries. Small-scale studies of the publishing histories of lesser-known poets and novelists will also be of importance. If you are interested in local literary history, there might be a dissertation topic just waiting for you at your local reference library or record office.

If you were interested in such a topic, what sort of questions might you ask? (Remember, one of the best ways of writing a dissertation is to ask an interesting question, or set of related questions, and then try to answer them by your research.) As this book, by way of illustration, uses *Moll Flanders* and Tennyson's *Selected Poems*, the following questions are also based on these texts. Similar questions, with suitable amendments, could be asked of other texts and of other periods.

Questions that you might be thinking about

We are not wanting here to raise questions about historical determinism in literature, about how far one can explain the particular properties of each work of art by referring to the social and economic circumstances in which it was produced. Rather we are saying: if you talk about a collection of poems or a novel being 'popular', or 'read widely', or 'innovative', or 'firing the imagination of a generation' (if you can't resist such a dismal cliché), then you really ought first to ask yourself some questions. The following – in relation to *Moll Flanders* and *Selected Poems* – illustrate the point:

1 What was the format (i.e. size and number of volumes) of the first edition of *Moll Flanders*? Did all the volumes appear simultaneously? Was this a common form of publication? In other words, did many other works of fiction, appearing around the same time, adopt the same pattern?

2 Was *Moll Flanders* the product of a single publisher, or was it the product of a group of publishers (sometimes called a 'conger')? Some seventeenth- and eighteenth-century books were such valuable properties that booksellers bought shares in them (for example, *Tom Jones*). Sales of these shares sometimes took place. Was the novel in question subject to this sort of speculation?

3 Did the printer or bookseller who produced *Moll Flanders* specialize in the publishing of novels? If so, how many did he/she publish, and of what type? If not, what prompted him/her to publish this novel? What was the profile of the novel's publisher? (In other words, what else did he/she publish in the year in which the novel you are studying appeared?)

4 How was *Moll Flanders* publicized? Where was it reviewed? How and where was it sold? (Booksellers' lists are a good source of information on this.) Did the novel get into the libraries of the time and, if so, in what quantities?

5 How popular was *Moll Flanders*? How frequently was it reprinted? Was it always reprinted as a complete text?

6 What happened to eighteenth-century novels in the nineteenth century? How frequently, for instance, was *Moll Flanders* or *Tristram Shandy* reprinted? What happened to their texts (abridged, bowdlerized, etc.)?

7 Were novels really popular? How, for instance, would their sales and their readership compare with those of religious works, or of broadside ballads, in the same period?

8 Where was Tennyson's poetry most likely to be first published? In a newspaper, a magazine, a book? What was the immediate context of the poem? (In other words, what piece of news or what sort of article was juxtaposed to it?)

9 Taking one major work by Tennyson (for example, *In Memoriam*, *Maud*, *Idylls of the King*), ask yourself the following questions: How many copies were printed? How much did a copy cost? How many were sold? Was it reprinted? If so, how often and when?

10 How was Tennyson's work advertised and where was it sold?

11 Did Tennyson's work appear in the circulating libraries? If so, for how long was it available, and how many copies did the libraries take? Is it found in public libraries of the period? In what quantities?

12   What was the relationship between Tennyson and his publishers? Take
     one major work by Tennyson and ask the following questions: How
     much money did Tennyson make out of it? How was his next major
     work marketed?

13   Did any Victorian poet achieve the level of popularity enjoyed by such
     popular novelists as Dickens or M.E. Braddon?

Suggested reading

Because Greetham is not particularly strong on book history, you would be
wise to look elsewhere for your reading. Below we offer a number of titles
and suggest that you select one and read through the sections identified. If
you cannot get hold of any of the books listed here, look over the long list of
'Selected reading' and choose a couple of titles that cover the area of your
research topic or deal with a historical period in which you are interested.

> *The Encyclopaedia of Literature and Criticism*, essays by Sutherland, Feather,
> Cressy, Eliot, Klancher, Madden, Patterson and Hawkes (Section VII, 'Produc-
> tion and Reception').

> Gaskell, *A New Introduction to Bibliography* ('The English Book Trade to 1800',
> pp.171–85; 'The Book Trade in Britain and America since 1800', pp.297–310).

> Altick, *The English Common Reader* ('The Book Trade, 1800–1850', 'The Book
> Trade, 1851–1900': Chapters 12–13).

> John Feather, *A History of British Publishing* (London: Croom Helm, 1988);
> ('Licence and Liberty, 1695–1800', 'The First of the Mass Media 1800–1900':
> Parts Two and Three).

Selected reading

What follows is an attempt, under a number of general headings, to identify
aspects of book history that might be of particular interest to those studying
topics in literary history. If you want to pursue a literary critical dissertation, the information below should allow you to put your criticism in a
broader cultural context. If you are considering some form of editorial,
bibliographical or book history study, it should provide you with a number
of possible approaches and techniques.

1   Bibliography

> Robin Myers (ed.), *The British Book Trade from Caxton to the Present Day*
> (London: André Deutsch, 1973); a useful compilation, which includes works on
> individual publishers and publishing houses.

> Check also NCBEL 1.11, 'Book production and distribution'.

> Check bibliographies in *Encyclopaedia of Literature and Criticism* (between
> pp.809–937) and in Greetham.

2   The history of printing

Sean Jennett, *Pioneers in Printing* (London: Routledge and Kegan Paul, 1958); a bit 'pop', but quite good on the various innovations which affected the eighteenth and nineteenth centuries.

James Moran, *Printing Presses* (London: Faber and Faber, 1973); a comprehensive history of the evolution of printing machines.

Michael Twyman, *Printing 1770–1970* (London: Eyre and Spottiswoode, 1970); very helpful on how the developments in printing technique affected and reflected social changes over the period. Twyman is particularly good on ephemera; lots of magnificent illustrations.

3   Publishing and general book trade history

R.D. Altick, *The English Common Reader* (Chicago: University of Chicago Press, 1957); many editions since. Altick gives a witty and comprehensive introduction to the social history of the mass reading public in the period 1800–1900. There is a useful bibliography, and an index listing production runs for some of the nineteenth century's bestsellers, including a few poetry titles. Not always reliable, it nevertheless provides a good starting point for discussions about the relative popularity of poetry. Despite being rather limited on poetry, and somewhat out of date, Altick is still one of the best introductions to the subject.

Patricia J. Anderson and Jonathan Rose, *British Literary Publishing Houses 1820–1880* (London and Detroit: Gale, 1991); a very useful collection of short histories of British publishers of the period.

Lucy Brown, *The Victorian Newspaper* (Oxford: Clarendon Press, 1985); interesting short survey of an under-explored area.

Nigel Cross, *The Common Writer* (Cambridge: Cambridge University Press, 1985). In creating this study of minor and commonly impoverished writers of the late eighteenth and nineteenth centuries, Cross derived most of his information from the archives of the Royal Literary Fund.

Michael Crump and Michael Harris (eds), *Searching the Eighteenth Century* (London: The British Library, 1983); a series of essays which discusses how the ESTC can be searched for book history data, which it illustrates through a number of eighteenth-century topics.

Robert Darnton, *The Kiss of Lamouvette* (London: Faber and Faber, 1990); particularly Section 3, 'The printed word'.

Elizabeth L. Eisenstein, *The Printing Press as an Agent of Change* (Cambridge: Cambridge University Press, 1979).

Simon Eliot, *Some Patterns and Trends in British Publishing 1800–1919* (London: Bibliographical Society, 1994); quantitative book history, with detailed production figures (some per year) for poetry/drama, religion, fiction, etc.

John Feather, *The Provincial Book Trade in Eighteenth-Century England* (Cambridge: Cambridge University Press, 1985); a good, if brief, summary of what is known about this subject. Feather has been criticized for not using computer searches of the ESTC in his work.

John Feather, *A History of British Publishing* (London: Croom Helm, 1988); sometimes a little simplistic, but short and readable.

John Feather, *Publishing, Piracy and Politics* (London: Mansell, 1994); a useful introduction to the history of copyright in Britain.

Lucien Febvre and Henri-Jean Martin, *The Coming of the Book* (London: Verso, 1984). This is the English paperback version of a work originally published in Paris in 1958.

G.A. Glaister, *Encyclopaedia of the Book* (1960; London: Oak Knoll Press and The British Library, 1996). A useful reference work which concentrates on the physical aspects of the book.

June Steffenson Hagen, *Tennyson and his Publishers* (London: Macmillan, 1979). Not very impressive, but worth looking at, not so much for the interpretation of the data as for the data itself.

James Hepburn, *The Author's Empty Purse and the Rise of the Literary Agent* (London: Oxford University Press, 1968). Although concentrating on nineteenth-century novelists, Hepburn is very illuminating on the uneasy relationship between writers and their publishers.

John O. Jordan and Robert L. Patten (eds), *Literature in the Marketplace* (Cambridge: Cambridge University Press, 1995); a mixed bunch of essays, but provides a useful context.

Peter Keating, *The Haunted Study* (London: Secker and Warburg, 1989). This social history of the English novel, 1875–1914, is mostly about fiction, but is very good on the social context of late Victorian literature in general.

James Lackington, *Memoirs of the First Forty-Five Years of the Life of James Lackington* (London, 1791); marvellous confessional account of the types and techniques of bookselling in the eighteenth century.

Douglas C. McMurtrie, *The Book* (London: Bracken Books, 1989); 1st edn, 1943. This gives a broad introduction to the book as a physical object.

F.A. Mumby, *Publishing and Bookselling* (London: Jonathan Cape, 1954); 5th edn with additional material by Ian Norrie, 1974. Though a rather old-fashioned survey, this is at present all we have in this area.

Michael Olmert, *The Smithsonian Book of Books* (Washington, DC: Smithsonian Books, 1992); not always accurate, but superbly illustrated.

Marjorie Plant, *The English Book Trade*, 2nd edn (London: George Allen and Unwin, 1965). Though now out of date, this is the only book available if you want a broad survey of the trade.

Isabel Rivers (ed.), *Books and their Readers in Eighteenth-Century England* (Leicester: Leicester University Press, 1982).

J. Shattock and M. Wolff (eds), *The Victorian Periodical Press: Sampling and Soundings* (Leicester: University of Leicester Press, 1982).

J.A. Sutherland, *Victorian Novelists and Publishers* (London: Athlone Press, 1976); a seminal work in publishing history which reveals how a writer negotiates with a publisher and how the result can affect the way in which literature gets marketed.

Charles Wilson, *First with the News* (London: Jonathan Cape, 1985). This history of W.H. Smith and Son, written by a distinguished Cambridge business historian, is very good on bookselling and newspaper distribution; interesting on Smith's circulating library.

4   The history of libraries

Luciano Canfora, *The Vanished Library* (London: Hutchinson, 1989); a remarkable discussion of the Museum and Library at Alexandria and its impact on the canon.

G.L. Griest, *Mudie's Circulating Library and the Victorian Novel* (Bloomington and London: David and Charles, 1970). This is the best currently available introduction to that highly influential Victorian literary institution, the circulating library.

Raymond Irwin, *The English Library: Forces and History* (London: George Allen and Unwin, 1966); a brief but useful (though dated) introduction to the subject.

Paul Kaufman, *Libraries and their Users* (London: Library Association, 1969); an interesting series of studies of the wide variety of libraries available in the eighteenth century, and of the borrowers who used them.

Thomas Kelly, *A History of Public Libraries in Great Britain 1845–1975*, 2nd edn (London: Library Association, 1977). See particularly Books I and II. Kelly gives an interesting appendix which lists libraries and their dates of foundation.

Thomas Kelly and Edith Kelly, *Books for the People* (London: André Deutsch, 1977); essentially a concise, illustrated version of the above, with some remarkable photographs.

Edward Miller, *Prince of Librarians* (London: André Deutsch, 1967); an interesting biography of Antonio Panizzi, the mid-Victorian reforming librarian of the British Museum Library.

5   The history of reading

C.M. Cipola, *Literacy and Development in the West* (Harmondsworth: Penguin, 1969); useful introduction to the subject – short and accessible.

Robert Darnton, *The Forbidden Best-Sellers of Pre-Revolutionary France* (London: Harper Collins, 1996); a brilliant and entertaining demonstration of how reading-history might be practised.

Harvey J. Graff (ed.), *Literacy and Social Development in the West* (Cambridge: Cambridge University Press, 1981); a useful collection, which deals with the general impact of printing on society as well as discussing literacy rates.

Joseph McAleer, *Popular Reading and Publishing in Britain 1914–1950* (Oxford: Oxford University Press, 1992); a very sound and useful study of a hitherto under-researched area.

Alberto Manguel, *A History of Reading* (London: Harper Collins, 1996); over-general and over-anecdotal but it does have a broad sweep.

David Vincent, *Literacy and Popular Culture: England 1750–1914* (Cambridge: Cambridge University Press, 1989); a fascinating study of the ways in which the English working classes became literate.

It is worth keeping an eye on the leading journals in related fields as they frequently record the most recent research findings in the subject. The most notable are:

> *The Library* (London: the Bibliographical Society)
>
> *Library History* (Leeds: Maney Publishing)
>
> *The Papers of the Bibliographical Society of America* (New York: Bibliographical Society of America)
>
> *Publishing History* (Cambridge: Chadwyck-Healey)

Primary sources

The most important primary material for the study of literature is obviously literature itself. For book history there is a range of additional sources you ought to consider. A short selection is listed below.

Manuscript material

Much of this comes in the form of publishers' letters, readers' reports, account books and other business papers. Some of the major archives have been put onto microfilm and (at least roughly) indexed. The following list of microfilm archives is not exhaustive, but it should give you an idea of what's being done in the field. If you have the time and opportunity, you might like to have a look at some of it.

> *The Archives of British Publishers* (Cambridge: Chadwyck-Healey, 1975–). This includes the archives of:
>
> > Cambridge University Press, 1696–1902
> >
> > Kegan Paul, Trench, Trubner and Henry S. King, 1853–1912
> >
> > The House of Longman, 1794–1914
> >
> > Macmillan and Co., 1854–1924
> >
> > Elkin Matthews, 1811–1938
> >
> > George Routledge and Company, 1853–1902.
>
> Robin Myers (ed.), *Records of the Stationers' Company 1554–1920* (Cambridge: Chadwyck-Healey, 1985–6). The Stationers' Company was a guild of printers, booksellers, paper-makers and allied trades. Until the nineteenth century, most printers and booksellers registered details of each title they produced with the company, so its archives are an invaluable source of information about what was produced in the earlier centuries of printing.
>
> *Archives of the Royal Literary Fund 1790–1918*, compiled by Nigel Cross (London: University Microfilms, 1982). The RLF was set up in 1790 as a charity for the support of writers who had fallen into poverty. Its archives are full of fascinating cases which detail the lives of an interesting group of late eighteenth- and nineteenth-century writers.

Printed material

There is an enormous amount of information to be gained from contemporary sources (for example, catalogues, bibliographies and literary or trade magazines), and a reasonable amount to be gained from the modern catalogues of copyright libraries. One aim of studying the publishing history of a given work is to establish the number and timing of its editions and reprints (this helps in assessing its popularity and its influence). A straightforward survey of, say, *The Gentleman's Magazine* or *The Publishers' Circular* may reveal a reprint or even a new edition hitherto unknown simply because no modern library happens to possess a copy of it. The most important sources for such a reprint survey, in chronological order, are:

D. Foxon (ed.), *English Bibliographical Sources* (London, 1964–). This series reprints a number of eighteenth-century periodicals and journals which listed new publications (for example, *The Monthly Catalogue*, 1723–30; *The Gentleman's Magazine*, 1731–51; *The Monthly Catalogues from the London Magazine*, 1732–66).

Bent's Monthly Literary Advertiser, 1801–60

The Publishers' Circular, 1837–1959; a trade journal issued fortnightly from 1837, and weekly from 1891. Each issue gave a list of books first issued or reprinted in the previous fourteen days (in the previous seven days from 1891). At the end of each year these fortnightly lists were compiled into an annual list which was printed as a supplement to the *Circular* early in the following year. A microfiche edition of this journal has now been published: Simon Eliot and John Sutherland (eds), *The Publishers' Circular* and *The English Catalogue* 1837–1900 (Cambridge: Chadwyck-Healey, 1988).

The English Catalogue of Books; *The Publishers' Circular* lists were compiled every few years into a separate volume, and a set of volumes called *The English Catalogue* was the result. Being a compilation, it is inevitably less accurate than the original *Publishers' Circular* material. However, it has the advantage of being more widely available as the whole series was reprinted by Kraus Reprints (New York) in the 1960s. The original fortnightly lists were accumulated into yearly volumes, also called *The English Catalogue*. For the annual volumes up to 1900, see the Eliot and Sutherland edition referred to above.

The Bookseller, 1858–present; provides monthly lists of newly published books.

The Times listed, under the heading 'Books of the Day', some of the books published each day.

Weekly and monthly literary and critical journals are very useful for tracing the career of a book (through listings of new books, advertisements and reviews). In particular, look at (for the eighteenth century) *The Gentleman's Magazine* and (for the nineteenth century) *The Athenaeum*.

If none of these sources is available, you might try some of the largest modern catalogues:

The British Library General Catalogue of Printed Books to 1975. Despite being the premier copyright deposit library in Britain, the BL catalogue does not record all the reprint editions (certainly not of minor authors); it would be of some use if nothing else were available. This catalogue may be available to you in printed, cd-rom or networked (Intranet) form at your research library. It is now also available on the Web.

National Union Catalog. Being a union catalogue, this draws on a very wide range of US libraries and thus is, potentially, a much better source, although inevitably biased towards North American authors and editions. (For this reason it is rather good for listing the US 'pirate' editions of English authors, i.e. those editions produced without paying the author any copyright fee.) As with all union catalogues, it contains its fair share of bibliographical ghosts.

If none of the above is available, you could work your way through the resources listed in the Checklist in Chapter 16, under 'National bibliographies' and 'Printed library catalogues' (pp.209–212).

Some book history research projects

1 The Book Production Database (1836–1936)
This is an attempt to establish the costs of producing a book in the nineteenth century, and is based on a survey of the surviving production ledgers of major nineteenth-century publishers and printers (for example, Macmillans, George Bell and Son, Chatto & Windus). One year has been taken in each decade (1836, 1846, 1856, etc.) and a complete survey of that year's production has been made. This is now being loaded into a database so that we shall be able to plot the effects of the Industrial Revolution on the way in which books were financed, produced and marketed. This is not an abstract matter: the cost of production and distribution of a book affects its price, which determines who can buy it (or how they can borrow it), which in turn determines the readership of a book, its size and its social/cultural composition.

2 The Reading Experience Database, 1450–1914 (RED)
This joint venture, launched in 1996 by the Centre for the Book in the British Library and The Open University, is an attempt to catalogue as many examples as possible of the historical evidence for reading experience and practices in the past. What people read, how they read and how they reacted to their reading are very difficult matters to establish. There are no official statistics, no ledgers that record such experiences. The only way in which we can recapture such things is by finding references to the reading of particular books, newspapers, broadside ballads or advertising hoardings; these references may occur in diaries, journals, autobiographies or – and this is a very important source – in the books themselves in the form of annotations, marginal notes and flyleaf comments.

Given that much of this evidence is discovered accidentally, many of the contributions to RED will come as by-products of other research. However, systematic surveys of such sources as Pepys's diaries and the letters of Charles Dickens will also be made. RED is currently interested in reading experiences within the British Isles or the reading experience of those born in the British Isles between 1450 and 1914. It is a large and long-term project but, when it has been going for some years, it should produce fascinating insights into a very important subject about which we currently know very little indeed. RED will have much to contribute to the debate centred on reader-response criticism and reception theory (see Chapter 10).

Should you discover evidence of reading of the texts you are studying, then you could become a scholarly contributor to RED. Write to RED, Centre for the Book, British Library, 96 Euston Road, London NW1 2DB for a copy of the record form on which you can give your evidence. Alternatively you can use an electronic version of the record form, which can be found on the RED home page on the Web:

> http://www.open.ac.uk/OU/Academic/Arts/RED/

Questions and exercises

Try to tackle one of the questions below when you next visit your research library. You may not have time to write a full answer, but see how much of the necessary material for an answer you can collect; or, at least, see if you can establish where such material might be found and how you might use it. These questions cover the two periods relevant to *Moll Flanders* and Tennyson's *Selected Poems*.

Defoe and the eighteenth-century book

1   As far as you can, plot the publishing history to 1800 of either *Clarissa* or *Tristram Shandy*. In other words, find out how many editions and/or impressions were issued during the period. Were different publishers involved? (You might find a search of the ESTC, if available, helpful here.)

2   At what price was the first edition of *Moll Flanders* published? Were its subsequent editions published at the same price? When did it begin, if ever, to appear at a lower price?

3   Are there any records of printers operating in your locality in the eighteenth century? What sort of things did they print? Alternatively, were there any local booksellers in the same period? (The archives of local papers, if they exist and if they go back far enough, are a useful source for this; local trade directories can also be helpful. Do not underestimate the usefulness of local history collections and of county record offices.)

4   Using the same sources as in 3, can you discover whether there were any commercial (subscription) or public libraries in your area? If so, what did they contain and to whom did they lend?

5   If you have a great eighteenth-century house near you, does it still have its library? Perhaps the catalogue still exists. What can you learn of the

book-buying (if not book-reading) habits of the eighteenth century from such evidence?

6 Take one year of *The Gentleman's Magazine* and make a survey of its literary content. What books were discussed, and what books were listed? What are the limitations of using such evidence to establish the reading tastes of the time?

7 Using Gaskell's chapter on 'Presswork' (pp.118–41), write a brief description of how a book was printed on a common (wooden) press in the eighteenth century. Then set this technical process into its social context by reading Robert Darnton's entertaining essay, 'The Great Cat Massacre', in Robert Darnton, *The Great Cat Massacre* (Harmondsworth: Penguin, 1985).

Tennyson and the nineteenth-century book

(Note: inevitably, being a compilation, *The English Catalogue* is inherently less reliable than the lists originally printed fortnightly – and reprinted annually – in *The Publishers' Circular*. If you can get hold of *The Publishers' Circular*, use it in preference to *The English Catalogue*.)

1 Plot Tennyson's publishing history between 1840 and 1890 by referring to the entries in *The English Catalogue*. How many collections of his poems were issued? How frequently were they reprinted? How many publishers were involved? What can one infer about their respective popularity, and does that popularity (expressed in numbers of editions) vary from decade to decade?

2 Taking Tennyson as an example, discuss the pricing of books between *c*.1830 and *c*.1890. Are there evident changes? What is the price differential between first editions and reprinted editions? Does that differential change over the period?

3 With reference to one or two contemporary critical magazines (such as *The Athenaeum*, *The Saturday Review*), make a survey of one publisher's advertisements over a few months. How do they present poetry? Does it feature significantly in the advertisements, or is it overwhelmed by more marketable prose? How frequently are new books of poetry promoted? Is the poetry which receives most publicity the sort of poetry we now consider most worth reading?

4 Using *The Athenaeum*, take any five years between 1860 and 1900 and make a survey of Mudie's advertisements. Attempt to establish the circulating library's policy towards poetry by asking the same sort of questions as posed in Question 3.

5 See if you can find a printed catalogue issued by any public library in your area founded before 1900. Make a survey of its holdings in poetry, and from this try to infer the librarian's buying policy. If you can find the annual library reports for the same period, see what additional information, if any, these provide.

6 On what sort of machinery would Tennyson's *Oenone* have been printed in 1833? On what sort of machinery would Browning's *Asolando* have been printed in 1889?

7 Using the volumes of the *English Catalogue* which cover the years 1850–89, and taking Tennyson, Elizabeth Barrett Browning, Robert Browning, Clough, Arnold, Swinburne, Christina Rossetti, Dante Gabriel Rossetti and Meredith as a sample, find out the four publishers who issued the largest amount of poetry in terms of editions listed.

8 Using *The Publishers' Circular,* work out the publishing history of Tennyson's *The Princess* between its first edition and 1860. When precisely was it first issued? How many times was it reprinted, and what was the average gap between reprints? How much did its first edition cost, and how much was its cover price in 1860?

9 Using *The English Catalogue,* make a study of the publishing history of Fitzgerald's *Omar Khayyám* between 1859 and 1890. Remembering that, of the first edition of 250 copies, only 50 were sold at the asking price (the others were remaindered at a penny), what was the fate of the reprints? Try to find out the original price of the first edition and record the cover price of subsequent editions. Were any really cheap, popular editions (i.e. under a shilling) issued before the 1890s?

10 As a contrast, look at the history of a once popular but now all-but-forgotten poet – Martin Tupper. Can you compile a list of editions of his *Proverbial Philosophy* from 1838 to 1880? You could make a good start by looking at Appendix B of Altick, which has a reference to Tupper's work. How would Tupper's sales (based on the number of editions issued) have compared with Tennyson's or Browning's?

6 EDITING LITERARY TEXTS

by W.R. Owens

The preparation of reliable, scholarly texts is one of the most valuable tasks a literary scholar can undertake. Both general readers and professional literary critics concentrate on texts, and their work of interpretation or evaluation will be gravely damaged if these are corrupt or imperfect. The more detailed a critic's attention to the words of the text, the greater the need for textual accuracy. The US critic F.O. Matthiessen was famously caught out when he wrote admiringly of what he took to be a brilliantly incongruous image in Herman Melville's *White Jacket* – the 'soiled fish' of the sea. Unfortunately for Matthiessen, 'soiled' was the printer's invention: Melville had actually written 'coiled'.

Many important literary works are still read and studied in woefully undependable texts. The reasons why texts become corrupt are manifold. Consider some of the processes that an author's work may have gone through before it is finally published. First of all there is the author's manuscript or typescript, which may be full of scribbled deletions or additions, in indecipherable handwriting or wretched typing. This document is then 'edited' by someone at the publishers who will make various changes, including applying a 'house style' in matters of spelling and punctuation. When this 'copy edited' text comes before a compositor to be set in type, there are almost limitless opportunities for mistakes to creep in – in misreading the manuscript; in well-meant but mistaken attempts to 'correct' the author; or in setting wrong types. Words or whole sections may be left out, added, or set in the wrong order. Some of these mistakes may be corrected at proof-reading stage, but the author may also take this opportunity to change or add to the original text; and, in setting this fresh material, further errors may occur. All this means that even the first edition of a book seldom presents to readers the exact words as intended by its author. When it goes through subsequent editions, the errors of the first edition are often reproduced, and more errors introduced when it is reset, so that the longer texts are in print, the more corrupt they may become.

The job of textual scholars and editors, then, is to work towards the production of accurate editions of literary texts. This can be a highly complex and laborious task, requiring specialized skills, but it can also be very enjoyable and rewarding, and if you are attracted to it there may be opportunities for you to edit a text, or part of a text, yourself. As a postgraduate student, in any case, it is important that you have some general knowledge of the methods and aims of editors and textual scholars, so that, if for no other reason, you are able to assess the relative authority of the various available texts of the works you will be studying.

Let us begin by considering a specific example. I want you to imagine that you are preparing a scholarly edition of Daniel Defoe's novel *Moll Flanders*. Your aim is to present as accurate a text as possible of the novel as Defoe

(12)

At last one of the Ladies took so much Fancy to me, that she would have me Home to her House, for a Month she said, to be among her Daughters.

Now tho' this was exceeding kind in her, yet as my old good Woman said to her, unless she resolv'd to keep me for good and all, she would do the little Gentlewoman more harm then good: Well, says, the Lady, that's true, and therefore I'll only take her Home for a Week then, that I may see how my Daughters and she agree together, and how I like her Temper, and then I'll tell you more; and in the mean time, if any Body comes to see her as they us'd to do, you may only tell them, you have sent her out to my House.

This was prudently manag'd enough, and I went to the Ladies House, but I was so pleas'd there with the young Ladies, and they so pleas'd with me, that I had enough to do to come away, and they were so unwilling to part with me.

However, I did come away, and liv'd almost a Year more with my honest old Woman, and began now to be very helpful to her; for I was almost fourteen Years old, was tall of my Age, and look'd a little Womanish; but I had such a Taste of Genteel living at the Ladies House, that I was not so easie in my old Quarters as I us'd to be, and I thought it was fine to be a Gentlewoman indeed, for I had quite other Notions of a Gentlewoman now, than I had before; and as I thought, I say, that it was fine to be a Gentlewoman, follow'd to be among Gentlewomen, and therefore I long'd to be there again.

About the Time that I was fourteen Years and a quarter Old, my good old Nurse, Mother I ought rather to call her, fell Sick and Dyed; I was then in a sad Condition indeed, for as there is

(13)

no great Bustle in putting an end to a Poor Bodies Family, when once they are carried to the Grave so the poor good Woman being Buried, the Parish Children she kept were immediately remov'd by the Church-Wardens; the School was at an End, and the Children of it had no more to do but just stay at Home, till they were sent some where else; and as for what she left, her Daughter a married Woman with six or seven Children, came and swept it all away at once, and removing the Goods, they had no more to say to me, than to Just with me, and tell me, that the little Gentlewoman might set up for her self if she pleas'd.

I was frighted out of my Wits almost, and know not what to do, for I was, as it were, turn'd out of Doors to the wide World, and that which was still worse, the old honest Woman had two and twenty Shillings of mine in her Hand, which was all the Estate the little Gentlewoman had in the World; and when I ask'd the Daughter for it, she huft me and laught at me, and told me, she had nothing to do with it.

It was true, the good poor Woman had told her Daughter of it, and that it lay in such a Place, that it was the Child's Money, and had call'd once or twice for me, to give it me, but I was unhappily out of the way, some where or other; and when I came back she was past being in a Condition to speak of it: However, the Daughter was so Honest afterward as to give it me, tho' at first she us'd me Cruelly about it.

Now was I a poor Gentlewoman indeed, and I was just that very Night to be turn'd into the wide World; for the Daughter renov'd all the Goods, and I had not so much as a Lodging to go to, or a bit of Bread to Eat: But it seems some of the

(14)

the Neighbours who had known my Circumstances, took so much Compassion of me, as to acquaint the Lady in whose Family I had been a Week, as I mention'd above; and immediately she sent her Maid to fetch me away, and two of her Daughters came with the Maid tho' unsent; so I went with them Bag and Baggage, and with a glad Heart you may be sure: The fright of my Condition had made such an Impression upon me, that I did not want now to be a Gentlewoman, but was very willing to be a Servant, and that any kind of Servant they thought fit to have me be.

BUT my new generous Mistress, for she exceeded the good Woman I was with before, in every Thing, as well as in the matter of Estate; I say, in every Thing except Honesty; and for that, tho' this was a Lady most exactly Just, yet I must not forget to say on all Occasions, that the First tho' Poor, was as uprightly Honest as it was possible for any One to be.

I was no sooner carried away as I have said by this good Gentlewoman, but the first Lady, that is to say, the *Mayoress* that was, sent her two Daughters to take Care of me; and another Family which had taken Notice of me, when I was the little Gentlewoman, and had given me Work to do, sent for me after her, so that I was mightily made of, as we say; nay, and they were not a little Angry, especially, Madam the *Mayoress*, that her Friend had taken me away from her as she call'd it; for as she said, I was Hers by Right, she having been the first that took any Notice of me, but they that had me, won'd not part with me; and as for me, tho' I shou'd have been very well Treated with any of the other, yet I could not be better than where I was.

(15)

HERE I continu'd till I was between 17 and 18 Years old, and here I had all the Advantages for my Education that could be imagin'd: the Lady had Masters home to the House to teach her Daughters to Dance, and to speak *French*, and to Write, and others to teach them Musick; and as I was always with them, I learn'd as fast as they; and tho' the Masters were not appointed to teach me, yet I learn'd by Imitation and enquiry, all that they learn'd by Instruction and Direction. So that in short, I learn'd to Dance, and speak *French* as well as any of them, and to Sing much better, for I had a better Voice than any of them; I could not so readily come at playing on the Harpsicord or Spinnet, because I had no Instrument of my own to Practice on, and could only come at theirs in the intervals, when they left it, which was uncertain, but yet I learn'd tollerably well too, and the young Ladies at length got two Instruments, that is to say, a Harpsicord, and a Spinnet too, and then they Taught me themselves; But as to Dancing they could hardly help my learning Country Dances, because they always wanted me to make up even Number; and on the other Hand, they were as heartily willing to learn me every thing that they had been Taught themselves; as I could be to take the Learning.

By this Means I had, as I have said above, all the Advantages of Education that I could have had, if I had been as much a Gentlewoman as they were, with whom I liv'd, and in some things, I had the Advantage of my Ladies, tho' they were my Superiors; but they were all the Gifts of Nature, and which all their Fortunes could not furnish. First, I was apparently Handsomer than any.

HERE

Figure 6.1(a)
Moll Flanders: extract from the first edition

(10)

if they would give her leave, she would keep the Gentlewoman as she call'd me, to be her Assistant, and teach the Children, which I was very well able to do ; for I was very nimble at my Work, tho' I was yet very young.

But the Kindness of the Ladies did not end here, for when they understood that I was no more maintain'd by the Town as before, they gave me Money oftener ; and as I grew up, they brought me Work to do for them ; such as Linnen to Make, Laces to Mend, and Heads to Dress up, and not only paid me for doing them, but even taught me how to do them ; so that I was a Gentlewoman indeed, as I understood that Word ; for before I was Twelve Years old, I not only found my self Cloaths, and paid my Nurse for my keeping, but got Money in my Pocket too.

The Ladies also gave me Cloaths frequently of their own or their Childrens ; some Stockings, some Petticoats, some Gowns, some one thing, some another, and these my old Woman managed for me like a Mother, and kept them for me, obliged me to mend them, and turn them to the best Advantage, for she was a rare House-Wife.

At last one of the Ladies took such a Fancy to me, that she would have me Home to her House, for a Month, she said, to be among her Daughters. Now tho' this was exceeding kind in her, yet as my good Woman said to her, unless she resolv'd to keep me for good and all, she would do the little Gentlewoman more harm than good : Well, says the Lady, that's true, I'll only take her Home for a Week then, that I may see how my Daughters and she agree, and how I like her Temper, and then I'll tell you more ; and in the mean time, if any Body comes to see her as they us'd to do, you may only tell them, you have sent her out to my House.

This

(11)

This was prudently managed enough, and I went to the Lady's House, but I was so pleased there with the young Ladies, and they so pleased with me, that I had enough to do to come away, and they were as unwilling to part with me.

However, I did come away, and liv'd almost a Year more with my honest old Woman, and began now to be very helpful to her ; for I was almost fourteen Years old, was tall of my Age, and look'd a little Womanish ; but I had such a taste of Genteel living at the Lady's House, that I was not so easy in my old Quarters as I us'd to be, and I thought it was fine to be a Gentlewoman indeed, for I had quite other Notions of a Gentlewoman now, than I had before ; and as I thought that it was fine to be a Gentlewoman, so I lov'd to be among Gentlewomen, and therefore I long'd to be there again.

When I was about fourteen Years and a quarter Old, my good old Nurse, Mother I ought to call her, fell Sick and Dy'd ; I was then in a sad Condition indeed, for as there is no great Bustle in putting an End to a poor Body's Family, when once they are carried to the Grave ; so the poor good Woman being Buried, the Parish Children were immediately remov'd by the Church-Wardens ; the School was at an End, and the Day-Children of it had no more to do; but just stay at Home, till they were sent some where else ; as for what she left, a Daughter, a married Woman, came and swept it all away, and removing the Goods, they had no more to say to me than to Jest with me, and tell me, that the little Gentlewoman might set up for her self, if she pleased.

I was frighted out of my Wits almost, and knew not what to do ; for I was, *as it were*, turn'd out of Doors to the wide World. and that which was still worse, the old honest Woman had two and Twenty Shillings of mine in her Hand, which was

Figure 6.1(b)
Moll Flanders: extract from the second/third edition

(12)

was all the Eſtate the little Gentlewoman had in the World; and when I ask'd the Daughter for it, ſhe huſht me, and told me, ſhe had nothing to do with it.

IT was true the good poor Woman had told her Daughter of it, and that it lay in ſuch a Place, that it was the Child's Money, and had call'd once or twice for me to give it me, but I was unhappily out of the way, and when I came back ſhe was paſt being in a Condition to ſpeak of it: However, the Daughter was ſo Honeſt afterwards, as to give it me, tho' at firſt ſhe us'd me Cruely about it.

Now was I a poor Gentlewoman indeed, and I was juſt that very Night to be turn'd into the wide World; for the Daughter remov'd all the Goods, and I had not ſo much as a Lodging to go to, or a bit of Bread to Eat: But it ſeems ſome of the Neighbours took ſo much Compaſſion of me, as to acquaint the Lady in whoſe Family I had been; and immediately ſhe ſent her Maid to fetch me; and away I went with them Bag and Baggage, and with a glad Heart you may be ſure: The fright of my Condition had made ſuch an Impreſſion upon me, that I did not want now to be a Gentlewoman, but was very willing to be a Servant, and that any kind of Servant they thought fit to have me be.

BUT my new generous Miſtreſs had better Thoughts for me, I call her generous, for ſhe exceeded the good Woman I was with before in every Thing, as in Eſtate; I ſay, in every Thing except Honeſty; and for that, tho' this was a Lady moſt exactly Juſt, yet I muſt not forget to ſay on all Occaſions, that the firſt, tho' Poor, was as uprightly Honeſt as it was poſſible.

I was no ſooner carried away as I have ſaid by this good Gentlewoman, but the firſt Lady, *that is*
to

(13)

to ſay, the *Mayoreſs* that was, ſent her Daughters to take care of me; and another Family which had taken Notice of me when I was the little Gentlewoman, ſent for me after her, ſo that I was mightily made of; nay, and they were not a little Angry, eſpecially the *Mayoreſs*, that her Friend had taken me away from her; for as ſhe ſaid, I was hers by Right, ſhe having been the firſt that took any Notice of me; but they that had me, would not part with me; and as for me I could not be better than where I was.

HERE I continued till I was between 17 and 18 Years old, and here I had all the Advantages for my Education, that could be imagined; the Lady had Maſters home to teach her Daughters to Dance, and to ſpeak *French*, and to Write, and others to teach them Muſick; and as I was always with them, I learn'd as faſt as they; and tho' the Maſters were not appointed to teach me, yet 'l learn'd by Imitation and Enquiry, all that they learn'd by Inſtruction and Direction. So that in ſhort, I learned to Dance, and ſpeak *French* as well any of them, and to Sing much better, for I had a better Voice than any of them; I could not ſo readily come at playing the Harpſicord or Spinnet, becauſe I had no Inſtrument of my own to Practiſe on, and could only come at theirs in the Intervals when they left it; but yet I learned tollerably well, and the young Ladies at length got two Inſtruments, that is to ſay, a Harpſicord and a Spinnet too, and then they Taught me themſelves; but as to Dancing they could hardly help my learning Country Dances, becauſe they always wanted me to make up even Number; and on the other Hand, they were as heartily willing to learn me every thing that they had been Taught themſelves, as I could be to take the Learning.

BY

intended it. (We will return to the concept of 'intention' later, for it is a highly contentious one.) Your first task, evidently, is to examine all the versions of the novel to have appeared during Defoe's lifetime. You discover that it was first published in January 1722, but that it was obviously a popular work, for as early as July the same year there appeared 'The Second Edition Corrected', followed a few months later by a 'Third Edition, Corrected'. (There were in fact various other editions, serializations and abridgements during Defoe's lifetime, but these need not concern us for the purposes of the present exercise.)

The first problem facing you as an editor is how to decide which of these three editions to follow or, to use the technical term, which you should adopt as your 'copy-text'. You establish by close inspection that the first edition differs significantly from the second, but that the second and third editions are identical except for the title-pages (I will refer to them in what follows as the second/third edition). As a result, you decide to compare the first with the second/third edition to try to establish which is the more authoritative.

In Figures 6.1(a) and 6.1(b) you saw, reproduced in facsimile, extracts from the first edition, followed by the same extracts as they appear in the second/third edition. I'd like you to examine them both carefully, noting down any differences between them.

'Moll Flanders': facsimiles

As you can see, there are a number of small, but significant, differences between these two early versions of *Moll Flanders*. Quite a few words and phrases are cut in the second/third edition. There are also one or two additions. In particular, as you will have noticed, the sentence in the first edition (p.14) beginning 'But my new generous Mistress ... ' is obviously incomplete, and makes no grammatical sense as it stands. This error is corrected in the second/third edition (p.12).

The question you now have to consider is whether there is any reason to believe that Defoe himself was responsible for introducing the changes in the second/third edition. If you come to the conclusion that he was, you might decide to base your new edition on the text of this rather than on the first edition.

So what decisions have modern editors of *Moll Flanders* come to? If you have access to G.A. Starr's edition of *Moll Flanders* published in the Oxford World's Classics series (1981), you will find that, as well as including an 'Introduction' to the novel, Starr also includes a 'Note on the Text', pp.xxiii–xxix. Here Starr gives reasons for his choice of text and changes he has made to his chosen copy-text. Starr argues that, although most reprints of *Moll Flanders* have been based on the third edition, a close comparison of the early texts leads him to the conclusion that Defoe 'probably had no hand in the revisions' (p.xxv). It seems that the main reason for making the numerous small changes in the second/third edition was simply to shorten the text and thus reduce the cost of reprinting the book.

But although he uses the first edition as copy-text, Starr makes a number of important textual emendations (the term 'emendation' is used of any alteration made to a copy-text by a critical editor), some incorporating changes made in the second/third, some as a result of his own judgement. Details are given in footnote 13, p.xxvi, and footnote 15, p.xxviii. For example, as he explains, he has emended a sentence on p.281 where the first edition reading was clearly mistaken.

Oddly, though, if you compare the text of the passage from the first edition reproduced in Figure 6.1(a) with the same passage in Starr's text, you will see that Starr has chosen not to emend the equally defective sentence beginning 'But my new generous Mistress' (compare p.17 in Starr's edition, and see his explanatory note on p.352). My own view is that it would have been more consistent to have emended this sentence, either by deleting 'for she' or by incorporating the second/third edition reading, but – and this is an important point – including a note explaining to the reader exactly what the emendation is and why it had been made. The reader would then be in no doubt that there had been a departure from the copy-text in this instance, and would be in a position to make a judgement on the correctness or otherwise of the editor's decision.

This business of the presentation of textual variants and editorial emendations (usually referred to as the 'textual apparatus') brings me to an unfortunate weakness in the World's Classics edition of *Moll Flanders*. You may have noticed that Starr, in his Note on the Text (p.xxvii), says that 'In the Textual Notes (p.344 below)' he has selected 'approximately a third' of the 3,000 variants between the first and second/third editions to give readers an idea of the nature of these variants. If you turn to p.344 looking for these 'Textual Notes', you will find that it is a blank page! The explanation is that Starr's edition was originally published in 1971 as a volume in the Oxford English Novels series, and in that edition the 'Textual Notes' occupied pp.344–54, with the 'Explanatory Notes' following from p.355 on. When Oxford University Press reissued the edition in the World's Classics series, they obviously decided to cut out the Textual Notes but, although they repaginated the Explanatory Notes so that they follow straight on from the end of the text, they did not correct the mistaken reference to the non-existent 'Textual Notes' in the Note on the Text.

If you get hold of a copy of the 1971 edition in a library, you will be able to examine the Textual Notes; but the following extract will give you an idea of what they looked like. The references are to page and line number, and the first and second editions are represented by italic *1* and *2*. Thus, for example, the first note below refers to the phrase 'is made' on p.2, line 7, of the Oxford edition; the note following the square bracket tells you that Starr has followed the first edition reading, 'is made', but that in the second/third edition the words 'to be' were added between 'is' and 'made'. Next, on p.2, line 32, Starr has followed the first edition reading, 'other', though this was changed to 'another' in the second/third edition. In contrast, his third note – referring to p.3, line 29 – tells you that he has substituted the second/third edition's 'first or last' for the first edition's 'first and last', presumably on the grounds that it makes more sense. In cases where he follows neither the first nor second/third edition reading, as on 7.12 and 13.27, this is indicated by 'ed.'.

> 2.7 is made] is to be made *add*. 2.   2.32 other] another 2.
> 3.29 first or last 2: first and last 1.   5.10 Thieves purchase ...
> say, of]*om*. 2.   7. *title* HISTORY]FORTUNES 2.   7.12 Steps ...
> String, *ed*.: Steps, ... String 1: Steps ... String; 2.   7.13 knew 2:
> know 1.   8.12 nor] but 2.   8.25/6 in ... again,] after which 2.
> 8.28 Favour of] Favour afterward of *add*. 2.   9.35 had also
> 2: had also had 1.   10.4 Religiously] Religiously also *add*. 2.
> 10.28 where 2: were 1.   10.31 set] had set *add*. 2.   11.11
> Service,] Service at all *add*. 2.   11. 30 get at] get a Day at
> *add*. 2.   12.8 keep] find 2.   12.9 will] would 2.   13.2/3 took
> up] look'd upon 2.   13.4 any body knows,] I know; 2.
> 13.5 Gentlewoman's] Lady's 2.   13.16 that terrible Bug–bear]
> *om*. 2.   13.27 pleas'd to be familiar [with] me *ed*.: pleas'd to be
> familiar me 1: mightily pleased 2.   13.35 I understood by it no
> more *ed*.: I understood by it to no more 1: it was no more 2.
> 14.17 myself] my self besides *add*. 2.   14.22 and Humble;] *om*.
> 2.   14.30 and always Clean;] *om*. 2.   15.2/3 it ... say,] I was past
> it; for 2.   15. 4 she ... it] was enough 2.   15.8/9 and ... Needle,]
> *om*.2.   15.10 of the Town] *om*. 2.   15.28 so much] such a 2.
> 16.25 Children] Day-Children 2.   17.16/17 away, ... unsent] om.
> 2.   17.23 Mistress,] Mistress had better Thoughts for me, I call
> her generous, *add*. 2.   17.34/5 and had ... do,] *om*. 2.   18.4/5,
> tho' ... yet] *om*. 2.   18.33 but they] *Viz*. that mine 2.   19.7/8
> could ... sometimes] happened often 2.   20.2 begun] begin 2.
> 20.8 opener] open 2.   20.26 have] has 2.   20.27 have] has 2.
> 20.28 as 2: has 1.

From this example, let us draw together what we have learned about the work of scholarly editors. We have seen that they have to examine in minute detail copies of all surviving editions of the work published in the author's lifetime – and if any manuscripts are extant, these would have to be taken into consideration also. The aim of all this often very laborious comparison is to decide which of these early versions should be selected as the copy-text upon which a single new edition can be based. The question of how to select a copy-text has been much debated. In a famous essay, 'The Rationale of Copy-Text', first published in *Studies in Bibliography*, 3 (1950–51), pp.19–36, W.W. Greg drew a distinction between the 'substantives', that is the words of a text, and the 'accidentals' – the punctuation, spelling, capitalization and such typographical matters as the use of italics. In the majority of cases,

Greg argued, while an author may change words and whole passages in editions after the first, he or she is unlikely to scrutinize the accidentals in subsequent editions.

In such cases, assuming that the manuscript has not survived and that there is no convincing evidence that the author substantially changed the punctuation etc. in a later edition, the editor will usually choose as copy-text the first published edition, since it will transmit most accurately the accidentals of the manuscript from which it was set. This is not to say that the first edition reproduces the manuscript without alteration. There will almost certainly be changes and errors in it, but in the absence of other evidence to the contrary it must, according to Greg, be regarded 'within reason' as the basic authority. What the editor then does is to emend this copy-text in various ways, notably by substituting readings which seem likely to have been introduced or sanctioned by the author in later editions, and by correcting obvious errors and supplying new readings where the editor believes that these represent more faithfully the author's intended meaning.

An edition produced in this way is called a 'critical' edition, which is to say that every word and 'accidental' of the text has been examined critically by the editor, who may have altered certain readings in the copy-text after a considered assessment of all the available evidence. Such an edition will include a 'textual introduction' (or 'Note on the Text'), which will describe all the texts that have textual authority or significance, indicate the reasons for the choice of copy-text, and point out the nature and scope of the editor's emendation of the copy-text.

Also included will be an amount of textual apparatus. This will vary between editions, but essentially it will comprise a record of all emendations, and all significant variant readings in texts which carry textual authority. Such apparatus may be presented at the foot of the page, or gathered together at the back of the book, but the purpose of recording it is to provide all the information necessary to enable the reader to evaluate and reconsider the textual decisions made by the editor. In addition to the provision of textual information, which is of primary importance, the editor will usually provide an introduction to the work being edited and such explanatory annotation as seems appropriate.

The most influential exponent of Greg's editorial principles has been the US scholar Fredson Bowers. What has come to be called the 'Greg–Bowers' school of textual scholarship dominated the practice of Anglo-American scholarly editing for most of the twentieth century, and the edition of *Moll Flanders* which we have been examining is an example of this approach. However, in recent years there has been a growing body of dissent from the 'Greg–Bowers' emphasis on the production of a single, 'eclectic' edition in which certain readings are 'privileged' by being incorporated into the 'definitive' reading text, while others are relegated to the textual apparatus

as 'variants'. There are certainly some literary works which do not seem to
be amenable to an approach aiming at a single definitive text.

One such example, which I would like you to consider briefly, is Samuel
Richardson's famous novel *Pamela* (1740). Richardson had his own printing
business, and not only printed his own novels but was continually revising
them, so that there are changes in the text of nearly every edition published
in his lifetime. The three facsimile extracts in Figures 6.2(a)–(c) are (a) from
the first edition of 1740; (b) from a modern edition based on an edition
which appeared *c.*1810, which in turn was based on the 'eighth' edition of
1762; and (c) from a modern edition based on an edition not published until
1801, but which reproduced a text that had been extensively revised by
Richardson before his death in 1761. I'd like you to read each version, noting
variations in the text, and also making some notes about what effect these
changes have on the literary style and content of the passage.

Figure 6.2(a)
Pamela: extract from the
first edition, of 1740

I was hush; but she said, Pr'ythee, my good Girl, make haste to-bed. See if the Door be fast. So I did, and was thinking to look in the Closet; but hearing no more Noise, thought it needless, and so went again and sat myself down on the Bedside, and went on undressing myself. And Mrs. *Jervis* being by this time undrest, stept into Bed, and bid me hasten, for she was sleepy.

I don't know what was the Matter; but my Heart sadly misgave me; but Mr. *Jonathan's* Note was enough to make it do so, with what Mrs. *Jervis* had said. I pulled off my Stays, and my Stockens, and my Gown, all to an Under-petticoat; and then hearing a rustling again in the Closet, I said, God protect us! but before I say my Prayers, I must look into this Closet. And so was going to it slip-shod, when, O dreadful! out rush'd my Master, in a rich silk and silver Morning Gown.

I scream'd, and run to the Bed; and Mrs. *Jervis* scream'd too; and he said, I'll do you no harm, if you forbear this Noise; but otherwise take what follows.

Instantly he came to the Bed; for I had crept into it, to Mrs. *Jervis*, with my Coat on, and my Shoes; and taking me in his Arms, said, Mrs. *Jervis*, rise, and just step up Stairs, to keep the Maids from coming down at this Noise; I'll do no harm to this Rebel.

O, for God's sake! for Pity's sake! Mrs. *Jervis*, said I, if I am not betray'd, don't leave me; and, I beseech you, raise all the House. No, said Mrs. *Jervis*, I will not stir, my dear Lamb; I will not leave you. I wonder at you, Sir, said she, and kindly threw herself upon my Coat, clasping me round the Waist, you shall not hurt this Innocent, said she; for I will lose my Life in her Defence. Are there not, said she, enough wicked ones in the World, for your base Purpose, but you must attempt such a Lamb as this!

He was desperate angry, and threaten'd to throw her out of the Window; and to turn her out of the House the next Morning. You need not, Sir, said she; for I will not stay in it. God defend my poor *Pamela* till To-morrow, and we will both go together.—— Says he, let me but expostulate a Word or two with you, *Pamela*. Pray, *Pamela*, said Mrs. *Jervis*, don't hear a Word, except he leaves the Bed, and goes to the other End of the Room. Aye, out of the Room! said I; expostulate To-morrow, if you must expostulate!

I found his Hand in my Bosom, and when my Fright let me know it, I was ready to die; and I sighed, and scream'd, and fainted away. And still he had his Arms about my Neck; and Mrs. *Jervis* was about my Feet, and upon my Coat. And all in a cold, clammy Sweat was I. *Pamela, Pamela!* said Mrs. *Jervis*, as she tells me since, O—h, and gave another Shriek, my poor *Pamela* is dead for certain!——And so, to be sure, I was for a time; for I knew nothing more of the Matter, till about three Hours after, as it prov'd to be, I found myself in Bed, and Mrs. *Jervis* sitting up on one side, with her Wrapper about her, and *Rachel* on the other; and no Master, for the wicked Wretch was gone. But I was so over-joy'd, that I hardly could believe myself; and I said, which were my first Words, Mrs. *Jervis*, Mrs. *Rachel*, can I be sure it is you? God be prais'd! God be prais'd!—— Where have I been? Hush, my Dear, said Mrs. *Jervis*, you have been in Fit after Fit. I never saw any body so frightful in my Life!

I was hush; but she said, "Pr'ythee, my good girl, make haste to bed. See if the door be fast." I did, and was thinking to look into the closet; but, hearing no more noise, thought it needless, and so went again and sat myself down on the bed-side, and went on undressing myself. And Mrs. Jervis, being by this time undressed, stepped into bed, and bid me hasten, for she was sleepy.

I don't know what was the matter, but my heart sadly misgave me: indeed, Mr. Jonathan's note was enough to make it do so, with what Mrs. Jervis had said. I pulled off my stays, and my stockings, and all my clothes to an under-petticoat; then hearing a rustling again in the closet, "Heaven protect us! But before I say my prayers I must look into this closet." And so was going to it slip-shod, when, O dreadful! out rushed my master in a rich silk and silver morning-gown.

I screamed, ran to the bed, and Mrs. Jervis screamed too; he said, "I'll do you no harm if you forbear this noise; but otherwise take what follows."

Instantly he came to the bed (for I had crept into it, to Mrs. Jervis, with my coat on and my shoes), and taking me in his arms, said, "Mrs. Jervis, rise, and just step up stairs, to keep the maids from coming down at this noise: I'll do no harm to this rebel."

"O for Heaven's sake! for pity's sake! Mrs. Jervis," said I, "if I am not betrayed, don't leave me; and, I beseech you raise all the house."—"No," said Mrs. Jervis, "I will not stir, my dear lamb; I will not leave you. I wonder at you, Sir," said she; and kindly threw herself upon my coat, clasping me round the waist. "You shall not hurt this innocent," said she; "for I will lose my life in her defence. Are there not," said she, "enough wicked ones in the world, for your base purpose, but you must attempt such a lamb as this?"

He was desperate angry, and threatned to throw her out of the window; and turn her out of the house the next morning. "You need not, Sir," said she; "for I will not stay in it. God defend my poor Pamela till to-morrow, and we will both go together."—Says he, "Let me but expostulate a word or two with you, Pamela."—"Pray, Pamela," said Mrs. Jervis, "don't hear a word, except he leaves the bed, and goes to the other end of the room.","—"Aye, out of the room," said I, "expostulate to-morrow, if you must expostulate!"

I found his hand in my bosom, and when my fright let me know it, I was ready to die; I sighed, screamed and fainted away. And still he had his arms about my neck; Mrs. Jervis was about my feet, and upon my coat. And all in a cold dewy sweat was I. "Pamela! Pamela!" says Mrs. Jervis, as she tells me since,—"Oh!" and gave another shriek, "my poor Pamela is dead for certain!" And so I was for a time; for I knew nothing more of the matter, one fit followed another, till about three hours after, I found myself in bed, and Mrs. Jervis sitting up on one side, with her wrapper about her, and Rachel on the other; but no master, for the wicked wretch was gone. I was so overjoyed that I hardly could believe myself; I said, which were my first words, "Mrs. Jervis—Mrs. Rachel, can I be *sure* it is you? Tell me, can I?—Where have I been?" —"Hush, my dear," said Mrs. Jervis; "you have been in fit after fit. I never saw any body so frightful in my life!"

Figure 6.2(b) *Pamela*: extract from the 'Everyman'/early nineteenth-century edition

I was hush! but she said, 'Pr'ythee, my good girl, make haste to-bed. See if the door be fast.' I did, and was thinking to look in the closet; but hearing no more noise, thought it needless, and so went again and sat myself down on the bed-side, and proceeded to undress myself. And Mrs Jervis, being by this time undressed, went into bed, and bid me hasten, for she was sleepy.

I don't know why, but my heart sadly misgave me: indeed, Mr Jonathan's note was enough to make it do so, with what Mrs Jervis had said. I pulled off all my clothes to an under petticoat; and then hearing a rustling again in the closet, I said, 'Heaven protect us! but I must look into this closet, before I come to bed.' And so was going to it slip-shoed,[62] when, O dreadful! out rushed my master, in a rich silk morning gown.[63]

I screamed, and ran to the bed; and Mrs Jervis screamed too; and he said, 'I'll do you no harm, if you forbear this noise; but other-wise take the consequence.'

Instantly he came to the bed-side (for I had crept into it, to Mrs Jervis, with my coat[64] on, and my shoes); and, taking me in his arms, said, 'Mrs Jervis, rise, and just step up stairs, to keep the maids from coming down at this noise: I'll do no harm to this rebel.'

'O, for heaven's sake! for pity's sake! Mrs Jervis,' said I, 'if I am not betrayed, don't leave me; and, I beseech you, raise all the house!'

'No,' said Mrs Jervis, 'I will not stir, my dear lamb; I will not leave you. I wonder at you, sir!' and kindly threw herself upon my coat, clasping me round the waist. 'You shan't hurt this innocent; for I will lose my life in her defence. Are there not,' added she, 'enough wicked ones in the world for your base purpose, but you must attempt such a lamb as this!'

He was in a rage, and threatened to throw her out of the window; and to turn her out of the house the next morning. 'You need not, sir,' said she; 'for I will not stay in it. God defend my poor Pamela till to-morrow, and we will both go together.' 'Let me, Pamela,' said he, 'expostulate with you but one moment.' 'Pray, my dear,' said Mrs Jervis, 'don't hear a word, except he leaves the bed, and goes to the other end of the room.'

Mrs Jervis was about my feet, and upon my coat. The wicked wretch still had me in his arms. I sighed, and screamed, and then fainted away.

'Pamela! Pamela!' said Mrs Jervis, as she tells me since, 'O—h!' and gave another shriek, 'my poor Pamela is dead for certain!'

And so, to be sure, I was for a time; for I knew nothing more (one fit following another) till about three hours after, as it proved to be, I found myself in bed, and Mrs Jervis sitting up on one side, with her wrapper[65] about her, and Rachel on the other; and no master, for the wicked wretch was gone. But I was so overjoyed, that I hardly could believe myself; and I said, (which were my first words), 'Mrs Jervis, can I be *sure* it is you? Rachel, can I be *sure* it is you? Tell me! can I? Where have I been?'

'Hush, my dear,' said Mrs Jervis; 'you have been in fit after fit. I never in my life was so frightened.'

Figure 6.2(c)   *Pamela*: extract from the latest text revised by Richardson

'Pamela': facsimiles

I would guess that the first thing to strike you is that version (c) is very unlike the first two versions. Much of the overtly sexual impact of the encounter has been toned down: her master no longer puts his hand in Pamela's 'bosom', for example. Pamela's language has become more restrained: 'He was desperate angry' becomes 'He was in a rage'; her vigorous rejoinder to her master's offer to 'expostulate a Word or two' is omitted altogether; her frequent use of the word 'God' is changed or dropped after the first edition. These changes affect the presentation of the leading characters significantly. The actions of her master in the final version seem less reprehensible, while Pamela seems more refined, less like a young servant.

I imagine that, after doing this little exercise, you will agree that the text of *Pamela* from which the (c) extract comes is so different from the text of the first edition in extract (a) that it is impossible to speak of *one* text of *Pamela*. This being the case, what is a prospective editor of the novel to do? It is obvious, I take it, that the existing texts cannot simply be amalgamated, because Richardson's revisions are far too numerous and extensive, amounting almost to a rewriting.

You might like to consider the editor's problem for a minute or two, and jot down which text (or texts) modern editions should be based on, and why you think this. Two things you might take into account are: first, the author's intentions; and second, the readership your modern edition is designed for.

The question of *author's intentions* enters into our thinking here because, as we have seen from our work on *Moll Flanders,* it is a pretty basic axiom of scholarly editing that the reproduction of a writer's work should fulfil as far as possible his or her intentions – which is usually, but by no means necessarily, interpreted to mean *final* intentions. It seems clear in this case that the version of *Pamela* published in 1801, after Richardson's death, most faithfully represents his final intentions. To some extent it can be seen as the culmination of a process of authorial revisions which was begun in the second edition. If you decided that this final version is the text upon which the editor should base a scholarly edition, you have made a defensible choice, and in fact extract (c) is taken from the 1980 Penguin edition, whose editor, Peter Sabor, has done just this.

On the other hand, you may have decided that the first edition should be the copy-text, and that the editor should prepare an edition which aims to reproduce as accurately as possible the text in which *Pamela* first appeared, correcting only obvious printer's errors, misspellings and so forth. This again would be an eminently defensible choice. Here you are concerned less with the author's final intentions than with offering to modern readers the opportunity to read the text which Richardson originally 'intended', the one which created such a sensation when it was first published. It is no doubt arguable that the final version of *Pamela* is in some respects a more polished work of art; the Richardson who carried out these revisions had behind him the vast experience of writing *Clarissa* and *Sir Charles Grandison*. Certainly anyone wishing to trace in detail the development of Richardson's art as a novelist will want to compare the various editions, but I think his biographers are right to conclude that the first edition 'is closer to the *Pamela* whom Richardson actually imagined, whereas all succeeding texts try to approach the *Pamela* he thought he should have imagined' (T.C. Duncan Eaves and B.D. Kimpel, 'Richardson's revisions of *Pamela'*, *Studies in Bibliography*, 20 (1967), 61–88).

The conclusion we've reached, then, is that *ideally* students of Richardson require two editions of *Pamela* – one of the first edition, the other of the final, 1801 edition. And it hardly needs saying, except that it is sometimes forgotten, that students ought to check carefully which edition they are using. It would be rather pointless to write a detailed account of the style of *Pamela*, drawing conclusions about Richardson's early craftsmanship, using an edition such as the Penguin – where the text is one that had been virtually rewritten at the height of his artistic maturity.

As we have seen with *Moll Flanders*, any good scholarly edition will have (as well as an introduction) a 'Note on the Text' where the editor will usually outline the printing history of the book, and will state which edition the text is based on. If you look at a copy of the Penguin *Pamela*, you will find this information on pages 21–2. The only other edition of *Pamela* available (at the time of writing) to British readers is the Dent 'Everyman' edition, first published in 1914 and reset, with a new introduction, in 1962. This edition gives no information about which text it is based on, and the absence of such information should be enough to make you avoid this text for scholarly purposes. In fact it has been shown that it reprints a version of *Pamela* which had been published early in the nineteenth century (Peter Sabor, 'The Cooke–Everyman edition of *Pamela'*, *The Library*, fifth series, 32 (1977), 360–66). This nineteenth-century version in turn derived from the 'eighth' edition of 1762, but the 1762 text was extensively cut, there were thousands of alterations of words, and direct speech was enclosed in inverted commas. The extract (b) above is from this 'Everyman'/early nineteenth-century edition, and you have noted the effect of introducing some of these changes. Philip Gaskell is perhaps being a shade melodramatic when he describes this as 'a text of hair-raising inaccuracy', but I hope you can now see why it is essential to use a properly edited, scholarly text wherever possible (Philip Gaskell, *From Writer to Reader: Studies in Editorial Method*, Oxford: Clarendon Press, 1978, p.77).

What this encounter with the text(s) of *Pamela* has brought up sharply is the vexed question of author's *intentions*, and the problem of intentionality has been at the heart of much of the recent debate about textual editing. You will find a useful outline of the various opposing points of view on this issue in D.C. Greetham, *Textual Scholarship: An Introduction* (New York and London: Garland, 1994) (see especially pp.335–46, 352–7). At the risk of oversimplifying, the two main sides in the debate may be labelled the 'intentionalist' and the 'social product' schools of thought.

Up to now, what I have been presenting to you is the approach that 'intentionalist' editors and textual critics have been taking for centuries. They might have argued among themselves about what to do when it seemed that authors had substantially changed their intentions over time (as in the case of Richardson), but it was accepted by all that the aim was to establish texts as intended by their authors. Where the surviving versions of the text were faulty or incomplete, it was the duty of editors to attempt to reconstruct what the author might plausibly be assumed to have intended. The emphasis of this approach, it will be seen, is on the individual creator, or 'author', of the work being edited.

More recently, however, a number of textual scholars have begun to question this emphasis on the intentions of a single author. Two of the scholars most prominently associated with this 'revisionist' school of thought are D.F. McKenzie, especially in his *Bibliography and the Sociology of Texts* (London: British Library, 1986), and Jerome J. McGann, especially in *A Critique of Modern Textual Criticism* (Chicago: University of Chicago Press, 1983; reprinted, Charlottesville: University Press of Virginia, 1992). Literary works, according to McKenzie and McGann and their followers, are not solely the productions of individual 'authors': they are presented to readers as a result of the efforts of a large number of people – copyists, editors, printers, publishers, etc. – all of whom may in various ways make alterations to the text. This 'social' process continues as new and different forms of a work appear, handled by different publishers and read in various forms by successive generations of readers.

This attempt to shift the focus of editing away from an emphasis on individual authors, and single 'canonical' works, may be seen to relate to larger developments in literary theory, for example deconstruction, New Historicism and reader-response or reception studies. A number of recent books have begun to explore in detail these connections between literary theory and theories of editing texts, for example *Devils and Angels: Textual Editing and Critical Theory*, ed. Philip Cohen (Charlottesville: University Press of Virginia, 1991). One such connection is the idea that texts are fundamentally unstable – that they are processes rather than fixed, single objects. If this were true, it would obviously have large consequences for the presentation of scholarly editions.

It is at this point that the computer really comes into the picture, offering the possibility of editions available on the Internet or on cd-rom, which would allow a reader interactive access to all the variant states of a given text, and associated materials for its study. Plans for several such 'hypertext' editions are under way, and there is no doubt that they will make an enormous amount of data available to readers. For example, an edition of Chaucer's *Canterbury Tales*, being published by Cambridge University Press as a series of cd-roms, will include digitized images and transcriptions of all 84 known manuscripts and the four pre-1500 printed editions of the work – some six million words and 30,000 manuscript pages. As the 'editor' of this work explains, 'the balance of power in editing has shifted from presenting the text as a single editorial artefact, to presenting the text as a series of manuscript objects' (Peter M.C. Robinson, 'Manuscript Politics' in *The Politics of the Electronic Text*, ed. Warren Chernaik, Caroline Davis and Marilyn Deegan, Oxford: Office for Humanities Communication, 1993, pp.9–15).

Proposals for hypertext editions of Shakespeare are moving in a similar direction. The 'Shakespeare Electronic Archive', founded at MIT in 1992, is promising to provide readers with all the surviving early texts of the plays together with documents charting the changing reception of each play, and records of Elizabethan and subsequent theatrical and cultural practice. Such 'editions' open up dizzying vistas of readerly freedom where, effectively, each reader will become a do-it-yourself editor! This, at least, is the argument of one enthusiast, who claims that, because of its interactive nature, hypertext may be said to empower the reader: 'the reader calls forth his or her own text out of the network, and each such text belongs to one reader and one particular act of reading' (Jay David Bolter, *Writing Space: The Computer, Hypertext, and the History of Writing*, Hillsdale, New Jersey: Lawrence Erlbaum Associates, 1991, quoted in *The Politics of the Electronic Text*, p.6).

The case in favour of what may best be described as 'hypermedia archives', rather than editions, has been put strongly by, among others, Jerome McGann. In an important essay entitled 'The Rationale of Hypertext' (in *Electronic Text*, ed. Kathryn Sutherland, Oxford: Clarendon Press, 1997), he argues that the shift now taking place from paper-based text to electronic text will come to be seen as a revolution comparable to the shift from manuscript to print. In his view, the physical constraints of printed scholarly editions have meant that the works of many authors have been represented very inadequately. He discusses the examples of Robert Burns, William Blake, Emily Dickinson and Laetitia Elizabeth Landon as authors who operated in more than one medium, and whose literary achievements are fundamentally misrepresented in traditional typographical editions.

The article also includes illustrations drawn from his own ambitious project, *The Complete Writings and Pictures of Dante Gabriel Rossetti: A Hypermedia Research Archive*. This is designed to bring together digital images of manuscripts, printed texts, sketches, oil paintings and other documents in a decentralized 'hypertext' structure, in which no part is privileged over another, and the reader is encouraged to *make* order, rather than find order. A sample from the archive is available, as a demonstration model, on the Internet at

http://jefferson.village.virginia.edu/rossetti/rossetti.html

There is no doubt that the advent of the computer has changed the way in which textual editors work. For example, being able to store and manipulate texts in electronic form means that the laborious task of collating texts is easier and quicker. Whether it will change fundamentally the ways in which editions of literary works are published and read is another matter. For all the limitations of the print medium, the great critical editions are some of the most distinguished achievements of literary scholarship. It remains to be seen just how useful (or usable) the new electronic 'archives' will prove to be. The argument between those who see the function of scholarly editions as being to present works of art as *process*, and those who see it as being to present them as *product*, may be only just beginning.

Questions and exercises

1   'A correct text is the first object of an editor' (Wordsworth). Using a work (or works) by one author as an example, discuss some of the problems an editor may face in attempting to produce a 'correct' text.

2   Give an account of recent debates among textual scholars about the concept of authorial intentions.

3   Choose one literary work and compare several available editions (if possible including a full-scale scholary one), discussing how they differ.

4   Electronic hypertext editions of the works of several authors are currently being planned. Try to find out about one of these, and give an account of what such an edition might offer.

5   Take a look at Jerome McGann's sample of his editorial work on Dante Gabriel Rossetti on the World Wide Web:

    http://jefferson.village.virginia.edu/rossetti/rossetti.html

    How effective is it in presenting a scholarly argument? Is the use of hypertext and multimedia on the WWW or on cd-rom the way forward for the next generation of scholarly editions? Are there any drawbacks to the use of this technology as far as the editor or his or her readers are concerned?

6   Choose one literary work and illustrate with examples what a knowledge of its textual history might tell us.

Selected reading

Fredson Bowers, *Essays in Bibliography, Text and Editing* (Charlottesville: University Press of Virginia, 1975). Bowers has been a powerful influence on textual scholarship over the past thirty years or so, and these essays will give you a good impression of his style and the nature of his work.

Philip Cohen (ed.), *Devils and Angels: Textual Editing and Literary Theory* (Charlottesville and London: University Press of Virginia, 1991).

Philip Gaskell, *From Writer to Reader* (Oxford: Clarendon Press, 1978). A fascinating introduction to the problems of editing literary texts, illustrating the surviving textual evidence for twelve works.

D.C. Greetham, *Textual Scholarship: An Introduction* (New York and London: Garland, 1994). The final two chapters give an excellent account of developments in textual editing, and there is an extremely useful bibliography.

D.C. Greetham (ed.), *Scholarly Editing: A Guide to Research* (New York: Modern Language Association of America, 1995). A collection of twenty-five essays describing editorial work on texts from ancient times through to the twentieth century.

D.C. Greetham, *Theories of the Text* (Oxford: Clarendon Press, 1998). An account of debates within textual scholarship in the light of contemporary literary theories.

Jerome J. McGann, *A Critique of Modern Textual Criticism* (Chicago and London: University of Chicago Press, 1983). An influential statement of the view that texts are not the communications of autonomous individual authors but the products of a variety of social forces operating over time.

Jerome J. McGann (ed.), *Textual Criticism and Literary Interpretation* (Chicago and London: University of Chicago Press, 1985). Includes important essays by Donald Pizer on 'Self-censorship and Textual Editing', and by McGann on 'The Monks and the Giants: Textual and Bibliographical Studies and the Interpretation of Literary Works'.

Jerome J. McGann, *The Textual Condition* (Princeton, New Jersey: Princeton University Press, 1991).

D.F. McKenzie, *Bibliography and the Sociology of Texts*, The Panizzi Lectures (London: The British Library, 1986).

Peter L. Shillingsburg, *Scholarly Editing in the Computer Age* (Athens, Georgia and London: University of Georgia Press, 1986).

Ian Small and Marcus Walsh (eds), *The Theory and Practice of Text-Editing* (Cambridge: Cambridge University Press, 1991).

Kathryn Sutherland (ed.), *Electronic Text: Investigations in Method and Theory* (Oxford: Clarendon Press, 1997). A very useful collection of essays, including Jerome J. McGann on 'The Rationale of Hypertext', Peter M.W. Robinson on 'New Directions in Critical Editing', Julia Flanders on 'The Body Encoded: Questions of Gender and the Electronic Text' and Peter S. Donaldson on 'Digital Archive as Expanded Text: Shakespeare and Electronic Textuality'.

G. Thomas Tanselle, *A Rationale of Textual Criticism* (Philadelphia: Pennsylvania University Press, 1989). An elegant defence of 'intentionalist' editing.

G. Thomas Tanselle, 'Textual Criticism and Literary Sociology', *Studies in Bibliography*, 44 (1991), 83–143. A lengthy and detailed reply to the arguments of McGann and McKenzie. Earlier essays published by Tanselle in *Studies in Bibliography* have been collected in three volumes published by the University Press of Virginia: *Selected Studies in Bibliography* (1979); *Textual Criticism since Greg* (1987); and *Textual Criticism and Scholarly Editing* (1990).

James Thorpe, *Principles of Textual Criticism* (San Marino, California: The Huntington Library, 1972). An attractively written general account, arguing that textual editing cannot be reduced to a science or have a single methodology.

Part 3

LITERARY RESEARCH AND LITERARY THEORY

From New Criticism to Structuralism

Literature, gender, feminist criticism

Deconstruction

Reader-response criticism and reception theory

New Historicism

Post-colonial theory

7 FROM NEW CRITICISM TO STRUCTURALISM

by Graham Martin

What *is* literary research? And what has literary theory to do with it? A Ph.D. thesis by a postgraduate student in literature, as in other subjects, is expected to offer 'a contribution to knowledge': this is the phrase employed by universities to define the criterion by which such a thesis must be judged. And though a Master's degree is much less demanding than a Ph.D., nevertheless the same criterion applies in some measure; so if we explore what is meant by 'a contribution to knowledge', this will have an immediate bearing on your work.

In the pages that follow, I will attempt such an exploration: what is literary research and what kind of knowledge is it intended to produce? This is where literary theory is relevant. Theory involves a consideration of the principles governing practice, and different theories will point to different kinds of practice. Recent decades have witnessed an extraordinary upsurge of theorizing about literature – what it is and what its study requires – which brings into question earlier, familiar and still-dominant assumptions. Before you go further, you need to know something about the implications for literary research of such thinking.

The necessity for close reading

Until the early years of the present century, detailed aesthetic analysis of literary texts – despite a long tradition in classical scholarship, and rabbinical interpretation of Holy Writ – was not considered a legitimate aspect of literary research in the form that we now accept. Research was dominated by models derived from historical investigation and, to a certain degree, from nineteenth-century science. Both the interpretation of literary texts and questions of their evaluation were considered either not susceptible of sufficiently exact standards to deserve the term 'scholarship', or only to be practised, as a sort of hard-earned indulgence, by those who had already proved their qualifications as 'scholars'.

A strong motive in the development of literary theory was to challenge such a position, not (except in some extreme cases) to deny the importance of literary scholarship but in order to assert the equal claims of a different intellectual discipline according to which literary texts themselves became directly the objects of attention. Traditional scholarship, it was argued, while appearing to address literary texts, effectively ignored them in its preoccupation with secondary concerns – the principles of good editing; or biographical discussion that transformed the text into an appendage of the writer's life; or cultural history that reduced the text to one of a number of pieces of evidence for a political or philosophical or social trend.

How, then, was the literary text to establish its independent claim to attention? Here is a Wordsworth poem from *Lyrical Ballads* (1805), as illustration:

A slumber did my spirit seal;
    I had no human fears:
She seemed a thing that could not feel
    The touch of earthly years.

No motion has she now, no force;
    She neither hears nor sees,
Rolled round in earth's diurnal course
    With rocks, and stones, and trees.

The scholar would ask of this poem such questions as: Who wrote it? How do we know? When was it first published? When first written? Is there a manuscript version? Are there any textual variants between manuscript and printed versions? Between versions printed at different dates? If so, how do we decide between them so as to establish the most authoritative text? Who is 'she'? When did she live and die? Why did she die? What was the relationship between her and the author? Are the poem's philosophical or moral ideas characteristic of the author, and of the period in which it was written? Does the poem reveal any literary or philosophical influence, and can these be related to what we know about the author's reading? What did the original readers of the poem think about it?

What issue or issues about the poem do such questions fail to touch? Briefly, the issue of *meaning* (save glancingly in the questions about philosophical and moral ideas and about influence) and the issue of *form*. Twentieth-century literary theory of the kind now known as 'New Criticism' may be broadly characterized by its determination to put these two closely related issues at the centre of literary study. Referring to our example, what this amounts to in practice can be described as the necessity for 'close reading'.

One key assumption of New Criticism is that the poem's meaning resides in the words actually appearing on the page, in the order in which they appear, set out in lines of that particular length, metrically arranged and (in this case) with rhymes. The poem is, in effect, conceived as a unique 'word' naming a unique experience. All other accounts of the poem's meaning, however useful they might be in helping us to understand it, amount to no more than an approximate paraphrase of the actual words arranged as the author arranged them. 'Close reading' of the poem requires scrupulous attention to these words – individually and in their interactions with each other.

A second assumption is that the poem is in no sense directly biographical. Its narrator 'I' is a fictional character, different from the author, existing only in this poem; similarly 'she' has no direct analogue in the real world. The poem, in other words, is a *fiction*, invented, made up, and its relationship with actual events in the author's life is complex, indirect, perhaps not traceable – since the significant sources would be mental and emotional, whose only recorded 'trace' might well be the poem itself. The poem's meaning is thus to be explored, not by asking questions which lead off into biography, but by questions about the verbal structure which provides its two fictional characters ('I' and 'she') with their only mode of existence.

A third assumption of New Criticism is that the poem is a unity, carrying within its structure all the information necessary to understand it. This assumption has the effect of making certain questions about it beside the point. Thus, of the relationship between 'I' and 'she', it is relevant to stress that it greatly mattered to the narrator; but it is not relevant to ask: is that because they were married, or had they only been having a love affair? It is relevant to notice that the second verse shows that 'she' had died and been absorbed into the cyclical rhythms of nature, but it is not relevant to wonder what she died of (falling off a mountain, pneumonia, bad treatment by the narrator), or where she lies buried.

The autonomy of the text

Why are such questions ruled out? For two reasons: the negative reason, namely that the poem provides us with no way of answering them, one way or the other; and the positive reason, that the poem focuses our attention elsewhere. According to this view, a poem's meaning is unified: the words exist within 'a field of force', constraining them into distinctive patterns of implication. Understanding the poem means grasping these patterns, and not distracting ourselves with what they exclude. Relevant questions thus might be: in what sense did the narrator's spirit 'slumber', and what is the force of the phrase 'I had no *human* fears'? Why did he call her 'a thing' when she was still alive? To describe a dead person as having neither 'motion' nor 'force' is unexpected: what effects are aimed at in such a phrase? Why in the last lines does the poet convey a notion of the earth's daily gravitational rotation? What does this imply about the fate of the dead woman? And in comparing the situation sketched in the first and second stanzas, is the narrator mourning the woman's death or reconciled to it? Is he blaming himself for not realizing that she might die? Such questions about the poem remain within the field of implications set up by its particular language, and in that sense they are relevant to its meaning.

There is also the issue of *form*. Traditional scholarship had tended to deal with the formal properties of literary texts in a manner both abstract and historical – as, for example, noting the predominance in different literary periods of certain general formal traits (epic, pastoral, satire, sonnet, heroic couplets, blank verse, Spenserian stanzas, etc.). Twentieth-century New Criticism has attempted closer and more specific accounts of the way in which *form* contributes to *meaning*, and in which particular constellations of *meaning* are a specific result of particular handlings of *form*. A traditional account of the poem we have looked at would be content with providing a general description of the metre (octosyllabic or four-stress, alternating with hexasyllabic or three-stress) and rhyme-scheme (abab/cdcd). Modern discussions would go on to ask how these formal properties contributed to *meaning*. Thus, does the rhythm of the first line permit reading it at speed? And if not, what contribution does a measured reading-pace make to the poem's mood? Does the two-stanza pattern of the poem help to give an effect of narrative finality to the second verse, and if so, what does this add?

Such an approach is a logical extension of the view that the poem's meaning derives from the arrangement of a particular set of words in a particular order. Words, singly and in groups, have phonetic as well as semantic characteristics. Rhythm, rhyme, verse-stanzas, line lengths, are established largely by the phonetic aspect of the poem's language. The poem's *form*, therefore, can be read as an aspect of its meaning. Here, too, the notion of the poem's *unity* comes into play and as a potentially evaluative criterion. The more it can be shown that different elements in the poem contribute to a single complex effect, the more clearly the poem emerges as a *unity*. It then follows that formal characteristics which make no contribution to this unity, or even set up distracting influences, are signs of the poet's failure to control the different ways in which arrangements of language can coalesce in a single complex meaning. A mis-match between form and meaning thus can be held to be a significant defect.

We can sum up this approach to poems as deriving from a primary insistence upon the *autonomy of the text*. Whatever source materials went into its creation – biographical, literary, political, cultural, philosophical, linguistic – were taken over by the poetic text and reassembled in a new set of relationships intrinsic to that poem alone, delivered to the reader by means of discernible linguistic formal, phonetic and semantic properties. Armed with this theory of the literary text, critics went on to elaborate an impressive variety of interpretative techniques, making use of the findings of literary scholarship but nevertheless working to independent analytical procedures. Poems provided the initial material for such criticism, and poems of a particular kind – as a rule, lyrics of moderate length, of a semantically dense verbal texture, formally elaborate.

But long poems whose verbal texture was different proved less amenable to this approach, as did satirical poems where the explicit attention to a contextual political and social condition necessarily challenged the assumption that literary texts were intrinsically autonomous. A convenient illustration of this is Tennyson's *In Memoriam* (1850), a poem directly engaging the implications for Christian belief of the scientific claim that the world of nature, far from offering evidence of a benevolent deity, was 'red in tooth and claw' (*In Memoriam*, LVI). Tennyson's poem, that is, tackles moral and spiritual problems keenly interesting to its first readers who, as products of a Christian culture, were beginning to react anxiously to new knowledge being systematized in the geological and biological sciences. To consider *In Memoriam* as 'an autonomous text' is to rule out such aspects of the poem's meaning. A.H. Clough's *Amours de Voyage* (1858), with its satirical reflections on the role of money in Victorian society, raises the same difficulty. One effect of the New Critical insistence on textual autonomy was that poems of this kind, for which autonomy could not effectively be claimed, were devalued, relegated to the category of having merely historical interest, as evidence of the superannuated tastes of a past epoch.

Form in the novel

What was the effect – of this concept of 'textual autonomy' – on the discussion of novels? Poetic language, in the sense that we have been considering, is not a prominent feature of most novels. Where it is, as in some twentieth-century fiction, the tested methods for analysing poems proved enlightening, if not wholly satisfactory. But for the genre as a whole, textual autonomy had to be sought in structural principles of organization. Thus, the role of the narrator of the novel came under scrutiny. A key distinction was made between the author, as a biographical entity, and the teller of the tale. Different kinds of teller could thus be discerned:

- the 'omniscient' narrator, as in *Tom Jones* (1749) – knowing from the start how events will turn out and why the characters behave as they do, and having privileged access to their private thoughts

- the first-person narrator, as in *Great Expectations* (1861), conceived as one of the characters in the novel, finding things out as the tale unfolds, knowing little more than the reader about the private thoughts of other characters

- or sometimes the 'unreliable narrator', as in Ford Madox Ford's *The Good Soldier* (1915), who leads the reader up the garden path by concealing his own responsibility for events.

The unity of the text might then be shown to derive from the consistency with which the novelist managed the narrator's role. We can take an illustration from Defoe's *Moll Flanders* (1722), a first-person novel – in effect, her life-story. Critical debate about this novel has turned on the question of whether Defoe expects us simply to *accept* his heroine's view of her life, which is full of inconsistencies and unresolved contradictions, or whether he expects us to develop independent judgements, to view Moll as not only self-deceived but also self-exculpatory about deeds of her own that invite a less flattering explanation. Is *Moll Flanders* a novel in which Defoe offers a series of individually interesting events whose relations with each other are casual? Or is it a novel in which events have an internal logic that Moll fails to see, her failure then becoming the *raison d'être* of the novel? Critics committed to the idea of 'the autonomy of the text' would find the latter account obligatory if the novel is to be granted a high evaluation.

Jane Austen's *Emma* (1816) provides a useful comparison. Here, we have an omniscient narrator, telling us about a heroine whose self-deceptions and self-discoveries are an important organizing principle of the novel. The narrator directs us towards these by means of a subtly ironic prose style, which prompts the reader's awareness of Emma's failures of insight. Indeed, the very concept of 'irony' has been extensively adopted for critical discussions of novels because it names the effect of those narrative devices that establish two conflicting levels of meaning: one level consists in what the characters think and feel 'to be the case', the other in what the reader, prompted by the conduct of the narrative, discovers to be a more comprehensive and penetrating account. Austen's high reputation has been justified precisely on the grounds of her skill, subtlety and *consistency* in developing an 'ironic' position from which the reader is offered a unifying view of the novel's events. The critical argument about *Moll Flanders* has turned on the question of whether or not Defoe did indeed manage Moll's tale in a comparable manner.

We can pursue this issue of textual autonomy by considering another aspect of narrative structure – the relationships between sets of events distinct enough to strike the reader as independent 'stories', small diversions from the main 'story'. In the case of *Moll Flanders* we move from one mini-narrative to the next, representing different stages in Moll's life, the significant connecting thread being Moll's part in each of them. But in Henry Fielding's *Tom Jones* we meet a more complex and sophisticated handling of narrative. The apparently separate 'stories', centred on Tom as he journeys from Somerset to London, turn out to reveal further unsuspected interconnections. The narrator makes this entirely explicit to the reader by failing to complete some of these minor narratives, and leaving it an open question as to whether the rest of the main narrative will provide a completion.

The dénouement of *Tom Jones* has been compared to that of an orchestral symphony in which certain motifs, present in variously explicit degrees in earlier parts of the work, are finally restated and synthesized in the final movement. *Tom Jones* also differs from *Moll Flanders* in the sense that Fielding encourages in the reader a high degree of critical consciousness about the structure of his text, where Defoe is content with a less sophisticated narrative procedure. The narrator of *Tom Jones* repeatedly invites the reader to conceive the narrative as a single, complexly planned construction, possessing its own internal logic, and to take pleasure in discovering what this logic is.

Such narratorial explicitness about the principles on which a novel is constructed exists even more emphatically in Laurence Sterne's *Tristram Shandy* (1759–67), where the narrator repeatedly raises the question of how 'stories' relate to the 'real events' they purport to set out. Where does the 'story of man's life' actually begin? When he is an adult, first responsible for the conduct of his life? When he is a child, being shaped by parents and education in ways that will later constrain his ability to act as an independent adult? When he is born? When he is first conceived by his parents? Should the 'story' not then begin with his parents' life? Sterne thus obliges us to face the arbitrariness of any narrative construction. 'Stories' must begin somewhere, but that is always to cut into the continuum of historical time from a pre-conceived point of vantage. *Tristram Shandy* is not so much a 'story' as a comic demonstration of the difficulty of telling one.

Samuel Richardson tackled the problem of narrative construction by writing 'epistolary novels', where the narrative is carried by means of letters written by the chief characters. We may say that Richardson's method in his novels *Pamela* (1740–41) and *Clarissa* (1747–8) is to convert his heroines *into* 'novelists', drawing upon the common practice whereby we all make stories out of the disparate events of our own lives. Unlike Fielding and Sterne, he reduces the reader's consciousness about narrative to zero, attempting to merge the text with the events it reports. The 'autonomy of the Richardson text' thus requires a different sort of analysis than does *Tom Jones*.

Questions and exercises

1   Before reading the next section, 'Questions of meaning', you might now return to p.86 and examine the questions about Wordsworth's 'A slumber did my spirit seal'. Work out your answers according to the kind of analysis practised under the aegis of New Criticism.

2   If you have read *Moll Flanders,* you could look again at her account of the pickpocketing episode (World's Classics edition, pp.211–14). What does this make us think about Moll? Is it Defoe's way of encouraging us to take a sharply critical view of her? Or is it merely another of the mini-stories that make up her novel as a whole, with no special significance? Your view here would figure in a discussion about the kind of narrative unity – or dis-unity – that the novel possesses.

Questions of meaning

We have looked briefly at the way in which twentieth-century conceptions of the literary text have led to an analysis of poetic and novelistic *form*. But what of *meaning*? Literary texts prompt both 'internal' and 'external' questions. 'External' questions lead towards matters of biography, and other contextual determinations arising from the social, cultural and intellectual conditions under which the 'texts' were composed. 'Internal' questions have been the particular concern of New Critical practice, following its theorization of literary texts as entities in themselves, not to be reduced to the complex of causes that bore upon their production.

'Internal' questions must, however, also confront the issue of meaning, and from two angles – for the original readers, and for the present readers. To illustrate this distinction we may take an example from the late sixteenth century, John Donne's poem beginning:

> Sweetest love, I do not goe
> For weariness of thee,
> Nor in hope the world can show
> A fitter love for me.
> But since that I
> Must die at last, 'tis best
> To use myself in jest
> Thus by fained deaths to die.

We need to notice that 'die' involves a standard Elizabethan sexual pun, but we find otherwise little suggestion that historical change has interposed a distance between what the verse meant for Donne's first readers, and for us. But with the majority of poems and novels the matter is more complicated. We may take as an example the fact that the hero of Defoe's *Robinson Crusoe* (1719) spends a remarkable amount of time in prayer – something it would be difficult to imagine a twentieth-century castaway doing. The meaning of these prayers for Defoe's first readers – or indeed for his Victorian readers, also habituated to prayer – differs from their meaning for us, or at least for those of us for whom prayer is no longer a common practice.

Some argue that whatever contemporary readers may choose to make of past literary texts, the scholar's job is to concentrate simply on what the author intended it to mean. A more complex position was offered by E.D. Hirsch, in *Validity in Interpretation* (New Haven: Yale University Press, 1967), who proposed to confine the concept of 'meaning' to the authorial intention for the text when first completed, and to use 'significance' for the series of different meanings that later generations of readers have discovered in it. Hirsch was here arguing against a widely held view – made current in an essay by W.K. Wimsatt and Monroe C. Beardsley called 'The Intentional Fallacy' (1946; in W.K. Wimsatt, *The Verbal Icon*, Lexington: University of Kentucky Press, 1954, pp.3–18) – that the meaning of a text could only be known by an examination of the text itself, and that no extra-textual evidence (say, letters or essays by the author offering his or her view of the text's meaning) could be used to delimit the implications of the text for a modern reader.

The view elaborated in 'The Intentional Fallacy' conceives the author as simply another reader of his or her text, one to whom attention should be paid, but always of a critical kind, since the fact that the author *intended* the text to have such-and-such a meaning was no guarantee of his or her success in having established it. This is a strong argument, but Hirsch's position has the advantage of addressing directly the problem raised by Robinson Crusoe's prayers. In place of the notion of an original unitary 'meaning', it substitutes the more flexible notion of a 'plurality of signifi-cances' whereby texts signify differently to different generations of readers, a state of affairs richly illustrated by the history of critical opinion (to be readily inspected in the 'Critical Heritage' series, which assembles a selection of comments on important writers' work from date of first publication till the present century).

However, one could raise another objection to Hirsch's position: *why* read the text ourselves if its meaning for us, today, is to be set aside in favour of what the author originally meant? Literary texts, on this view, become indistinguishable from other historical documents, and literary research simply a branch of historical research. As we have seen, it is this kind of thinking that twentieth-century criticism began by contesting.

Matthew Arnold and value

Some mention should be made here of two general approaches to 'meaning' which further involve the question of 'evaluation'. Matthew Arnold (1822–88), an influential figure in the development of twentieth-century thinking about literature, proposed in his essay 'The Study of Poetry' a distinction of value between those works deserving attention for historical reasons, because they illustrated a certain stage in the development of a national literature, and those which belonged to 'the class of the truly excellent' (*Essays in Criticism*, 2nd series, London: Macmillan, 1888, p.16).

The first group would be works worth examining in the light of their importance for their original readers. Such works from our point of view might be the minor poems of Pope, or a widely read eighteenth-century poem by James Thomson entitled *The Seasons* – evidence of the growing preoccupation of eighteenth-century readers with 'Nature', in contrast with the social world which provided Pope's main subject. Or, as we have seen, another such work might be Tennyson's *In Memoriam*. The question which Arnold suggests we should ask of these works is: what conditions, *no longer present for modern readers*, account for the high value which past readers, implicitly and explicitly, allotted to them?

But it was in the second, much smaller group of poems that Arnold's chief interest lay – 'the class of the truly excellent' (by which he primarily meant Homer, Dante, Shakespeare, Milton). Studying these would indeed require the assistance of some historical knowledge, but the reason for studying them lay elsewhere. Such poets offer commanding examples of what Arnold calls 'truth and seriousness' (op. cit., p.22), qualities that writers of merely historical interest cannot match.

Truth to what? Seriousness about what? It is reasonable to ask. Arnold is elusive when pressed with such questions. He considered general discourse on these themes unhelpful, and offered only a selection of quotations from the great poetic masters to illustrate his meaning in concrete terms. But we can descry behind, or within, his essays an implicit conception of an *ideal* human nature to which we should all aspire, and in whose direction 'the class of the truly excellent' poets could be influential in pointing us. Such poets, in Hirsch's terms, had 'significance' of a rare kind. Their work offered representations of 'truth and seriousness' about an ideal human nature by whose means we can learn to evaluate not only other writers in any particular period, but the quality of our own lives.

Evidently we meet here a theorization of literary texts more specific than the one we have so far identified as influential in modern literary study. Arnold conceives literary texts (primarily poems) as suasive representations of moral ideas which require of the reader something more complex than 'understanding'. But from the angle of our discussion, he illustrates an argument adopted by many twentieth-century critics to the effect that the value of a literary text must be linked with its success in articulating what is permanent in 'human nature', as distinct from what is merely transient and 'historical'.

To return to our example of Robinson Crusoe's prayers: it may be that we cannot enter into these in the spirit of an original, or even a Victorian, reader, but since religious experience is (or, at least, has been claimed as) a permanent need in human nature, we can 'read' Crusoe's prayers as an expression of this trait. The effect of this argument is to collapse Hirsch's distinction between 'intentional meaning' and 'significance' in favour of a permanent core of intrinsic 'meaning' variously expressed by different works and in different ages. It is then this a-historic 'meaning' that we look for in the literature of different periods, and (if we follow Arnold) proceed to evaluate for its greater or lesser approximation to the fullest expressions of such 'meaning' in the work of the great masters.

A comparable insistence on the 'evaluation' of literary texts was a striking feature of the work of both I.A. Richards (1893–1979) and F.R. Leavis (1895–1978), whose extensive influence gave the 'Anglo' branch of Anglo-American criticism a highly distinctive character. For Leavis, a study of literature which did not bring its evaluative potential to bear upon contemporary culture and education was little short of worthless. Though no uncritical admirer of Arnold's thought, Leavis nevertheless may be thought of as Arnold's twentieth-century heir. 'Literature', in his view, could not in the end be studied alone, and theories of literature implying anything of the kind could only encourage forms of research that would eventually prove sterile.

Meaning and history

A different approach to this problem of 'meaning' adopts a historical view, in marked contrast with Arnold's, and is particularly germane to the discussion of the novel. The novels of Defoe, Richardson and Fielding all reveal a detailed attention to the daily texture of eighteenth-century life: clothing, streets, commercial transactions, eating and drinking, houses, forms of travel, the different kinds of place – countryside, villages, market towns, cities – through which the characters pass. We prize such details for conveying to us something of the authentic flavour of life in eighteenth-century Britain – persuading us that, in contrast with the no-time and no-place of 'romance', we are in touch with a particular time and a particular place. The term 'novel' continues to hold this implication in its connection with 'news': as an adjective, 'novel' still means 'new'. 'Novels' have always been directly responsive to those aspects of social life that strike its readers as being of the *present moment*, and interesting precisely for that reason.

But as the novel as a genre grew and developed, the question arose: does its connection with 'novelty' mean that the works of each generation of novelists automatically lose their interest? Or can a continuing interest only be defended on the same lines as an interest in last year's newspapers, the objects of a merely historical curiosity about the habits and prejudices of a vanished time? If the principal interest of the novels of Defoe, Richardson and Sterne lies in a long-vanished 'novelty', why spend time reading them today? One way of answering this question is, of course, with Arnold's argument that literature continues to matter in more than merely historical terms because it presents admirable versions of an unchanging human nature which it is proper for us to take as a model. But a different argument was developed round the concept of 'realism', whereby some novels were held to represent, not just the changing surfaces of social existence but an understanding of the forces of historical change which underlay the social appearances. This argument, too, has an evaluative force. Novels become more valuable in the degree to which their 'realism' penetrates beyond the surfaces of an ever-changing society to the deeper currents of historical causation. You will meet this argument in its application to Defoe's and Richardson's work in Ian Watt's *The Rise of the Novel* (London: Chatto and Windus, 1957), where the emergence of the genre is related to the growth of a capitalist economy and the classes of readers which that society brought into being.

We saw that the Arnoldian argument collapsed Hirsch's distinction of 'meaning' and 'significance' by dismissing the former to the category of a merely historical existence and basing the work's claim to our attention on an a-historical account of the latter. The argument based on degrees of 'realism' collapses Hirsch's dichotomy from the opposite direction: it claims that 'meaning' derives from the work's engagement with its specific historical moment, and that this should continue to control the subsequent readings that Hirsch calls 'significance'. The work matters because it addresses historical determinants which, though in different forms, still bear upon contemporary life.

An aspect of this argument also worth mentioning here is its significance for discussions of *form:* if novelistic form is conceived as an aspect of meaning, then the deeper 'realism' that engages dominant historical determinations will demand expression in different forms in different periods. Thus, it has been claimed that the eighteenth-century Gothic novel, in breaking with the practice of 'realism' begun by Defoe, Richardson and Fielding, spoke to areas of life which that 'realism' had refused to consider. In broaching a new novelistic form, such writers found a way of expressing previously ignored experiences.

Questions and exercises

1   Again, if you have read *Moll Flanders* and/or *Tom Jones*, you could turn here to browse through the chapters in Ian Watt's *The Rise of the Novel* which relate these works to the deeper 'reality' of eighteenth-century society. Alternatively, you might spend some time listing the kind of information about eighteenth-century society which a critic would have in mind in proposing that some novels in a given historical period have a better claim to 'realism' (in the sense discussed above) than others.

2   Do you agree with Arnold's claim that the best literature is the kind that presents us with images of an ideal human nature? Is that, or something on those lines, what attracts you to the study of literature?

Structuralist criticism

In sketching this approach to the 'internal' structure of literary texts, I have used the term 'twentieth-century criticism', or 'New Criticism'. Critics who elaborated such analyses are: I.A. Richards, William Empson, F.R. Leavis, John Crowe Ransom, Kenneth Burke, Cleanth Brooks, Robert Penn Warren (whose joint anthology *Understanding Poetry*, New York: Holt, Rinehart and Winston, 1976, may be quarried for an impressive array of poems discussed along the lines that I briefly illustrated in my comments on 'A slumber did my spirit seal'), W.K. Wimsatt, and – in respect of novels – Wayne Booth (in *The Rhetoric of Fiction*, Chicago: University of Chicago Press, 1961).

Yet, a different approach towards literary texts was being developed, not by these Anglo-American critics but in the work of French critics influenced by the view of language proposed by a Swiss linguist, Ferdinand de Saussure (1857–1916). In the longer perspective this approach draws on a school of Russian critics writing in the 1920s, now known as the Russian Formalists because of their concentration on literary *form*. The Russian Formalists, like the exponents of New Criticism, were reacting against a view of literary study that bypassed the specificity of literary texts, and that treated them as mere grist to the mill of cultural and intellectual history, or of the biographies of authors – the latter practice being nicely caricatured, by one Russian Formalist, as an obsession with the question 'Did Pushkin smoke?'

Their approach, in contrast, was to set up a formal definition of 'literariness', whereby texts could be analysed in an objective spirit for the features which made them 'literary'. This was not a search for some essence or spirit of literature mysteriously secreted within some texts and not others, but for discernible formal properties which could be theorized as constituting the 'literariness' of these texts. Noting that the claim to 'realism' made by one generation of writers (and indeed of painters) involved them in contesting the 'realism' of the preceding generation, the Formalists argued that such claims depended upon formal devices that had the effect of 'foregrounding' (i.e. bringing into the forefront of the reader's conscious-

ness) artistic conventions that had remained invisible in work of the preceding generation.

We may again take an illustration from Defoe and Fielding. In *Moll Flanders*
and *Robinson Crusoe*, the narrative is supposedly the life-story of the
heroine/hero. Defoe establishes their *bona fides* as narrators by
presenting their stories as, in effect, life-confessions to the reader. Why
is Moll telling us her story? Because she wants to establish the fact that,
at this late stage in her life, she is now an admirably moral and upstanding
person whom life has taught a variety of useful lessons that she wants to
pass on. Thus is the 'realism' of her tale validated for the reader. But of
course this is simply a narrative device. It is Defoe's way of *pretending* that
the narrator – the inventor of all Moll's escapades, the source of all her
moralizing – is not himself.

Fielding, on the other hand, makes it entirely clear that *he* is the narrator of
Tom Jones's history. His novel lays claim to a different kind of 'realism', the
constant narratorial presence insisting upon the distance between literary
narrative and the world. 'I am, of course, only telling a story,' is the implicit
message of the narrator of *Tom Jones*, 'and we all know that stories, unlike
life, turn out happily.' Thus Tom can be saved from hanging without an
effect of 'unreality'. By thus foregrounding the over-arching role of the
narrator in all story-telling, Fielding distances his work from the 'realism'
claimed by Defoe's style of narrative construction, and demonstrates (by
implication) its fictional character.

For the Russian Formalists, what matters is not the allegedly superior
'realism' of one kind of writing over another – all 'realism' has to be
constructed on the basis of some conventions, some arrangement of fictional devices. What makes for 'literariness' is the authorial self-conscious-
ness that rearranges the devices to create an effect of a new 'realism' – new
in contrast with the 'realism' of the previous generation of writers. The
student of literature must therefore concentrate on the devices themselves,
and the succession whereby one deployment of them challenges another.
On this argument, George Orwell's *Animal Farm* (1945) is 'literary', not
because of its content or meaning but because it makes use of the early
history of the Russian Revolution to revive the device of the Aesopian fable
(where animals play human roles) in an unexpected way. Its content is
certainly significant – but only for those interested in politics, cultural
influences, the history of the Cold War. All that matters for the student
of literature is its fresh manipulation of an apparently abandoned literary
device.

In *Tristram Shandy*, a novel very interesting to the Russian Formalists, Sterne
'lays bare the devices' of story-telling in the most radical way, by
contrasting the pace of a narrative account of events with the time
which would really be filled by these events. Here is where the 'literariness'
of *Tristram Shandy* can be identified. We noticed in our previous comments
on Fielding and Sterne that the notion of the 'autonomy of the text' has the

effect of putting a high valuation on novels or poems which display – and invite the reader's awareness of – the fact that works of *literary art* is what they are. Russian Formalism is equally concerned with such works, but with a difference. Whereas Anglo-American criticism invites attention to the uniqueness of each text, Formalism regards 'literariness' as a relational concept, pointing to the way in which different texts contrast and compare with each other in their formal aspects. According to this view, we are not to spend time on the individual qualities of Defoe, Richardson, Fielding and Sterne, but only on their relationships conceived, not in terms of 'meaning' (whether historical or moral or social) but in terms of their deployment of 'formal devices'.

Yet the Formalist preoccupation with the role of 'devices' is not wholly abstracted from the connection between literature and life. It also depends on an important further idea, translated from the Russian as 'defamiliarization'. A given artistic practice persuades readers, through habit and repetition, that its formal structure is a true reflection of reality. The artistic practice that then challenges its predecessor by foregrounding familiar artistic conventions, so revealing their conventional nature, releases us to a fresh 'defamiliarized' perception of the reality. This is the value of 'literariness': it keeps reminding us of the arbitrary character of art, and of its power to impose upon us fixed and therefore impoverishing conceptions of reality.

Nevertheless, the key aspect of Russian Formalism was the notion that literary texts must be studied as *a closed system*, whereby the important stimulus to literary production is not the individual author's interest in communicating with readers, nor his or her response to the moral, social or political issues of the day, but his or her reaction against earlier styles of literary practice. In this way, the study of literature was to be made *objective*, no longer affected by the individual critic's subjective response to texts, but confined to elements open to the observation of anybody prepared to study the text carefully. This ideal of objectivity is of further interest in that it is shared by those who argue that the study of literature, if it is to qualify for academic respect, must attend primarily to matters of fact which are publicly available – as distinct from issues involving subjective response (such as Arnold's emphasis on evaluation; or more generally, a concern with textual meanings where individual interpretation comes strongly into play).

Saussure: language and the world

The notion of studying a closed system governed by internal rules lies at the centre of Saussure's thinking about language. Words, according to Saussure, *signify* (i.e. derive their ability to mean something) not from their relationships with things in the world, outside the language system, but from their relationships with other words. A word is a *sign*, composed of a *signifier* (spoken or written) and a *signified* – a concept, as distinct from an object in the world, as *tree* is a concept distinguishing one kind of object from the kind conceptualized as *bush*. Language is a system of such signs which divide up the world of perception; and, far from 'reflecting' it, language always stands between us and that world.

Language, that is, constructs what we know as 'the world', and since different languages construct the world differently, complete one-to-one translation between languages is an impossibility. The individual words in each particular language are inextricably related to each other, and it is these relationships that enable each word to 'mean' differently from another word. 'Bat' is able to signify its concept only because of its differences from 'pat', 'bit', 'bam', not because it reflects or conveys the bat-like character of bats. 'Tree' signifies its concept by means of its differences from 'free', 'trek', 'thee', and so forth. The relationship between the sign 'tree' and its referent (the particular object in the world to which it refers) is arbitrary, not a product of any natural or intrinsic connection between sign and object.

This arbitrary relationship between language and the world may be illustrated by the fact that *tree* is the sign in English for the same concept signified in French by *arbre*. A language is thus a system in which there are *no positive terms*, no terms deriving their significance from relationships with what lies outside the system.

Arithmetical numbers provide a certain analogy. What does the number 3 *mean*? It means any of: 2+1, or 1+1+1, or 4–1, or 5–2, etc. Each of these numbers takes its meaning from its relationship with others. Numbers are therefore a closed system, and that is Saussure's central point about language. Meaning, signification, is provided by *difference*: it is purely relational.

Saussure's concern was with language as a whole, not with literature, but his ideas have become powerfully influential in literary criticism. One influence, the more noticeable though also the less radical, has led to so-called *structuralist* criticism, the application to literary texts of the idea of language as a closed system to be analysed for the underlying rules governing the correct interrelationship of signs. If words are only able to 'mean' in terms of their relationship with other words – so that what needs to be studied are the rules which establish these relationships and account for the structure of the language system – then, by analogy, literary texts might be considered as 'second-order' language systems, similarly constructed in terms of underlying rules.

Applied to novels, such an approach involves seeking out an underlying *grammar of narrative*, a set of rules whereby all narratives are constructed. The aim here is not to arrive at the interpretation of a particular narrative, but to analyse its structure as an example of the general grammar shared by all narratives. Thus the simple sentence 'He went to the station.' can be conceived as narrative – admittedly short and unexciting – which works because the rules connecting different kinds of word (nouns, verbs, prepositions, articles) have been followed. 'He station to the went.' is neither sentence nor narrative because it fails to follow these rules.

Barthes's narrative coding

Roland Barthes (1915–1980), among other French critics who have responded to Saussure's influence on these lines, attempted to analyse a grammar of narrative. Noting the small progress that was achieved by the inductive approach to narrative (that is, by empirical inspection of large numbers of actual stories with a view to arriving at a sound generalization about their structure), he proposed instead the deductive approach, a hypothesis to be tested against a variety of cases. In 'Introduction to the Structural Analysis of Narratives' (1966) he outlined a basic paradigm or model, of which individual narratives were variants, in the same way that all rainbows – wherever they take place, and however varied they appear in shape, size, intensity or clarity of coloration – are variants of the same set of physical interactions between light, water and the human retina.

Saussure had distinguished between *la parole*, particular acts of speech or writing, and *la langue,* the shared network of linguistic relationships without which no *parole* could take place. Barthes's analysis of narrative offered to identify the common *langue* on which each specific act of narration (i.e. each particular narrative *parole*) depended. It is important to notice here that, for Barthes, the actual words of a literary text are manipulated by their position and function within the *langue* of narrative into a *second-order* language. Barthes's attention is thus not focused on words or sentences, as normally understood, but on sequences of such sentences deployed according to the structural patterns of narrative. Such language grouping built up a narrative *syntagm*, responsible for the effects which traditional criticism would call 'suspense', or 'narrative pace', or 'atmosphere'.

One of Barthes's purposes was to question what we might call 'the reality effect' of narratives. If all stories depended on a common narrative paradigm, their claim to *reflect* reality could no longer be sustained. The tradition of the European realist novel had claimed to offer a *mimesis*, or imitation, of 'the real'. It was of course conceded that novels involved invention – fictional characters and episodes, manipulated plots, happy endings. But (as Fielding's case indicates) it was assumed that readers could treat the fictional elements as if these functioned in the manner of the wrapping paper for a parcel, to be tossed aside as the reader proceeded to uncover the 'truth' about the world contained in the story.

But if the wrappings proved to be the parcel itself, if a paradigmatic narrative structure always determined the arrangement of the story's parts according to a small number of patterns, the notion of conveying particular truths about the world became difficult to accept. Just as a scientific analysis of the natural world produces explanations that common-sense observation could not begin to envisage, so a structuralist approach to narrative undermines commonsensical notions about its relation with 'the real'. Common sense tells me that my desk is solid, impenetrable, and static, whereas modern physics explains that it is made up of electrons, neutrons, atoms, molecules, whizzing about and around at various speeds, in otherwise empty space, collectively constituting a field of electrical forces in a dynamic interactive balance. Structuralist analysis in general is similarly directed at replacing our ordinary common-sense notions about narrative.

Barthes's second contribution to an understanding of narrative, also directed at the novel's claim to 'realism', is considerably more devastating to common-sense views. It is more concerned with the act of reading than with the structure of narratives. Narratives succeed in 'meaning', Barthes proposed, only because they are interpreted by means of codes already learned by readers from the culture which provides their education.

How do such codes work? Suppose you are driving along a street, and a man steps off the pavement, faces your car, and agitatedly waves his arms back and forth above his head. You understand that he wants you to stop, because there is some emergency for which he needs help. How do you understand that? Why do you not just think 'He's mad', or 'He'd better get out the way or I'll run him down'? Because you interpret his signals to mean 'an emergency'.

If he just stood in the road without waving his arms, the signal would certainly be different, and probably not understood, because there is no *code* to help you interpret it, whereas in the first case such a code exists. You assume that the man intends such an interpretation because you and he share the code and he relies on that knowledge. This will be clearer if we imagine that when you stop the car and get out, he pulls a gun on you, demands your money and drives off in your car. He would in that case have successfully used the code which says that 'waved arms' in that situation means 'emergency', because he would have used it to deceive you. A code, then, is a set of shared assumptions which enables people to send and to interpret understandable signals to each other.

Barthes claimed that narrative 'realism' was entirely an effect of the manipulation of a variety of codes which organize information and assumptions already in the reader's possession. Novels, therefore, consist entirely of the 'already-read' (Barthes, *S/Z*, 1970; trans. Richard Miller, London: Cape, 1975, p.19). For example, stories begin by posing an enigma which, after various delays and false turnings they proceed to solve, conveying an effect of a 'truth' that the process of the narrative has uncovered. Detective stories – the dead body, the puzzling and imperfect set of clues, several suspects, the privileged interpreter (the detective), the false solutions, concluding in the true solution that ends the narrative – offer the clearest example.

There are few novels which do not make use of this pattern, which readers accept as a basic rule about narrative leading to the production of truth. Barthes's point is that the notion of a discovered 'truth' is entirely the product of the code, having nothing to do with reality. This particular code works not because of any special knowledge delivered to the reader by the author of the narrative, but because, as readers, we enter into his or her use of the code. Barthes also proposed the existence of a 'cultural code' – a body of shared knowledge about society whereby the narrator could supply effects of 'knowledge' about characters and events, through allusions to fashions, historical events, psychological ideas about behaviour and motive. The 'knowledge effect' derives not from authorial perception but from the code shared with readers that such and such allusions established the veracity and probability of the episodes. If you think of your first efforts to read heavily allusive texts, where you were not in possession of the code in the sense of not recognizing the allusions or knowing what to make of them, you will see Barthes's point clearly. What makes such a text 'mean' to a reader is, precisely, knowledge of the cultural code. Imagine a novel which begins:

> The date was 3 September 1939, the time 11 o'clock in the morning. They had turned on the wireless just in time for the thin austere voice to confirm their fears. It had finally come. The waiting that seemed to have begun five years ago was finally at an end.

This will read differently according to whether the allusions – to Britain's declaration of war on Germany, to the then Prime Minister Neville Chamberlain, and to the political alarms and tensions of the 1930s – are picked up. In so far as those sentences convey knowledge, they depend on their invocation of material assembled by the 'cultural code'. A British reader, for example, will not find the same 'meanings' as a French reader, for whom the allusions are unlikely to work in the same way.

There is a metaphor underlying Barthes's theory of codes, which is that we are to think of a literary text as a *textile*, produced by weaving (i.e. by interweaving of a number of codes). His most famous demonstration of the idea is in *S/Z*, which systematically breaks down a short story by Balzac, *Sarrasine*, into the five codes composing it: *viz.* the enigma or 'hermeneutic' code; the signified code or code of semes (in more familiar English, themes); the symbolic code; the proairetic code (i.e. the code concerned with actions); and the 'cultural' code. To help indicate how Barthes's method works, here is an illustrating analysis from *Tom Jones*.

First read through this passage from Book I, Chapter 3:

> Mr Allworthy had been absent a full quarter of a year in London, on some very particular business, tho' I know not what it was; but judge of its importance, by its having detained him so long from home, whence he had not been absent a month at a time during the space of many years. He came to his house very late in the evening, and after a short supper with his sister, retired much fatigued to his chamber. Here, having spent some minutes on his knees, a custom which he never broke through on any account, he was preparing to step into bed, when, upon opening the cloaths, to his great surprise,

he beheld an infant, wrapt up in some coarse linen, in a sweet and profound sleep, between his sheets. He stood some time lost in astonishment at this sight; but, as good-nature had always the ascendant in his mind, he soon began to be touched with sentiments of compassion for the little wretch before him. He then rang his bell, and ordered an elderly woman servant to rise immediately and come to him, and in the mean time was so eager in contemplating the beauty of innocence, appearing in those lively colours with which infancy and sleep always display it that his thoughts were too much engaged to reflect that he was in his shirt, when the matron came in.

Now read through the passage again as analysed in terms of Barthes's codes: HER = hermeneutic code; SEM = signified code; SYM = symbolic code; ACT = proairetic code; REF = cultural code. The comments explain how the different codes work.

1   *Mr Allworthy had been absent a full quarter of a year in London, on some very particular business, tho' I know not what it was; but judge of its importance, by its having detained him so long from home, whence he had not been absent a month at a time during the space of many years.* We shall be told eventually what this 'very particular business' is, no doubt (HER). His not having been absent from home for any length of time for many years (SEM: provinciality). The name Allworthy (SEM).

2   *He came to his house very late in the evening, and after a short supper with his sister, retired much fatigued to his chamber.* (ACT).

3   *Here, having spent some minutes on his knees, a custom which he never broke through on any account,* Orthodox piety of the old school (SEM).

4   *he was preparing to step into bed, when, upon opening the cloaths, to his great surprize, he beheld an infant, wrapt up in some coarse linen, in a sweet and profound sleep, between his sheets.* Antithesis of coarse linen (= poverty and disadvantage) versus sweet sleep (= advantage of innocence) (SEM). Who is this baby? (HER).

5   *He stood some time lost in astonishment at this sight; but, as good-nature had always the ascendant in his mind, he soon began to be touched with sentiments of compassion for the little wretch before him.* Philanthropy (SEM).

6   *He then rang his bell, and ordered an elderly woman servant to rise immediately and come to him, and in the mean time was so eager in contemplating the beauty of innocence, appearing in those lively colours with which infancy and sleep always display it* Well-known characteristics of infancy and sleep (REF).

7   *that his thoughts were too much engaged to reflect that he was in his shirt, when the matron came in.* Good nature; sexual innocence (SEM).

You might try a similar analysis of a short paragraph from another novel to make sure you have grasped Barthes's method.

Barthes further proposed two kinds of fictional writing distinguished by the degree to which they invited the reader to become conscious of the codes offered for 'reading' the text. The first kind, so he claimed, was typical of the 'realist' tradition of the novel. Such novels were *lisible*, or 'readerly', because they invite the reader's passive consumption of the text as a direct reflection of 'the real', whereas in truth they are no more than a manipulation of the codes in which literary culture had already educated the reader.

In direct contrast are the *scriptible*, or 'writerly', texts which invite the reader to 'write' the novel in the sense of recognizing the plurality of significances offered by the play of codes (*S/Z*, pp.4–9). A modern example, John Fowles's *The French Lieutenant's Woman* (1969), offers the reader two alternative endings, one happy, one sad, each a plausible consequence of the preceding events. The effect is to push the reader into writing the novel's conclusion by choosing one or other of these alternatives, the novel in this respect becoming 'writerly'. In 'readerly' texts, where the narrator has made the choice and ensured its 'inevitability', we are soothed into a passive child-like condition whereby the narrator has decided for us what, in respect of its conclusion, the 'meaning' of the tale shall be.

Barthes's distinction, it should be stressed, describes 'pure' cases: actual novels combine 'readerly' and 'writerly' practices in varying proportions. To return to *Tom Jones* and *Tristram Shandy*: both these novels are 'writerly' in some degree, whereas *Moll Flanders* is, by and large, a 'readerly' text. Barthes also intended an evaluative force to his *lisible/scriptible* distinction, again as part of his considered campaign against 'realism'. Novels whose 'realism' claimed to address specific social problems, could be held to encourage an illusory attitude towards them by building in a logic of narrative harmony, wholly dependent on the 'truth-producing' code – a harmony rendering invisible the conflicts inherent in the social reality allegedly addressed. 'Realism', in Barthes's thinking, articulates an ideological position *within the actual narrative structure* more powerful than the express social or political views allotted to this or that character. 'Writerly' texts, on the other hand, maintain an absolute distinction between *écriture* (writing) and the world of events, perceptions and social actuality. Barthes extended his argument to autobiography, underlining the fact that these too are structured as narratives with a hero called 'I'. He warns the readers of his own autobiographical sketch that the narrator must be considered a character in a novel.

Macherey: literature and ideology

Mention should be made here of the work of Pierre Macherey (1938–), a French critic whose best-known work is *A Theory of Literary Production* (1966; trans. Geoffrey Wall, London: Routledge, 1978). Like the Russian Formalists, Macherey conceives the author of a text not as a creator who, like a potter, moulds the clay of his materials into a finished and unified individual work to be contemplated in its formal perfection, but as a producer or labourer who assembles pre-existing material (literary conventions, language, ideologies) into a product for consumption. The traditional task of the critic had been to interpret literary texts, to get as close to them as possible in order to reproduce their meaning. Macherey proposed, to the contrary, that the critic's task was to stand away from the work and diagnose it as a 'production' bearing the unmistakable signs of its origins.

This argument has a certain resemblance to that of the Anglo-American New Critic for whom the literary work was to be closely inspected as an independent entity, as it were a 'thing' made out of language. As we have seen, for such a critic 'meaning' derived from the individuality of the verbal construct. But for Macherey the 'meaning' derives not from what the individual work consciously 'says', but from what it doesn't say, from its silences, fractures and absences. A literary text for Macherey works to conceal its origins within the process of cultural production, a key element of which is *ideology*.

It is Macherey's emphasis on *ideology* that principally distinguishes his approach from the 'formalist' conception of a text that derives from structuralism and Saussurean linguistics. He conceives *ideology* as a set of imaginary beliefs about reality endlessly produced and reproduced by the conditions of life and the institutions (legal, educational, familial) of the capitalist state. Ideology, in other words, penetrates every detail of actual life. The literary text takes over *ideology* in this sense and 'works' on it in such a manner as to reveal its illusory, or at least fragmentary and self-contradictory, character. Where the mere reader or consumer of the text 'reads' its ideological aspects as reflections of 'the real', the critic brings to bear his or her theoretical – Marxist – knowledge of reality, showing up the contradictions that the fictional 'working-over' of the ideology betrays. The fiction, in other words, reveals in its self-contradictions deeper meanings than its surface composition shows.

Such meanings, however, only emerge from a process of reading *against* the grain of the text. Thus, in *Tom Jones*, while the text *offers* a complex narrative unity endorsing the good values of the ideal country gentleman, Squire Allworthy, it can be seen to contain unresolved contradictions which tacitly question that 'official' ideology. In the relationship between the two landowners in William Godwin's *Caleb Williams* (1794), a comparable contradiction can be noticed.

Common to such approaches to literary texts is their distance from ordinary reading. Anglo-American criticism supposes that the skilled and attentive critic is an *ideal* reader, performing more completely and comprehensively the activities of response and interpretation and judgement undertaken by a normal reader. (Normal readers have, of course, often protested that this is not the case, that nobody 'normally' reads in the New Critical manner.) Structuralist criticism makes no such claim; on the contrary, it distinguishes itself sharply from normal reading, much as the linguistic analyst of language is distinguished from the ordinary language-user. Barthes and Macherey go further, proposing that 'normal reading' is to be willingly locked into a complex set of illusions or deceptions from which it requires the special skills of their reading-practice to be liberated. Where the normal reader plunges into narrative in happy abandon of critical self-awareness, the structuralist critic analyses, abstracts and dissolves the particular narrative into the elements that it shares with all narrative. This, indeed, is the more radical influence emanating from the Saussurean concept of language. It brings into serious question an evaluative distinction – which Anglo-American criticism has always maintained – between texts which deserve formal study and those which do not. For if *all* narratives have a few patterns in common, then the usual reasons for discussing Thomas Hardy rather than Barbara Cartland, Joyce rather than Ian Fleming, Fielding rather than Frederick Forsyth, begin to look marginal.

What is 'a story'?

A different vein of structuralist criticism has concentrated on the formal properties of narrative. Take, for example, that aspect of a novel that we call the 'story'. Is this to be wholly identified with the particular set of words that constitute the novel? Or can it be distinguished from its actual verbal formulation, so that we can reasonably talk about 'the story of the novel' on the clear understanding that the novel as a whole is something other than 'the story' it tells? Here is the story of *Moll Flanders* as summarized by the entry in *The Oxford Companion to English Literature* (1985):

> The story relates her seduction, her subsequent marriages and liaisons, and her visit to Virginia, where she finds her mother and discovers that she has unwittingly married her own brother. After leaving him and returning to England, she is presently reduced to destitution. She becomes an extremely successful pickpocket and thief, but is presently detected and transported to Virginia in company with one of her former husbands, a highwayman. With the funds that each has amassed they set up as planters, and Moll moreover finds that she has inherited a plantation from her mother. She and her husband spend their declining years in an atmosphere of penitence and prosperity.

The bizarre flavour of this account results from the absence of Moll's own narrating presence. In Defoe's novel, she is the teller of her tale. It is her language, her way of 'telling the story', which lends plausibility to such an extraordinary sequence of relationships and events, partly by providing crucial information about early eighteenth-century English society, partly by explaining why she did what she did, to say nothing of what she didn't, and so how one event led to another. Nevertheless, if you were transferring this 'story' to another medium – film, opera or ballet – some such summary would be your starting point. Indeed, for any opera, the programme-note's terse précis of what you are about to see and hear portrayed on the stage demonstrates the same point, that while 'story' *is* an abstraction from actual narratives, it's not an idea we can do without.

Russian Formalist thinking about this problem proposed a distinction between *fabula* and *sjuzet* – between, roughly, 'the fable' and its specific treatment. Emile Benveniste, in his *Problèmes de linguistique générale* (Paris: Gallimard, 1966), made a similar contrast between *histoire* and *discours*, concepts subsequently familiarized in Anglo-American discussion by Seymour Chatman as *story* versus *discourse* (see his *Story and Discourse*, Ithaca: Cornell University Press, 1978). The former term was used to mean the succession of linked events that would figure in any adequate summary of a novel, film or play, and the latter was used to cover the way these events were presented. *Discourse*, in other words, refers to the novel's descriptions of places and people, how people behave towards each other, their dialogue and its motivation, together with any commentary and analysis of their predicaments supplied by the narrator and, more generally, the narrator's relationship with his tale – omniscient, first-person, 'unreliable', and so forth.

Thus if, in a production of *Hamlet*, the producer cut out one or more of the famous soliloquies where the hero meditates on the reasons for failing to enact his revenge upon Claudius, he would be altering the 'discourse' of Shakespeare's play, but not the 'story'. To do that, some event would have to be omitted – say, Hamlet's stabbing of Polonius. This event gave Claudius his excuse for sending Hamlet to England, seemingly to his death; and when that scheme failed, the same event gave Laertes a motive for his revenging role in the catastrophic conclusion.

Changes in 'story' are likely to be more radical than changes in 'discourse' but, as this last example shows, the two categories are interrelated, as well as distinct. A character's motive, not itself being an event, belongs to 'discourse', so that if the stabbing of Polonius (an event) is cut, Laertes would need to be provided with some other justification for his contri- bution to the final Act. Without this change in the 'discourse', the play's conclusion (its 'story') would have, in some way, to be revised. But a producer intent on cutting out the death of Polonius and yet preserving the Shakespearian ending of the 'story', could choose instead to work up the scene of Ophelia's burial as the catalyst for Laertes' agreeing to play Claudius's treacherous game. In which case, despite altering an item in the 'discourse', he or she would not further have revised the 'story'.

Narrative time

Formal descriptions of this kind have the signal advantage of recognizing individual differences between one narrative and another, especially with regard to 'discourse'. In any particular case, how its several aspects are treated can provide an account of a narrative considerably more precise than traditional discussion of 'characterization', 'suspense', 'atmosphere', etc. One such aspect is the handling of 'time', not as a theme for elegiac moralizing but as an intrinsic dimension of all narrative.

Consider again the minimal example we met earlier – 'He went to the station.' The verb builds in the notion of passing time in two ways: any journey takes some time, and for the reader this journey happened in the past. Now consider some elaborations: 'Just before he arrived at the station, he realized that he'd forgotten his season ticket.' The reader is still being told about something in the past, but that past now contains its own past, the forgetting of the ticket which preceded its own present.

Or consider: 'Just before he arrived at the station, he realized that he'd forgotten his season ticket again.' This extends the narrative's past well beyond its beginning, the moment of leaving home for the station, to incorporate several previous weeks, months, perhaps a year. We can complicate matters in the other time-direction: 'He realized that, having forgotten his season ticket, he would have to buy a daily return which would make him short of cash for the evening's entertainment.' The narrative's present now has a future as well as a past, an addition which makes explicit that all-important feature of narrative, the forward-looking dimension experienced by the reader as curiosity about 'what happens next?'

The point of these elementary examples is to bring out the way in which our sense of narrative time is inextricably linked to the linear form of grammatical sentences. By evoking a journey in the verb ('went'), the original sentence moves us through a passage of time, while the variants, by means of subordinate clauses and by shifting the emphasis from the journey to the journeyer, add to the initial evocation of a present moment something of its past and its future – all of which are still conceived as in the reader's past. And as to that, a simple change of tenses would make a difference, as you might like to prove for yourself.

How this bears upon narrative time in the novel was exhaustively analysed by Gérard Genette in *Narrative Discourse* (1980; trans. Jane E. Lewin, Oxford: Blackwell, 1986), a detailed discussion of Proust's *A la recherche du temps perdu*, a novel whose central theme is the way memory can sometimes overcome the inexorable and onward-flowing passage of time. Formally, Proust's narrative interpolates an account of past time with its own anticipations of a future episode, a future stretching well beyond the narrating present, to which both past and present will lead, and in which one or the other will be then remembered. Genette uses two primary technical terms – *analepsis* and *prolepsis* – though he greatly elaborates them as he proceeds. The first refers to information or episodes introduced into the narrative's present time which refer to its past, while the second refers to anticipations of some future event, similarly introduced into the narrative's present.

Analepsis will be familiar enough from the way characters are developed in most novels by reference to their past. In, for example, Chapter 10 of *Middlemarch* (1871–2), George Eliot casually introduces the new character Dr Lydgate; we learn nothing of his past, until Chapter 15 provides an *analeptic* account of his life – not only before his arrival in Middlemarch, but long before the story opened. *Prolepsis* is in some ways more interesting, especially when the narrator uses it as a form of implicit commentary. Four chapters into *Howard's End* (1910), E.M. Forster informs us that Helen Schlegel's life

> was to bring nothing more intense than the embrace of this boy who played no part in it. ... In time his slender personality faded, the scene that he had evoked endured. In all the variable years that followed she never saw the like of it again.

The second chapter of Muriel Spark's *The Prime of Miss Jean Brodie* (1961) describes the death of Mary Macgregor, some eight years later than the events with which the novel has begun. In each case the narrator briefly interrupts the linear progression of the novel's present time with news about its distant future. The effect is to counter the reader's preoccupation with the hermeneutic code whereby 'truth' will only be provided by the narrative's conclusion. These *prolepses* make immediately available, as it were, a final truth, a key perspective from which to consider everything else we will shortly read about the characters.

Poetic language

The influence of structural linguistics also led to new thinking about poetic language. Successors to the Russian Formalists pointed out that the 'devices' of poetry (alliteration, rhyme, rhythm, metaphor) could, in practice, be found in language-use for which 'literary' qualities could not be claimed. The force of the relational definition of 'literariness' depended on the clear identification of norms against which successors could develop new defamiliarizing devices. In fact, such norms could not easily be discovered. Prominent among those who went on to develop a more sophisticated account of 'poetic language' was Roman Jakobson (1896–1982), who proposed a linguistic model of which the 'poetic' function was one of six functions. Any message might reveal linguistic evidence of the 'poetic' function in a minor way, but only when this function dominated the others could the message be 'poetic'. This 'poetic' function could be discerned when the language of the message prompted in the receiver an awareness of the texture of that language (as distinct from its referential or other function) when, in Jakobson's phrase, the reader became aware of 'the palpability of the signs'.

Jakobson had studied the defective use of language by people with brain damage, and discovered two distinct kinds of failure – *syntagmatic* and *paradigmatic*. Syntagmatic failure meant an inability to utter connected sentences with all the necessary grammatical parts: nouns, or verbs, or adjectives would be omitted. Paradigmatic failure meant mistakes about the appropriate selection of these grammatical parts. From this he deduced that sentence construction was governed by two underlying rules – one for connecting words in meaningful chains, one for selecting the correct word from several grammatically equivalent possibilities. One rule governed the connecting and combining of words, the other the selecting and substituting of words.

Let us take a simple case: 'I went down to the station'. Each word belongs to a class of similar words, so that if we substitute 'We climbed up onto this roof', we have a syntactically identical sentence; or, again, in 'You fell over a cliff' the same is true. Failure to find the correct set of words from the various groups (I, we, you, he, they, she; down to, up onto, over; station, roof, cliff; and so forth) produces the paradigmatic form of language failure. Failure to connect the words properly, or to ensure that each kind is present (as in *I down station*, or *climbed roof*) produces the syntagmatic failure.

Most language-use is governed by an emphasis on the principle of *combination*. Jakobson proposed that poetic language resulted when the governing principle was that of *equivalence*, or substitution. In ordinary language-use, we are not made conscious of the potential equivalence of terms selected from the same set, or paradigm. The sentence 'means', however, only because we have learned that 'I' takes *its* meaning from its difference from equivalent or substitutable terms such as 'we', 'they', etc.

When this sense of potential equivalence is made actual, when we are thus obliged to *recognize* equivalences within the linguistic texture, then, argues Jakobson, we are being presented with the 'poetic' use of language. A characteristic effect derives from phonetic equivalences which play upon semantic terms not in themselves potentially equivalent. A simple example Jakobson used was the 1958 election slogan about President Eisenhower, 'I like Ike', where the phonetic resemblances between the terms overcome the non-equivalent single words and establish an identity between all three: voter, voted-for, and the political commitment connecting them all fuse in a single phonetic arrangement. The principle of equivalence here overbears the principle of combination, which is responsible for connecting the words in a linear syntagm. Rhyme – between lines, or internal rhymes within lines ('I like Ike') – is the most familiar form of such equivalence.

Jakobson's intention, structuralist in spirit, was to provide an objective method for describing the linguistic features that characterized a poetic text, without attention to meaning or value. He analysed poems to show that relationships of equivalence and parallelism, already recognized in traditional criticism to some degree (for example, rhyme, metrical patterning), were far more extensive and detailed than had been supposed. The effect of these equivalences was to complicate and make ambiguous the ordinary meanings of the words used in a poem. The linguistic patterning produced an awareness of the materiality of language, of the existence of linguistic signs as signs, within a system of signs. Or to follow Saussure's analysis of the sign into signifier and signified, poetic texts establish complex relationships between signifiers, 'floating free' of their conventional signifieds.

Let us look yet again at the first verse of the Wordsworth poem:

A slumber did my spirit seal;
  I had no human fears:
She seemed a thing that could not feel
  The touch of earthly years.

Phonetic equivalences in the first line play against the syntactical and semantic differences between *slumber* (slb), *spirit* (sp), and *seal* (sl). (Remember that *b* and *p* are very similar sounds – *p* is a breathed *b*.) The words, we may say, curve back upon each other by means of these phonetic links, so that *slumber* appears to contain the other two. Then, metre and lineation create a structural equivalence, dividing the verse into two equal halves, which the rhyme words link together. *Seal/feel* underlines the point that neither *I* in the first half of the verse, nor *she* in the second, paid normal attention to the world.

We can now read the two halves as linked both 'combinatively' and by 'equivalence'. A combinative reading suggests that 'I had no human fears *because* she seemed a thing, etc.' An equivalent reading plays against the notion of causal link, suggesting 'I had no human fears, and neither did she; both of us were cut off from ordinary awareness of mortality'. Rhythmically, this gets further support from the similar position in their respective lines of *my spirit seal/that could not feel*. Or again the second and fourth lines, linked by a rhyme, invite us to consider a similarity of meaning. Notice that all these equivalences do not have the effect of statements. Is *sealing the spirit* the same as *not being able to feel*? Is *having no human fears* the same as not recognizing *the touch of earthly years*? The linguistic pattern prompts questions, not the production of answers.

Probably the most striking word in the verse is *thing*. Why? Because it reminds us of the set of equivalent, or paradigmatic words, that *might* have been there – person, creature, woman, friend, etc. *Thing* is, as it were, haloed by the rejected possible equivalents. Then, this has its effect on *she*. Grammatically, *thing* is ungendered, and should be introduced by *it*. *She* and *thing* are thus set in an unexpected relation of equivalence and, as in the phonetic patterning of the first line, this pulls together the two words which are at the same time pushed apart by the intervening verb.

If you now remember the second verse, when the dead woman is said to share the existence of rocks and stones and trees, you will again discover that between the verses there are relationships both of combination and of equivalence. *She seemed a thing* (verse 1); she now is a thing (verse 2): the combinative reading leads to 'she died *because* she was insensitive in a thing-like degree to the facts of human life'; and the equivalent reading leads to 'her thing-like qualities in life make her thing-like existence in death entirely fitting'.

Questions and exercises

1   Take a short paragraph from any novel, and try your hand at analysing the succession of codes as classified by Barthes.

2   Similarly, taking a couple of paragraphs, or maybe a page, from a novel, analyse it in terms of 'story' versus 'discourse', and note any examples of analepsis and prolepsis.

3   Consider again the stanza from Donne's 'Sweetest love, I do not goe' (p.92), and look for the kind of phonetic equivalences that Jakobson considers crucial in 'poetic' language, and the way these interact with or play against the semantic patterns.

Or, you could take a verse or two from any other poem, and use it to practise this kind of close reading.

Is 'criticism' also 'literature'?

In looking at the influence of Saussurean linguistics on literary criticism in the work of Barthes, Macherey, Jakobson and others, we need to recognize that such brief summaries can give no more than an indication of its range and interest. But I hope I have said enough to reveal its difference from the characteristic approaches of Anglo-American criticism. As we have noticed, the latter developed from the conviction that traditional scholar-ship – directed towards cultural and historical contexts, or towards bio-graphical, editorial and bibliographical issues – assumed that only through these relatively factual and objective emphases could the study of literature yield *knowledge*. Anglo-American criticism attempted to complement such study with an approach to the text itself on terms that would minimize the subjectivity of the interpreter or analyst, and so validate textual discussion as a sufficiently objective discipline, equally yielding knowledge – knowl-edge moreover of the actual literature, and not just of contingent and ancillary matters.

Structuralist analysis of narrative, or the linguistic analysis of poetic texts, represents a different attempt to make discussion of texts objective. This explains the preoccupation with descriptive techniques and scientific models, which particular texts merely exemplify, and whose individual differences then become matters of lesser interest. We might indeed think of much structuralist and linguistic criticism as a contemporary expression of one aim of traditional fact-oriented scholarship. Both approaches imply that literary research can only yield knowledge if questions of interpretation and judgement – where the individual and subjective reader cannot be dispensed with – are no longer central matters.

But, as I have suggested, Saussurean linguistics have had the further effect of bringing into question the very category of literature; and it will be appropriate to take up this more radical question. Consider, again, the problem of *meaning*. New Criticism insisted that texts (certain texts, at any rate) had meaning for readers *today*, whatever meaning they may have had in the past. If this was not the case, then why read them, save as historical documents, like birth certificates, entries in Hansard, or letters about the sale of property? The study of literature, as a respectable academic discipline, absolutely required that literary texts had special characteristics distinguishing them from a historian's collection of primary sources. Confronted with evidence that texts had for original authors a meaning different from that which they had for modern readers, New Criticism insisted that the author's intention, or sense of the text's meaning, could not be allowed to constrain that of subsequent readers.

New Criticism offered, instead of the constraint on meaning deriving from authorial intention, the notion of practised, responsible, experienced reading, to be learned in the academies. Such 'reading competence' distinguished the inexperienced or inattentive or careless readers from those who have learned the procedures taught in courses about literature. Hirsch, we have seen, alternatively proposed that authorial intention was the ultimate criterion for textual *meaning*, which should be kept distinct from *significance* – his term for the relevance or value which successive generations of readers found in a given text.

Now both these views assume that meaning exists in the mind (whether the author's, or the reader's), the text itself being conceived as a vessel for the author to pour meaning into, and for the reader to extract it from. The text is, so to speak, passive, malleable to the author's intention, or the reader's need. But if, as Saussure's view of language asserts, words can only mean because of their difference from other words, from their location within a structure of signs (*la langue*), the implication arises that meaning is never entirely in the control of either author or reader, but is always affected by the language system. Neither author nor reader can, that is, make words or sets of words mean entirely what they want them to. As language-users, whether offering or receiving communications, we have to enter into a system of verbal signs that, in some degree, takes over from us. Whatever we say or write, further meanings than those we plan are always possible, not because of the carelessness, lack of attention or wilful irresponsibility of listeners or readers, but because of the language system itself. If this is a characteristic of all language, then the special debate about the meaningfulness of literary texts, as to the respective roles of author and reader, looks rather different. For whatever the author intended, the writing itself will carry further unintended meanings; and whatever a particular generation of readers finds valuable and relevant in a text can never exhaust its meaning-potential for another generation.

We may also note a second consequence. Jakobson's account of the specifically poetic function of language undertook to explain ambiguity, contradictoriness and indeterminacy of meaning, as features peculiar to the linguistic texture of literary texts. But the implication of Saussure's conception of *la langue* means that indeterminacy of meaning is intrinsic to *all* language-use, and is not confined to literary texts. It then becomes impossible to mark off some language-use as 'literary' or 'poetic', from other use as 'ordinary', or 'rational', or 'functional', so that the ambition to discover in linguistics an objective way of identifying 'the literary', free from the value-laden subjectivity of particular readers, is frustrated from the start. So, too, for narrative: the structuralist aim of identifying under-lying patterns which finally constrain and determine the ability of particu-lar novels to have meaning, to block off the particular language effects of individual stories, cannot succeed. The narrative model or paradigm exists only in the form of certain sets of words, and if – like all other words – they can only *mean* within the system of language, their meaningfulness cannot be closed off by a narrative paradigm.

For literary criticism itself, there is an even more remarkable implication. Both the scholar and the critic, in their familiar forms, jointly conceive the relationship of what they have to say about a text as secondary to it, a mere auxiliary to its better understanding. The assumption is that poems or novels exist in the world like other objects, open to comment and interpret-ation, but inherently different from them. A familiar metaphor in such thinking provided the title for an influential New Critical book – Cleanth Brooks's *The Well Wrought Urn: Studies in the Structure of Poetry* (London: Methuen, 1968). The poems there discussed are envisaged as having shape and solidity, as might an urn or statue. The scholar may be able to add a label, giving date and authorship, and point to resemblances with other urn-like objects. The critic may describe the contours, the interplay of curve and vertical, perhaps point to the presence or absence of handles, or the way surface decoration obscures or enhances the underlying shape. But all such commentary differs in kind from the text itself. It is 'about' the text, subject to it, its servant and devotee, even when it offers itself as commentary, interpretation, analysis. In a word, it is not 'literary' as the text is 'literary'.

But if there is no such creature as 'literary language', if there is only writing in some form or another, then writing about poems or novels, *whatever* the content, is nevertheless *writing*. And this writing, this interpretative or analytic or evaluative commentary, takes place under the conditions which determine all language-use, within the Saussurean language system, which (to put the point paradoxically) accommodates all language-users to its own laws, obliges them to mean in some degree what they do not intend to mean. Criticism, on this view, cannot be 'about' the text, in the sense of detached from, or subservient to, it; it can only be another text. 'Criticism' thus becomes one element in a system of which 'literature' is the other – complementary, not separate. The traditional priority allotted to 'literature' cannot be defended. Alternatively, we may say that 'literature' equals 'texts-plus-commentary' so that the humblest set of comments on a poem or a novel can claim a place in the domain of 'the literary'.

Selected reading

Matthew Arnold, *Essays in Criticism*, 2nd series (London: Macmillan, 1888).

Erich Auerbach, *Mimesis: The Representation of Reality in Western Literature*, trans. Willard R. Task (New Jersey: Princeton University Press, 1953).

Roland Barthes, *S/Z*, trans. Richard Miller (London: Cape, 1975). See pp.16–21 for Barthes's definition of the five codes; the book as a whole is a detailed analysis of the codes at work in Balzac's story *Sarrasine*.

Roland Barthes, *Image-Music-Text*, essays selected and trans. Stephen Heath (London: Fontana, 1977). See, especially, 'Introduction to the Structural Analysis of Narratives' and 'From Work to Text'.

R.P. Bilan, *The Literary Criticism of F.R. Leavis* (Cambridge: Cambridge University Press, 1979).

Wayne Booth, *The Rhetoric of Fiction* (Chicago: University of Chicago Press, 1961).

Cleanth Brooks and Robert Penn Warren, *Understanding Poetry*, 4th edn (New York: Holt, Rinehart and Winston, 1976).

Seymour Chatman, *Story and Discourse: Narrative Structure in Fiction and Film* (Ithaca: Cornell University Press, 1978).

Jonathan Culler, *Structuralist Poetics: Structuralism, Linguistics and the Study of Literature* (London: Routledge and Kegan Paul, 1975); an account of the linguistic theories on which structuralist criticism is based, together with chapters on the ideas of Jakobson, Barthes and others.

Victor Erlich, *Russian Formalism: History-Doctrine* (The Hague: Mouton, 1955).

E.D. Hirsch, Jnr, *Validity in Interpretation* (New Haven: Yale University Press, 1967).

Roman Jakobson, 'Two Aspects of Language and Two Types of Aphasic Disturbance', *Selected Writings of Roman Jakobson*, vol. 2, *Word and Language* (The Hague: Mouton, 1971).

Roman Jakobson, 'Linguistics and Poetics', *Selected Writings of Roman Jakobson*, vol. 3, *Poetry of Grammar and Grammatical Poetry* (The Hague: Mouton, 1981).

Frank Kermode, *Essays in Fiction, 1971–82* (London: Routledge and Kegan Paul, 1983). See Chapter 3 for an account of Barthes's *S/Z*.

Frank Lentricchia, *After the New Criticism* (London: Athlone Press, 1980); to be consulted *after* some basic reading in twentieth-century critical theory. It is notable for its exploration of the philosophical basis of New Critical ideas.

David Lodge (ed.), *Twentieth-Century Literary Criticism: A Reader* (London: Longman, 1972).

David Lodge (ed.), *Modern Criticism and Theory: A Reader* (Longman, 1988).

Pierre Macherey, *A Theory of Literary Production*, trans. Geoffrey Wall (London: Routledge, 1978).

Ladislav Matejka and Krystyna Pomorska, *Readings in Russian Poetics* (Cambridge, Massachusetts: MIT Press, 1971); a collection of essays by Formalist critics. See especially 'The Theory of the Formal Method' (Eichenbaum), 'On Realism in Art' (Jakobson), and 'Literature and Biography' (Tomasevski).

Robert Scholes, *Structuralism in Literature: An Introduction* (New Haven: Yale University Press, 1974).

J.P. Stern, *On Realism*, *Concepts of Literature* (London: Routledge and Kegan Paul, 1973); a valuable introductory account of 'realism'.

John Sturrock, *Structuralism and Since: From Levi-Strauss to Derrida* (Oxford: Oxford University Press, 1979).

Ian Watt, *The Rise of the Novel* (London: Chatto and Windus, 1957).

René Wellek and Austen Warren, *Theory of Literature*, 3rd edn (Harmondsworth: Penguin, 1963).

W.K. Wimsatt, Jnr, *The Verbal Icon* (Lexington: University of Kentucky Press, 1954).

W.K. Wimsatt, Jnr and Cleanth Brooks, *Modern Criticism*, vol. IV of *Literary Criticism: A Short History* (London: Routledge and Kegan Paul, 1970). See especially the chapters on 'Symbolism', 'I.A. Richards', 'The Semantic Principle' and 'Eliot and Pound: an Impersonal Art'.

8 LITERATURE, GENDER, FEMINIST CRITICISM

by Richard Allen

Defining terms

To be engaged with questions about gender and literary texts is to be engaged with gender politics, with difference and with discrimination. What we rather dispassionately call 'literary theory' comes close to our lives here, for we are all in some way involved from day to day in the politics of gender – given that politics is about power. We are all in some way different from each other, and we are all likely to be involved (willingly or unwillingly) in discrimination – perhaps in the workplace, perhaps at home. In the later parts of this chapter I shall aim to map out the main developments in feminist criticism, but I want to begin by asking you to think for a moment about the three terms in the title of this chapter – in isolation, and in relation to each other. It's clear that 'literature' is a far from simple term, a point that is amply made elsewhere in this Handbook. Being clear about what 'gender' means will be important to my argument, so I should begin by saying a little about how I use it and how it differs from 'sex':

sex is to do with an individual's biology; the words *male* and *female* are used here

gender describes a set of qualities that are defined – or socially constructed – in a particular society or culture; when speaking of a person's gender we use words such as *masculine* and *feminine.*

We are born with a sex which, except for a few people, remains unchanged throughout our lives; but we learn a gender as part of learning to live in a family and a society, and as part of how we see ourselves. Putting literature and gender together allows us to think, for example, about how individual texts or genres represent, and reflect on, these social processes.

Take the genre known as the *Bildungsroman*, or the novel of education and vocation. We can use this term (borrowed – as, some would say, was the form itself – from German writing) to describe a novel such as Charles Dickens' *Great Expectations,* but we do not get very far with the discussion unless we recognize that the sex of the hero/heroine is significant, and that his/her development is a process involving gender. The development of Pip as a 'gendered subject' – an individual with a developing masculine identity – is surely at the heart of the novel, and his masculine route to adulthood is plainly different from the feminine route portrayed in Estella or Biddy. But, equally important, there is variety within the development of the masculine subject: Pip's masculinity is constructed by Dickens and society in a quite different way from that of Orlick or Joe or Jaggers. Sex might seem a simpler matter. Although Pip is plainly male, there is no description of his biological maleness; no mention of his unclothed body, of his shaving, of his voice being deep in pitch etc. We might take this as a clue to ignore the matter, but would this be right? Should we not again think of the contrasts between the silence in the book about Pip's maleness and the much more noisy treatment of Orlick?

What about the third term in the chapter title – 'feminist criticism'? It refers to a now large but still loosely defined body of work written by people who think that learned gender differences – especially and sometimes exclusively those which mark out women's experiences as writers and readers – are crucial in our study of literary texts. Thinking about why feminist criticism should be so much more recognizable a term than, say, 'gender criticism' or even 'masculinist criticism' takes us straight back to the idea of discrimination – and also marks out one of the key features of the development of literary study based on gender. Poetry provides an interesting example here. Histories of English literature will regularly lead one to the conclusion that poetry is men's work; when women are involved in literature, it is far more likely to be as writers of novels. Does this mean that it is characteristic of the male (some might say masculine) writer to be able to use language in a dense and highly formed way, whereas it is characteristic of the female (some might say feminine) writer to use more loosely formed language?

Whatever your answers to this question, it is plain that value judgements – in favour of male writers and masculine styles of writing – run all through this kind of argument, canonizing poetry by men. This is a form of discrimination which feminist criticism aims to combat. But this combating involves – implicitly or explicitly – adopting a political position. The idea of feminist criticism as a common endeavour, championing women's writing as an apparently single thing, allows for a sense of solidarity and a sense of being empowered; hence, perhaps, the persistence of the unifying title 'feminist criticism' even though criticism by feminists has become extremely diverse. But there is a price to pay, because defining something as specifically feminist criticism also sets it apart from the activity we just call literary criticism. Literary criticism, apparently ungendered, seems somehow to include feminist criticism just as a gendered *sub*-category – rather than leading equally to masculinist and feminist criticism. The idea of masculinist literary criticism that overtly celebrates men's dominance, makes most people uneasy; so masculinist criticism often follows the paradigm of feminist criticism in looking for ways of presenting masculinity as somehow involving lack of power. As an example, see *Engendering Men: The Question of Male Feminist Criticism*, ed. J.A. Boone and M. Cadden (London: Routledge, 1990).

Thinking about women's writing

Feminist criticism is concerned, perhaps above all, with writing by women. The history of the English novel in the last decade of the nineteenth century can provide an interesting case study of the kinds of question and issue that might be raised. If in the past we had surveyed reading-lists for courses about the period, we would often have found that few women writers were listed. How come, when literature of the period was dominated by the novel, supposedly the genre most congenial to women authors? And, of course, in asking this question, we are asking two questions – one about the valuing and canonizing of writings, and one about the actual numbers of novels in the period written by women. This latter question might lead to the discovery that many women writers of the time – many household names of the time – are now hidden from literary history, and this in turn might lead to an investigation of the publishing market-place then and now, and the effect of literary critical valuations on the 'ordinary' reader. All this might be counted as a primarily historical or sociological investigation, although it is bound to raise questions about the standards by which critical judgements are being made.

Another set of questions is likely to focus much more on the way in which the novels are written. Conventional criticism might aim to answer the following: how is the writing, the characterization, the plotting and so on inferior to what we find in novels we have canonized? Feminist criticism would perhaps aim to reassess the way in which texts have been described and valued, and promote more texts by women into the canon.

A third set of questions might focus on issues of patriarchy and difference. Perhaps women's issues, written about by women, must just have a lower status – be discriminated against – in a patriarchal culture? If one is led to think in this way, the feminist slogan 'different therefore equal' might offer a way forward. We should ask, for example, not how such a text is inferior to something in the male/masculine canon, but how it is *different* from male/masculine writing. Or to put it another way, how do these works by women now hidden from history show a specifically female imagination at work which will find expression in a particularly female language and a particularly female way of writing? (There are similar questions to be asked about men's writing. Is it not the case that the writings of Thomas Hardy or Henry James, for example, reflect not some miraculously ungendered imagining and representing of the period, but rather something specifically different, male and masculine?)

Questions concerning the female and/or feminine imagination have great importance in feminist criticism, and it is worth spending a moment thinking about how they might be answered. There is an example in an article by Mary Jacobus, 'The Difference of View' (in *Women Writing and Writing about Women*, ed. Mary Jacobus, London: Croom Helm, 1979). Jacobus is discussing Mary Wollstonecraft, but I think her conclusions can interestingly be applied to the 1890s. Her answer turns into an argument about the separate nature of women. Put crudely, it goes something like the following. Patriarchy values the masculine, which is identified with the language of reason, government and administration – the language of realism. In contrast, the feminine is identified with sentiment, feeling, emotion, the irrational – even madness. If a woman writes in something akin to the language of men – makes herself even an honorary man as in the case of George Eliot – she may be admitted to the masculine-dominated canon of high literature. But if she writes in a way that foregrounds emotion, coincidences etc., she will be relegated to the feminine and to the popular – and forgotten.

But the situation can be conceptualized differently. Jacobus argues that 'madness' – or ways of writing that in conventional terms are not masculine – can be 'imagined as revolution, or the articulation of Utopian desire'. Imagining a non-patriarchal world is so difficult that it is hardly surprising if the results are sometimes marked by features that conventionally appear to be confusions and evasions, but that Jacobus sees as

> the transgression of literary boundaries – moments when the structures are shaken, when language refuses to lie down meekly, or the marginal is brought into sudden focus, or intelligibility itself refused ... [something which] reveals not only the conditions of possibility within which women's writing exists, but what it would be like to revolutionize them. (p.16)

We may ask further gender-based questions about literary history. For many years it seemed common sense to talk of the Gothic novel as superseded by the technically superior realist novel, which eventually lost its stylistic vitality and was superseded by Modernism. A gender-based enquiry notices that here two forms – the Gothic and the realist novel – predominantly associated with women are superseded by a style mostly associated with male writers; notices too, perhaps, that the Gothic style had a continuing life alongside realism. This way of thinking is enthusiastically explored in Ellen Moers, *Literary Women* (London, W.H. Allen, 1977). In a later discussion in *Between Men: English Literature and Male Homosocial Desire* (New York: Columbia University Press, 1985), Eve Kosofsky Sedgwick describes the basis on which Gothic writing has been revalued by feminist critics. Far from being escapist,

> the Gothic seems to offer a privileged view of individual and family psychology. Certain features of the Oedipal family are insistently foregrounded there: absolutes of licence and prohibition, for instance; a preoccupation with the possibilities of incest; a fascinated proscription of sexual activity; an atmosphere dominated by the threat of violence between generations. (p.91)

That sensational writing persists in novels by men and by women surely prompts us to ask further questions about the imaginations of writers and readers, and to resist the desire of the canon to banish such works to the lower categories of the 'sensational' or the 'popular'. These issues may also raise questions about canonized writings: for all his high reputation, Hardy is criticized for his occasional failings of style and realism. Perhaps we should, instead, see these as successes in representations that go beyond the realistic?

A note on Freud

Gender-based criticism, it will be seen, regularly operates in a kind of dialogue with the ideas of Sigmund Freud; the dialogue is sometimes friendly but sometimes vigorously hostile.

Why this is so is not difficult to understand. Gender-based criticism regularly gets involved with questions of gendered identity and, for better or worse, the ideas of Freud remain largely the basis of thinking about these issues in the West. Freud worked mostly in a medical framework, as a modern psychiatrist might, seeing individual people and attempting to 'cure' them. When he speaks in a particular case of the relationship between a child and a father, he is likely to be referring to particular individuals. Since his death, Freud's ideas have been – as it were – generalized, or seen as metaphors that explain how society as a whole works. Relations within an individual family become ways of understanding society: the rule of the father becomes the rule of patriarchy. Among those who have developed Freud's ideas, one name that crops up regularly in gender and feminist critical writing is that of Jacques Lacan because of his emphasis on language structures in understanding gendered development.

To get the most from feminist criticism, you will generally need to know something about Freud and Lacan. If you are unfamiliar with their ideas, a good starting point would be the opening section of Chapter 5 of Terry Eagleton's *Literary Theory: An Introduction*, 2nd edn (Oxford: Blackwell, 1996). Whatever they think of his ideas, most people find Freud's own writing quite approachable. Try, for example, *Three Essays on the Theory of Sexuality* (1905), or *Two Short Accounts of Psychoanalysis* (1909) or the case studies of 'Dora' and 'Little Hans'. (The case study of 'Dora' has been given considerable scrutiny by feminist writers: see, for example, Nina Auerbach, 'Magi and Maidens: The Romance of the Victorian Freud' in *Writing and Sexual Difference*, ed. Elizabeth Abel, Brighton: Harvester, 1982.) Lacan is much more difficult, and here an approach via a secondary source might be advisable. Joseph Bristow, *Sexuality* (London: Routledge, 1997) deals with both Freud and Lacan (and is interesting because of the focus on the erotic and on sexual desire, rather than on explanations of the development of personality). Elizabeth Grosz, *Jacques Lacan: A Feminist Introduction* (London: Routledge, 1990) is a more specialist study.

Feminist criticism

The sheer amount of specifically feminist criticism is both exciting and daunting; there is far more than I could list and describe here, so I shall be concentrating on a few books and offering an outline of the field. Additionally, if you haven't already done so it would be useful to work through one or more of the numerous anthologies of feminist criticism, in order to see the range of possibilities. Under 'Selected reading' (pp.129–30), I have listed collections edited by Elizabeth Abel, Mary Eagleton, Mari Evans, Mary Jacobus, Toril Moi and Elaine Showalter.

Most anthologies of literary theory now contain a section on feminist theory. To take an example, there is a chapter on 'Feminism' in *Modern Literary Theory: A Reader*, ed. Philip Rice and Patricia Waugh, 3rd edn (London: Edward Arnold, 1996). This contains extracts from a piece by Elaine Showalter, and from 'Women Writing: Jane Eyre, Shirley, Villette, Aurora Leigh' by The Marxist-Feminist Collective. This latter shows a number of characteristics of earlier feminist criticism. For example, it is set out in a way that is distinctly 'different' from most literary criticism, providing a series of paragraphs that are quite weakly linked; this is an expression of the feminist critique of the dominant orthodox style of writing as male and rational. There is a clear emphasis on intellectual enquiry – in the use of the French critic Pierre Macherey, the attention paid to social structures, and the use of analysis of the text – but there is a comparable emphasis on feeling. It is the work of a collective rather than a single individual, again something very much driven by feminist ideas (and also no doubt by Marxist ideas on the value of collectivity).

In introducing the extract from Showalter's article, 'Towards a Feminist Poetics', Rice and Waugh seem to suggest that Showalter stands apart from this emphasis on the collective; they say (p.99) that she works within an 'orthodox humanist belief in literature as the expression of a universal unity'. But this seems to me questionable: in *A Literature of Their Own: British Women Novelists from Brontë to Lessing* (London: Virago, 1978), for example, Showalter explores writing by women in relation to the idea that 'women ... have constituted a subculture within the framework of a larger society, and have been unified by values, conventions, experiences, and behaviours impinging on each individual' (p.11). Her approach in fact has much in common with that of another text, well worth exploring, which also suggested that women writers had a separable history of their own – Ellen Moers' *Literary Women* (London: W.H. Allen, 1977).

The Showalter extract is important because it shows her attempting to develop a distinct conceptual structure for feminist criticism which can define itself quite separately from other critical methods and give a fuller meaning to the term 'feminist critique'. Though Showalter preserves an allegiance to feminist assumptions – for example, by acknowledging that her work is the result of a collective 'sharing' of knowledge (see the note on p.108 of Rice and Waugh) – the desire to develop a theoretical frame also suggests a desire that feminist criticism be accepted within the dominant discourse of universities. In the extract, Showalter divides feminist criticism into two kinds; the distinction she makes is a generally used one, although the labels she coined for them have not really caught on. On the one hand there is a criticism based on 'historically grounded inquiry' (p.99), and on the other a criticism based on 'the psychodynamics of female creativity, linguistics and the problem of a female language' (p.100). Showalter's categories might also be described by reference to books that have acted as 'mother-figures' to feminist criticism; on the one side stands Virginia Woolf's *A Room of One's Own* (first published 1929) and, on the other,

Simone de Beauvoir's *The Second Sex* (first published 1949). In more philo-sophical terms the distinction is between, on the one hand, a UK and US empirical tradition (often associated with Marxist, historical, materialist thinking) and, on the other, a French theoretical tradition – particularly associated with psychoanalysis.

Both ways of thinking focus on language, power and control but they do so in different ways. To describe it in over-simple terms, empirical and materi-alist feminist ways of thinking are likely to construe 'language' as physical words on the page; to gain power and control here involves overcoming barriers in education, publishing, contemporary ideas of what is acceptable and so on. Feminist writers and critics who draw on psychoanalytic think-ing conceive of language in a different and, they might say, 'deeper' way. Particular emphasis is given to the notion that a child develops his or her identity through the process of learning to use language. This is not a neutral process: the child learns to understand, to think and to speak what is described as a general symbolic language which currently authorizes and embodies patriarchy. As the child grows up, she or he takes on a powerless or powerful role as a woman or a man just as naturally as we talk to members of our own families, colleagues at work etc. The gendered power process is so 'natural' that conceiving an alternative is extremely difficult. Striking against it can, for example, involve women in attempting to recover some kind of equal (but different) powerful semiotic language embodying femininity and matriarchy (see H. Cixous, '*Coming to Writing' and Other Essays*, London: Harvard University Press, 1991).

These two different ways of thinking in feminism are excellently discussed by Janet Todd in her *Feminist Literary History* (Cambridge: Polity, 1988). Todd is partial but very even-handed – not an easy achievement. She writes in the introduction that 'the confrontation of the two modes, the socio-historical American and the French psychoanalytical, is an exciting spec-tator sport ... the fight is not yet over' (p.6). Feminist critics might, in such circumstances, be tempted to take one side or the other, or even to attempt some kind of magic synthesis. Todd's approach is different: she argues that it is healthy if each pushes at the other so that each is enriched by the other. Her own work, for example, involves using historically based understand-ing to push against the transhistorical and universal categories that psychoanalytically based thinking all too often uses. In other words, she aims 'to turn history [loose] onto psychoanalysis, to historicize its dis-course, methods and aims and to contextualize its functioning in the history it likes to allegorize and abstract' (p.6). What this might mean in practice can be gauged by, for example, Sandra Gilbert and Susan Gubar's classic study of predominantly nineteenth-century literature, *The Mad Woman in the Attic* (London and New Haven: Yale University Press, 1979), and the three-volume sequel, *No Man's Land* (London and New Haven: Yale University Press, 1988).

The shelves of bookshops suggest that, especially in higher education, approaches that favour the psychoanalytical have achieved a very strong hold in feminist criticism. Perhaps this will seem a good thing. Since psychoanalysis 'explains' both masculine and feminine, the result will be to give feminist work a very wide reach. But there is also a risk that the political emphasis within feminism, which I have been stressing, will be weakened or lost. The risk can, to a degree, be seen in Terry Eagleton's *Literary Theory: An Introduction,* which contains no substantive reference to Millett, Showalter or Todd and engages with feminism *only* under the heading of psychoanalysis.

In the case of both Freud and Lacan, you will often find yourself picking through fierce arguments. Some of the fiercest relate to their actual clinical practice as psychiatrists/analysts, seen regularly as wrong-headed, sexist, even damaging to their patients; for many critics, faults here are sufficient to damn all their work. For many others, the various ways in which Freud and Lacan think about the development of identity remain valuable – particularly when understood in metaphorical terms. Freud himself encourages a metaphorical way of reading; when writing about how individuals and families work, he will often reach for a mythical or story-book example to show that the pattern he is describing is not new but something quite familiar.

As an example, one might cite the 'castration complex', a set of ideas developed around 1908. For the girl child, her 'lack' of a penis seems to indicate that she has been castrated. For the boy child, the threat of being castrated by his father is a source of deepest anxiety. This might perhaps still be understood literally, but for most people it is easier to read it as expressing metaphorically (but none the less clearly) the deepest problems of identity. The idea that femininity is constructed in society around a *lack* of something is at the heart of feminist struggle – and that something might just simply be called power. The notion that the son grows up threatened by his father and must overcome him is at the heart of the myths of many civilizations; progress comes from the most powerful, it would seem. Less often foregrounded is the view that masculinity is itself constructed with threat and, as a result, has anxiety at its centre. *Great Expectations* can again provide an example. The absence of Pip's actual father allows Dickens more easily to describe a series of 'fathers' whom Pip must in some way supersede. But together they present a composite portrait which definitely involves something like castration. Magwitch is the first to threaten to cut something from Pip's body, but perhaps Orlick is the most threatening: 'When I was younger, I had a general belief that if he had jiggered me personally, he would have done it with a sharp and twisted hook' (Chapter 17).

Men, gender and queer criticism

Men have been involved in the growth of contemporary gender-based literary study from the beginning, though in far smaller numbers than women. Broadly speaking their involvement is of two kinds – first, work that shares the aims of feminism; second, work that came from the gay liberation movement that developed at the same time.

One of the first examples of the former type of work is John Goode's 'Women and the Literary Text', which appeared in a collection titled *The Rights and Wrongs of Women*, ed. Juliet Mitchell and Ann Oakley (Harmondsworth: Penguin, 1976). Goode's aim is to ask 'whether literary analysis can be valuable to women's studies'; using *Tess of the D'Urbervilles*, he discusses the relation of the representations of women to Hardy's male narrating voice (and to a possible male reader) in a most interesting way. Implicitly, however, the male critic fits easily into women's studies: there is no explicit reference to the possibility of a difference between the feminine and the masculine point of view. The essay is written within an apparently objective or neutral academic framework, but the lesson of gender politics is that nothing can be entirely intellectual and detached: the critic is a gendered subject, and is a producer of texts as much as the writer she or he reads, and is as much engaged with gendered language and with the play of power around genre.

Taking my own work here as an example, my gendered subjectivity and difference of view mean perhaps that I write about feminist criticism in what you will find to be a detached way. This might show in the general way I approach the subject, but also in apparently small details of language: women writing about being feminine will often use the pronoun 'we' to construct a sense of shared experience with their women readers in a way that I cannot. In this subsection I am writing about men, studies of masculinity and particularly gay criticism. Here I have a much more 'subjective' involvement (i.e. an involvement more closely related to my own identity as a gendered subject).

The gay studies perspective has been instrumental in developing the most distinct critical perspectives on the relation between literature and the masculine. Within that perspective, the values and links with feminist criticism are, as I have suggested, often strong. In the preface to *Between Men: English Literature and Male Homosocial Desire*, Eve Kosofsky Sedgwick, for example, places herself within a community of 'gay female and male scholars' (p.x), just as Elaine Showalter places herself within a feminist group. Sedgwick also regularly acknowledges the direct influence of feminist thinking in her work. In the main body of *Between Men*, however, she adopts the detached tone of academic discourse, no doubt because she wants her work to be read within the mainstream of literary criticism; since her name has become established, her tone has changed to something more personal. I am dwelling a little on this because these shifts of tone have gender-political significance. In Sedgwick's case, some say the gendered community that is invoked – the meaning of 'we' as she might use it – glosses over too much difference. For some, there is not so much a difference as a gap between being a woman (even a lesbian woman) and the gay masculinity about which she writes; for others, there is just as much a gap between Sedgwick's avowed feminism and her subject-matter.

In essence, *Between Men* tracks various formations of literary plots common since 1700 in which a heroine is caught between different men; the plot is resolved when a correct choice between the men is made. On the face of it, these plots are about heterosexuality and the family; they are myths of what is proper for women to choose and how they should behave. In the novels of Jane Austen the plots constitute a system of social control for women. Using ideas about literature and language which emphasize what is *not* said as much as what is said, a masculine-focused approach might lead us to suggest that these plots exert powerful social control over men too. Both men and women readers are 'put in place' (see Pamela Morris, *Literature and Feminism*, Oxford: Blackwell, 1993, p.138) and their gender identity defined. From a gay perspective, however, although we know that there were immensely close sexual relations between men in certain classes of society, this fact is silenced. Sexuality is constructed only as part of the relations between men and women.

Sedgwick's approach is historically specific; in her later book *Epistemology of the Closet,* she focuses on the time around 1900, a period regularly explored by writers on male homosexuality and masculinity because, it is argued, this was when the modern boundaries between the homosexual man and the heterosexual man were mostly built. (See Jeffrey Weeks, *Sex, Politics and Society: The Regulation of Sexuality since 1800*, London: Longman, 1981.) For Sedgwick, this either/or way of defining sexuality

> has been a presiding master term of the past century, one that has the same, primary importance for all modern Western identity and social organization ... as do the more traditionally visible cruxes of gender, class, and race. (p.11)

As with those other systems, what is important is the way in which ideology and language silence possibilities; here, by way of example, is part of Sedgwick's discussion of Henry James, a writer now regularly claimed as part of gay literary history. The extract refers to James's story 'The Beast in the Jungle':

> For (the hero) Marcher, the presence or possibility of homosexual meaning attached to the inner, the future, secret has exactly the reifying, totalizing, the blinding effect we described earlier ...
> Whatever Marcher feels ... may be discovered along those lines, it is, in the view of his panic, *one* thing, and the worst thing, 'the superstition of the Beast'. His readiness to organize the whole of his life around the preparation for it – the defence against it – remakes his life monolithically in the image of *its* monolith of, in his view, the inseparability of homosexual desire, (and) yielding, discovery, scandal, shame, annihilation. (p.205)

A different approach, but with a focus on the same period, can be seen in Alan Sinfield's *The Wilde Century: Effeminacy, Oscar Wilde and the Queer Moment* (1994). The main issue in the book is the modern construction of male homosexuality and the role of literary texts in that process.

Summarizing his argument in the preface titled 'Queer Thinking', Sinfield declares that

> the villain of the piece is the masculine/feminine binary structure ... the supposition that masculinity and femininity are the essential, normative properties of men and women respectively ... heterosexuals ... don't in fact fall tidily into masculine and feminine attributes ... so it is perverse that lesbians and gay men should be interpreted as some kind of contorted variation upon it. (pp.vii–viii)

Tracing the history of male effeminacy leads Sinfield to Tobias Smollett's novel *Peregrine Pickle* (1751). Smollett has been accepted in a relatively minor way into the canon of the English novel largely on account of his comic skill and his realism; 'no one gives the thousand and one strokes of eighteenth-century practical life better, not even Defoe' (A.R. Humphreys, 'Fielding and Smollett' in *From Dryden to Johnson*, The Pelican Guide to English Literature, vol. 4, ed. Boris Ford, Harmondsworth: Penguin, 1957, p.327). Sinfield picks out a scene in which 'queer thinking' and reading discover a sub-text peeping through the apparently easy comic surface:

> [Another] episode may point us towards some of the anxieties that the instability of effeminacy, as a concept, was provoking. Pickle and Pallet wish to attend a masquerade: because Pallet is a stranger to the town and might get lost, he is persuaded to dress as a woman – on the altogether unconvincing pretext that this will oblige Pickle to attend him 'with more care...' The upshot of this strange project is ... that Pallet is accosted by a nobleman who takes him for a woman. In this incident (on the surface at least) no one is given to same-sex passion; cross-dressing is a convenience and then a mistake. There are legitimate reasons for cross-dressing, the episode seems designed to say; it may be all good clean fun, and conducted by the very men who in the previous episode punish 'abominable practices'. (p.42)

Conclusion

This last example illustrates many of the concerns of gender-aware criticism. A critic focuses on an apparently straightforward – often simply 'realistic' – piece of writing to show not only that the text is shot through with gender issues, but that investigation of the text is bound up with investigation of gender and power issues in society. Usually the critic is motivated by her or his own gendered position and agenda; Sinfield writes that 'my project of historical reconstruction has substantial implications for how we handle ourselves today' (p.viii), and Pamela Morris begins *Literature and Feminism* by declaring that her 'emphasis is on feminist literary criticism as an empowering practice of reading' (p.ix).

I will happily sign up to both of these programmes. When I reread Ibsen's play *A Doll's House* recently, I was ready for the feminist meanings that have accumulated around the text and made it famous: the heroine, Nora, is caught in a trap built of the economic and social order of society and patriarchal language. With my interest in gender-based criticism, I was able to join in modern feminist reading of the work. But I felt myself also empowered to read from my own different point of view, to reconstruct history in a different way and to see the play as part of a different ideological process still operating today. The play diagnoses the way in which femininity makes women subject to the power of father and then of husband. It seems to allow Nora to escape, but the line of force that runs from Ibsen himself to his character remains in place. That line of force coerces the reader and holds the woman and the nature of femininity at the centre of the stage, making it the 'problem'. In a strong feminist play it seems natural that, in an early scene, Nora shares her story in an intimate conversation with a woman friend – who is herself a widow. Nora's husband meanwhile talks with *his* friend *off*-stage. As I was reading, this scene assumed crucial significance: the off-stage conversation became a key to the play's silencing of the masculine. Ibsen's instructions for the design of the stage make the men's conversation take place almost literally in the closet. The play allows us to think of a bond existing between the men, but goes no further: we cannot think whether it is homosexual or homosocial. So the problem of the play so far as masculinity is concerned is exactly that: the nature of the relationship between men is silenced, and our attention is diverted because Nora is made the problem to be solved.

What I want to suggest through this anecdote is not that somehow my queer-thinking reading of *A Doll's House* has finally exposed the *truth* about the play, but that thinking of gender (Ibsen's and my own, as well as the characters' in the play) has empowered me to read the play in a different way. Gender-based criticism is nothing if it does not empower the reader to reread texts and bring out new meanings, enabling the silenced to speak and making silences disruptive.

Questions and exercises

1   Choose any novel written by a woman which contains an extended representation of a man. To what extent can it be said that the author genuinely represents masculinity? Is there evidence to support a claim that such representations of men by women are more revealing of femininity?

2   Poems by Christina Rossetti (1830–94) and Matthew Arnold (1822–88) come within a few pages of each other in Christopher Ricks, *The New Oxford Book of Victorian Verse*. That enables us to put together, for example, 'Goblin Market' (1859) and 'The Scholar Gypsy' (1852–3?), or 'A Better Resurrection' (1857) and 'Growing Old' (1864–7). What can such comparisons tell us about representations of gender in the mid-nineteenth century? Can the comparisons also tell us something about feminine and masculine ways of writing?

3   Consider some or all of the following relationships: that between Pip and Herbert Pocket in *Great Expectations*; between Illingworth and Gerald Arbuthnot in *A Woman of No Importance*; between Fielding and Aziz in *A Passage to India*; between Gerald Crich and Rupert Birkin in *Women in Love*; between characters in *A Boy's Own Story*. Taking the perspective of queer criticism, what similarities can you see between these relationships (or between similar relationships within other novels you have read)?

4   Find out what you can about the lives of two women writers (from the past or from the present). What similarities and differences can you discern between their lives (a) up to the point of their first publications, and (b) in their writing lives as a whole? Do your findings lead you to conclude that the women feel the same pressures and possibilities, or otherwise have any common cause?

Selected reading

Elizabeth Abel (ed.), *Writing and Sexual Difference* (Brighton: Harvester, 1982).

Nina Auerbach, 'Magi and Maidens: The Romance of the Victorian Freud', in Elizabeth Abel (ed.), *Writing and Sexual Difference* (Brighton: Harvester, 1982).

Simone de Beauvoir, *The Second Sex* (1949), trans. and ed. H.M. Parshley (London: Everyman, 1993).

Frances Bonner, Lizbeth Goodman, Richard Allen, Linda Janes and Catherine King (eds), *Imagining Women* (Cambridge: Polity, 1992).

J.A.Boone, M. Cadden (eds), *Engendering Men: The Question of Male Feminist Criticism* (London: Routledge, 1990).

Joseph Bristow, *Sexuality* (London: Routledge, 1997).

Helen Crowley and Susan Himmelweit (eds), *Knowing Women* (Cambridge: Polity, 1992).

Mary Eagleton (ed.), *Feminist Literary Criticism* (London: Longman, 1991).

Terry Eagleton, *The Rape of Clarissa* (Oxford: Blackwell, 1982).

Terry Eagleton, *Literary Theory: An Introduction*, 2nd edn (Oxford: Blackwell, 1996).

D. Elam, *Feminism and Deconstruction: Ms en Abyme* (London: Routledge, 1994).

Mari Evans (ed.), *Black Women Writers* (London: Pluto, 1985).

Sigmund Freud, *Three Essays on the Theory of Sexuality,* in The Pelican Freud Library, vol. 7 *On Sexuality*, trans. James Strachey and Angela Richards (Harmondsworth: Penguin, 1977).

Sigmund Freud, *Case Histories 1: 'Dora' and 'Little Hans'*, in The Pelican Freud Library, vol. 7 *On Sexuality*, trans. James Strachey, Angela Richards, Alan Tyson (Harmondsworth: Penguin, 1977).

Sandra M. Gilbert and Susan Gubar, *The Mad Woman in the Attic* (London and New Haven: Yale University Press, 1979).

Sandra M. Gilbert and Susan Gubar, *No Man's Land* (London and New Haven: Yale University Press, 1988).

John Goode, 'Woman and the Literary Text' in Juliet Mitchell and Ann Oakley (eds), *The Rights and Wrongs of Women* (Harmondsworth: Penguin, 1976).

Elizabeth Grosz, *Jacques Lacan: A Feminist Introduction* (London: Routledge, 1990).

Maggie Humm (ed.), *A Reader's Guide to Contemporary Feminist Criticism* (Hemel Hempstead: Harvester Wheatsheaf, 1994).

Mary Jacobus, 'The Difference of View' in Mary Jacobus (ed.), *Women Writing and Writing about Women* (London: Croom Helm, 1979).

Mary Jacobus (ed.), *Reading Woman: Essays in Feminist Criticism* (London: Methuen, 1986).

Jane Miller, *Women Writing about Men* (London: Virago, 1986).

Kate Millett, *Sexual Politics* (London: Virago, 1969).

Ellen Moers, *Literary Women* (London: W.H. Allen, 1977).

Toril Moi (ed.), *Sexual/Textual Politics: Feminist Literary Theory* (London: Methuen, 1985).

Franco Moretti, *The Way of the World: The Bildungsroman in European Culture* (London: Verso, 1987).

Pamela Morris, *Literature and Feminism* (Oxford: Blackwell, 1993).

Philip Rice and Patricia Waugh (eds), *Modern Literary Theory: A Reader,* 3rd edn (London: Edward Arnold, 1996).

Eve Kosofsky Sedgwick, *Between Men: English Literature and Male Homosocial Desire* (New York: Columbia University Press, 1985).

Eve Kosofsky Sedgwick, *Epistemology of the Closet* (Berkeley: University of California Press, 1990).

Elaine Showalter, *A Literature of Their Own: British Women Novelists from Brontë to Lessing* (London: Virago, 1978).

Elaine Showalter (ed.), *The New Feminist Criticism: Essays on Women, Literature and Theory* (London: Virago, 1986).

Alan Sinfield, *The Wilde Century: Effeminacy, Oscar Wilde and the Queer Moment* (London: Cassell, 1994).

Janet Todd, *Feminist Literary History* (Cambridge: Polity, 1988).

Alice Walker, *In Search of our Mothers' Gardens: Womanist Prose* (London: Women's Press, 1984).

Mary Wollstonecraft, *The Rights of Women,* ed. Miriam Krammick (Harmondsworth: Penguin, 1978).

9 DECONSTRUCTION

by Stuart Sim

Introduction

Deconstruction is a form of textual practice (one cannot really say 'analysis' or 'interpretation' since it rejects the assumptions such terms involve), derived from the work of the French philosopher Jacques Derrida, which aims to demonstrate the inherent instability of both language and meaning. Derrida is possibly best approached as the latest, and in many ways the most radical, exponent of philosophical scepticism, a tradition whose brief has been to undermine the time-honoured assumptions of Western philosophical enquiry – assumptions such as that truth is not a relative notion, or that words have determinate meanings.

Although its heyday is probably now past (postmodernism having largely eclipsed it as the major talking point in theoretical circles at the time of writing), deconstruction continues to inspire debate, and Derrida's claim that it is to be regarded as the heir to Marxism has succeeded in provoking fresh controversy. (In fact, deconstruction is now commonly regarded as an aspect of the postmodern movement.) The extent of deconstruction's influence in its heyday, particularly in academic circles in the USA, can be gauged from the following remarks by a US critic:

> There can be no denying that the representation of 'crisis' in criticism in the late 1960s is the work of deconstruction and those it influenced. Nor can it be denied that the polemical conflicts which resulted both from this declaration of crisis – to which deconstruction is the rigorously appropriate response – and the rising prominence of deconstructive techniques sustained the seeming vitality of the institution through the 1970s and into the 1980s. Careers have been made, books published, journals begun, programs, schools, and institutions founded, courses offered, reviews written, and conferences held. The point is simple: no matter which 'side' one takes in the battle, the fact is that deconstruction effectively displaced other intellectual programs in the minds and much of the work of the literary avant-garde.
>
> (Paul A. Bove, *The Yale Critics: Deconstruction in America*, ed. J. Arac, W. Godzich and W. Martin, Minneapolis: University of Minnesota Press, 1983, p.6)

Derrida's keenest followers have arguably been the 'Yale critics' – Geoffrey Hartman, Harold Bloom, Paul de Man and J. Hillis Miller – and, as Bove suggests above, a specifically 'American' school of deconstruction has grown up over the last few decades. It is worth noting, however, that Derrida himself is at best ambivalent about 'American' deconstruction, and has attacked it on several occasions. (See, for example, Jacques Derrida,

The Ear of the Other: Otobiography, Transference, Translation, Lincoln, Na. and London: University of Nebraska Press, 1988.)

Primary and secondary reading

Derrida's best-known, and in general most accessible, work is *Writing and Difference* (Chicago: Chicago University Press, 1978), a collection of essays which contains two of his most trenchant critiques of structuralist methodology, 'Force and Signification' and 'Structure, Sign and Play in the Discourse of the Human Sciences'. For a fuller picture of the work of this very prolific writer, one might also consult *Of Grammatology* (Baltimore and London: Johns Hopkins University Press, 1976), *Margins of Philosophy* (Brighton: Harvester Press, 1982), *Positions* (London: Athlone, 1981), *The Post Card: From Socrates to Freud and Beyond* (Chicago and London: University of Chicago Press, 1987), *The Truth in Painting* (Chicago and London: University of Chicago Press, 1987), or *Spectres of Marx: The State of the Debt, the Work of Mourning, and the New International* (London: Routledge, 1994). The Yale critics and Derrida can be found in action together in *Deconstruction and Criticism*, ed. Harold Bloom (London: Routledge, 1979). Geoffrey Hartman's *Saving the Text* (Baltimore and London: Johns Hopkins University Press, 1981) is worth exploring as a particularly exuberant example of deconstructionist criticism.

For a sound introduction to deconstruction, see Jonathan Culler, *On Deconstruction* (London: Routledge, 1983), or Madan Sarup, *An Introductory Guide to Post-Structuralism and Postmodernism* (London: Harvester Wheatsheaf, 1993). Christopher Norris has also written several useful studies on Derrida and deconstruction, including *Deconstruction: Theory and Practice* (London: Methuen, 1982), *The Deconstructive Turn* (London: Methuen, 1983), *Contest of Faculties* (London and New York: Methuen, 1985) and *Derrida* (London: Fontana, 1987). Norris is always good value on this subject, and the latter text is arguably the most impressive introduction to Derrida currently available. Henry Staten's *Wittgenstein and Derrida* (Oxford: Blackwell, 1985) usefully examines Derrida's work within the context of modern philosophical scepticism, while Michael Ryan's *Marxism and Deconstruction: A Critical Articulation* (Baltimore and London: Johns Hopkins University Press, 1982) is a pre-*Spectres of Marx* attempt to find common ground between Derrida and Marx. On the critical side, for a well sustained attack on Derrida's philosophical position, see Patrick Colm Hogan's *The Politics of Interpretation: Ideology, Professionalism and the Study of Literature* (New York and Oxford: Oxford University Press, 1990).

Deconstruction and structuralism

One of the most fruitful ways of coming to terms with deconstruction is to consider its relationship to structuralism; indeed it would not be fanciful to regard it as a form of *anti*-structuralism. Deconstruction is to some extent a development of structuralism and has common roots in semiotics and Saussurean linguistics, while rejecting most of the assumptions of structuralism – particularly its systematic approach to texts and methodical forms of analysis. Deconstruction also rejects the commitment to binary opposition in structuralism (a trait structuralism inherits from Saussurean linguistics) on the grounds that such oppositions always privilege one term over the other – signified over signifier, for example – in a relationship of domination. (In a wider cultural context, the assumed dominance of man over woman is another instance of a loaded binary opposition.)

In 'Force and Signification' and 'Structure, Sign and Play', Derrida's anti-structuralist credentials are clearly displayed for all to see. In the former essay, structuralism's tendency to assume an essential structure at the heart of all discourse is called into question through an attack on the critic Jean Rousset, whose application of structuralist methodology to the work of Jean Corneille results in *Polyeucte* being posited as the central text of the playwright's *œuvre*. Every other Corneillean play is then to be judged against the perfectly realized structure that is *Polyeucte*. To Derrida this is 'ultra-structuralism', a method that always finds exactly what it sets out to look for, and in this sense it is to be regarded as authoritarian and, indeed, totalitarian in intent (totalitarian here meaning the reduction of phenomena to a formula that is seen to govern them totally, as is the case with structuralism's linguistic model). Claude Levi-Strauss is taken to task in similar fashion in 'Structure, Sign and Play' for his belief that South American Indian myths are to be considered as variations of a central myth, where 'the apparent divergences between the versions are to be treated as the result of transformations within a set' (*The Raw and the Cooked*, London and New York: Cape, 1970, p.147). Again, it is a case of the theory's assumptions dictating the nature of the analyst's findings. There is also criticism of Levi-Strauss for admitting that the incest taboo seems to be both 'natural' *and* 'cultural', thus undermining the binary opposition of nature and culture on which so much of Levi-Strauss's work depends.

Structuralism is for Derrida merely the most blatant example of a questionable tendency found throughout Western cultural discourse – logocentricity, the belief that sounds, and words, are representations of meanings already present in the speaker's mind. Logocentricity in its turn depends on a commitment to what Derrida calls 'the metaphysics of presence' – the notion that meanings can be *fully* present to individuals in their minds, without slippage of any kind occurring. Derrida opposes such beliefs, arguing that 'meaning is neither before nor after the act ... the notion of an idea or "interior design" as simply anterior to a work which would supposedly be the expression of it, is a prejudice: a prejudice of the traditional criticism called idealist' (*Writing and Difference*, p.11).

In other words, meaning is not present *in* a text. At best it is a transitory phenomenon fleetingly experienced by the individual reader, which can never be recovered in its entirety nor in any sense fixed as a reference point for subsequent readers. (Paul de Man speaks of reading as an act that cannot be 'in any way prescribed or verified': *Blindness and Insight,* New York: Oxford University Press, 1971, p.107.) Derrida wants a free play of meaning, what Jonathan Culler has called 'the pleasure of infinite creation' (*Structuralist Poetics,* London: Routledge, 1975, p.248); this suggests that it is not just logocentricity that Derrida is setting himself against, but Western culture's commitment to rationality and linear thought. Taking his cue from Saussure's identification of the signifier as arbitrary, Derrida contends that linear thought is a constricting convention imposed on us rather than the ultimate goal to which all intellectual activity should aspire.

Structuralism is squarely within the idealist tradition for Derrida, and structuralists are held continually to commit the logocentrist heresy in their criticism, with the concept of 'structure' taking over from 'meaning' and the relationship between structure and text being an analogue for that between meaning and word. Derrida's argument is that structuralists are *imposing* a form on textual material, and that such a practice puts limits on human creativity: '*Form* fascinates', he claims, 'when one no longer has the force to understand force from within itself. That is, to create. That is why literary criticism is structuralist in every age, in its essence and destiny' (*Writing and Difference,* pp.4–5).

Derrida's concepts

Derrida's critique of structuralism, and of the assumptions it involves about the nature of meaning and language, is a powerful one, but it is not always easy to pin down the conceptual basis of his argument. In fact, defining Derrida's terms can be a thankless task (for one attempt, see Alan Bass's introduction to *Writing and Difference,* pp.xvi–xvii).

Critics and theorists are normally expected to use their terms in a consistent way; that is one of the heritages of the analytical bias in Western culture. Derrida, however, complicates matters by deliberately cultivating multiple reference in his terms – as in the notorious case of *différance,* a word coined by Derrida from the French word *différence* which means both 'difference' and 'deferral'. In speech, one cannot tell which meaning is intended, since the pronunciation remains identical. *Différance* becomes Derrida's way of demonstrating that there is always slippage of meaning, and he claims that it is operative at all times and all places within discourse. He also claims, somewhat ingeniously, that any term he uses is to be regarded as under erasure (*sous rature*), such that we cannot assume it has the status of a concept; in effect, each term cancels itself as it goes. Deconstruction, Derrida insists, has no concepts, and neither is it a form of analysis.

Derrida does not see himself as engaged in the business of explication – that is, of interpreting obscure meanings for the benefit of the puzzled reader – but of writing supplements to texts in such a way as to make meanings proliferate, and the inbuilt imprecision and self-cancelling nature of his terms considerably advances this process. The more meanings are encouraged to proliferate, the more texts demonstrate their inability to be reduced to any theoretical formula such as the linguistic model involves. In Derrida's work, to quote Hartman, 'interpretation no longer aims at the reconciliation or unification of warring truths' (*Saving the Text*, p.51). What deconstructionists set out to reveal is 'the strength of the signifier *vis-à-vis* a signified (the "meaning") that tries to enclose it' (Hartman, *Deconstruction and Criticism*, p.vii), thus problematizing the structuralist binary opposition that sees the signified as the dominant partner. Drawing attention to, and then ruthlessly undermining, such enclosures is one of the primary objectives of deconstruction, which seeks to show how signifiers resist and defer fixed meanings. Signifiers are to be considered instead as floating and unfixable, and signs as a result forever incomplete.

Deconstructive critical discourse

The critical discourse that results from this theoretical outlook is a heady mixture of wit, word-play, allusion and association of ideas, designed to exploit to the full the indeterminacy claimed to lie at the heart of language. Puns are a particularly favoured weapon because they are considered to have an inherent instability of meaning, being multi- (and possibly indeterminately) referential. Hartman has gone so far as to claim that puns are beyond value-judgement. (For a critique of deconstructionist theories of the pun, see Chapter 6, '"We Shall Catch at that Word": Hartman, the Pun and Deconstructive Criticism', of Stuart Sim, *Beyond Aesthetics: Confrontations with Poststructuralism and Postmodernism*, Hemel Hempstead: Harvester Wheatsheaf, 1992.) The following extract from *Saving the Text* is an entirely representative sample of what deconstruction aims at in the terms of critical practice:

> Near the beginning of *Glas* Derrida asks: 'What does the death knell of the proper name signify?' (27b) We can now answer: it signifies the birth of the literary text. The fading of the name leaves no legacy ('legs', homonym of *'lait'* and near-anagram of 'glas', as in 219b) except for the paranomasia of a text. 'Reste ici ou glas qu'on ne peut arrêter' (287b). Yet this movement without term incorporates 'terms' that displace the proper name. The terms are fixed or frozen particles (*glas* into *glace* and *classe*), coagulations in the stream of discourse, milk-stones (*galalithes*) or even body-stones ('le calcul de la mère' refers also to the organic, pathological kidney stone, *caillou*). They grow in language as in a culture; they are formed by a process analogous to introjection or incorporation; and there is a radical ambivalence about their value, whether they are blockage and detritus, or seminal and pregnant tissue. The letter *L*, signifying the pronoun 'Elle', is a mock-up of such a term; so is the reduction of 'savoir absolu' to *Sa*, which could be confused with another pronoun in the possessive case, also pointing to the

feminine gender. 'L'a', similarly, combines in Lacan's algebraic manner the capital *L* with what seems to be the *petit objet a* (standing for 'autre' instead of 'Autre', here within the feminine sphere).

(Geoffrey Hartman, *Saving the Text*, p.77)

The point of such writing, with its sudden and unpredictable shifts of topic, register and even language, is to sever the bond between signifier and signified, word and meaning, on which our discourses so crucially depend. In its very weakness as rational argument the extract is an excellent illustration of how *différance* is supposed to work, since *différance* 'introduces the idea of a differential play within language that everywhere prevents (or constantly *defers*) the imaginary coincidence of meaning and intent' (Christopher Norris, *Contest of Faculties*, p.82). The argument is that such a free-associative, almost stream-of-consciousness method of writing is less authoritarian than traditional criticism, where the critic is seen to mediate between text and reader: the argument is that it creates – rather than recovers, fixes, or closes off – meaning.

Derrida's writing similarly revels in its ability to defer criticism, analysis and the making of value-judgements. On the face of it *The Truth in Painting* is a work of aesthetic criticism, including chapters on such works of art as Van Gogh's *Old Shoes with Laces*. Derrida is at pains, however, to prevent anything like standard critical discourse from forming. We are treated instead to a series of cunning strategies designed to lead us away from the work in question:

> Here they are. I'll begin. What of shoes? What, shoes? Whose are the shoes? What are they made of? And even, who are they? Here they are, the questions, that's all ... Here it is. Questions about awkward gait (limping or shifty?), questions of the type: 'Where to put one's feet?' 'How is it going to work [*marcher*]?' 'And what if it doesn't work?' 'What happens when it doesn't work (or when you hang up your shoes or miss them with your feet)?' 'When–and for what reason–it stops working?' 'Who is walking?' 'With whom?' 'With what?' 'On whose feet?' 'Who is pulling whose leg? [*qui fait marcher qui*]' 'Who is making what go? [*qui fait marcher quoi*?]' 'What is making whom or what work?' etc., all these idiomatic figures of the question seem to me, right here, to be necessary.

(*The Truth in Painting*, pp.257, 263)

Most commentators would consider questions such as the above to be at best irrelevant, at worst intellectually irresponsible mischief-making, but they serve Derrida's purpose admirably in delaying, probably indefinitely, the moment of criticism ('performative supplementarity' being 'open to infinity': *The Truth in Painting*, p.3). At any one point the words can take off in any direction, demonstrating the chaotic potential always there under the surface of traditional analytically constructed discourse.

The politics of deconstruction

For all its philosophically serious purpose, deconstructive criticism often looks more like creative writing than criticism proper (*The Post Card* might even be considered an epistolary novel of sorts), although it can also be very learned in its breadth of allusion. What deconstruction has been notably successful in doing is making us more keenly aware of the openness of texts and their ability to elude definitive readings (to resist enclosure, as a deconstructionist would have it).

Perhaps the very best criticism has always done this, but there has been a noticeable tendency in modern schools of literary theory to hold out the promise of revealing what texts *really* meant (something about the class struggle, gender relations, human psychology, or the internal relations of language and grammar, for example). Deconstruction is a useful corrective to this all-too-common tendency, although its anarchic-looking procedures might themselves be seen to have their own socio-political commitments. To wish to escape from the world of authority and value into a world of 'innocence of becoming', as Derrida pictures it (*Writing and Difference*, p.292), has, one might suggest, definite ideological connotations. Derrida has pointedly avoided spelling out these commitments for most of his career (note his refusal to be pigeonholed politically by the assorted leftist interviewers in *Positions*, for example), but in *Spectres of Marx* he proceeds to argue for deconstruction as the inheritor of the liberationist credentials of Marxism – if not in a manner calculated to appeal to classical Marxists:

> It will always be a fault not to read and reread and discuss Marx ... and to go beyond scholarly 'reading' or 'discussion'. It will be more and more a fault, a failing of theoretical, philosophical, political responsibility ... There will be no future without this. Not without Marx, no future without Marx, without the memory and the inheritance of Marx: in any case of a certain Marx, of his genius, of at least one of his spirits. For this will be our hypothesis or rather our bias: *there is more than one of them, there must be more than one of them.*
>
> (*Spectres of Marx*, p.13)

The insistence on a plurality of meaning to Marx's intellectual heritage is typically deconstructionist (as well as counter to classical Marxism's ab-solutist bias), and has led to Derrida being appropriated to the post-Marxist movement (see, for example, Stuart Sim (ed.), *Post-Marxism: A Reader*, Edinburgh: Edinburgh University Press, 1998).

Conclusion

One's final attitude to deconstruction might well depend on whether one agrees that rationality and logocentricity really are the confidence tricks that Derrida insists they are. How far down this road one can follow Derrida without collapsing into a self-defeating solipsism and private language is, however, an interesting question to ponder. It might also be objected that if language is as marked by indeterminacy as deconstruction claims, then it is difficult to see how it can establish this indeterminacy through the use of language: some sort of logical paradox would seem to be involved at that point. Madan Sarup claims that Derrida can be exonerated from such an accusation:

> The usual superficial criticism of Derrida is that he questions the value of 'truth' and 'logic' and yet uses logic to demonstrate the truth of his own arguments. The point is that the overt concern of Derrida's writing is the predicament of having to use the resources of the heritage that he questions.
>
> (*An Introductory Guide to Post-structuralism and Postmodernism*, p.58)

But Sarup is unlikely to persuade too many doubters that the logical paradox has been explained away, although that rarely deters philosophical sceptics from proceeding with their enquiries.

For all its impact on critical discourse, it is most likely that deconstruction will be remembered as a particularly radical, if on occasion more than a little eccentric, form of philosophical scepticism that forced re-examination of the subject's foundations of argument.

Questions and exercises

1   Deconstructionists are very dismissive of the prominent role played by binary oppositions in Western thought. Can you think of any way of countering their arguments and *defending* binarism?

2   Is deconstruction no more than an abdication of critical responsibility?

3   How tenable a view is it that reading is an act that can in no way be prescribed or verified?

4   Is 'erasure' simply a form of cheating at argument?

5   If, as deconstructionists appear to believe, signs are forever incomplete, how can we ever have discourse?

6   'Like most forms of scepticism, deconstruction is a self-defeating exercise with nothing positive to offer the critical practitioner.' Discuss.

Selected reading

Jonathan Culler, *On Deconstruction* (London: Routledge and Kegan Paul, 1983).

Christopher Norris, *Derrida,* Modern Masters Series (London: Fontana, 1987).

Madan Sarup, *An Introductory Guide to Post-structuralism and Postmodernism,* rev. edn (Hemel Hempstead: Harvester Wheatsheaf, 1993).

Stuart Sim (ed.), *The A–Z Guide to Modern Literary and Cultural Theorists* (Hemel Hempstead: Harvester Wheatsheaf, 1995).

Stuart Sim (ed.), *The Icon Critical Dictionary of Post-Modern Thought* (Cambridge: Icon Press, 1998).

10 READER-RESPONSE CRITICISM AND RECEPTION THEORY

by Stephen Regan

One of the principal effects of 'New Criticism' in literary studies was to shift the focus of scholarly attention from 'author' to 'text'. The traditional assumption that 'authorial intention' was the source and guarantee of meaning in literature was effectively challenged and superseded by the notion of 'textual autonomy', with its insistence on the close relationship of form and meaning and its almost reverential acknowledgement of the literary work as 'a well-wrought urn'. With the explosion of new theoretical interests and procedures from the late 1960s onwards (feminism, psycho-analysis, structural linguistics, cultural materialism), the focus of interest shifted decisively towards the role of the reader or audience in the process of interpretation. The reader came to be seen not as the passive recipient but as the active producer of meaning. The idea of the text underwent a similar transformation: it was no longer to be regarded as a unified object with a single, determinate meaning, but a fractured, unstable entity with plural and perhaps indeterminate meanings.

Much of the impulse behind this theoretical revolution came from a set of critical interests and practices commonly referred to as 'reader-response criticism'. In the USA this kind of criticism is associated with the work of Stanley Fish, Norman Holland, David Bleich and others, though it overlaps significantly with the concerns of structuralist critics such as Jonathan Culler and Michael Riffaterre. In Germany, however, there exists a much more rigorous and well established philosophical tradition of reader-centred criticism, which is usually referred to as *reception theory* or *reception aesthetics*. The principal exponents of this tradition are two members of the 'Constance School' (both lecturers at the University of Constance) – Wolfgang Iser and Hans Robert Jauss. Although it is difficult to establish a single critical position or consistent theory among the various branches of reader-response criticism, it is possible to identify some prominent areas of investigation. Reader-response criticism and reception theory are principally concerned with:

- the kinds of reader that various texts seem to imply
- the codes and conventions to which readers refer in making sense of texts
- the mental processes that occur as readers move through a text
- and the sociological and historical differences that might distinguish one reading response from another.

This preoccupation with matters of textual interpretation is often referred to as *hermeneutics*, a word that was long associated with Holy Scripture but now has a widespread and commonly accepted secular usage. Modern literary theory, in bringing these hermeneutic concerns into the foreground of debate, has encouraged critics of all persuasions to declare their interests and be explicit about their intentions.

As a safe generalization, then, we might say that reader-oriented forms of criticism move the focus of attention in literary studies from the author and the work to the reader and the text. The idea that meaning is 'contained' in the words on the page is replaced by a more dynamic model in which the 'process' of meaning requires the active participation of the audience or reader. Let us look once more at the following short lyric by William Wordsworth:

> A slumber did my spirit seal;
>   I had no human fears:
> She seemed a thing that could not feel
>   The touch of earthly years.
>
> No motion has she now, no force;
>   She neither hears nor sees,
> Rolled round in earth's diurnal course
>   With rocks, and stones, and trees.

In Chapter 7, 'From New Criticism to structuralism', Graham Martin proposed a number of contrasting perspectives in relation to this poem. Traditional scholarship (with the emphasis mainly on the author) might ask: When was the poem written? When was it published? What can we deduce about the anonymous subject of the poem? What was her relationship to the poet? What moral or philosophical ideas does the poet put forward?

New Criticism would eschew the question of authorial intention and concentrate on those formal properties of the text – alliteration, metre, rhyme, stanzaic division, imagery – by which the poem resolves any internal ambiguity and strives for a unified meaning of timeless, universal significance. Graham Martin also indicated how structuralist readings of the poem might approach the text as a sign system, employing a specialized linguistic vocabulary to uncover its phonetic and semantic patterning.

Reader-response criticism is likely to concentrate on the ways in which a reader might encounter and experience Wordsworth's poem as a word-by-word, line-by-line activity. Raman Selden in *A Reader's Guide to Contemporary Literary Theory* (London: Harvester Wheatsheaf, 1993, p.48) offers Figure 10.1 as a way of illustrating how a text (even one as short as this) presents to its readers a series of shifting viewpoints. What the experience of reading reveals is not a kernel of meaning waiting to be dislodged from the outer shell of the poem, but a process or sequence of adjustments in perspective. With each adjustment of meaning, from (a) through to (d), the reader's assumptions and expectations are challenged and renewed.

A slumber did my spirit seal;
I had no human fears:
She seemed a thing that could not feel
The touch of earthly years.

No motion has she now, no force;
She neither hears nor sees,
Rolled round in earth's diurnal course
With rocks, and stones, and trees.

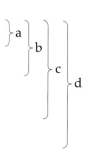

Figure 10.1

A number of questions arise, especially in relation to the contrary state-ments that might be deduced from the two stanzas of the poem: 'I thought she could not die' and 'She is dead'. What relationship exists between these statements? Has the speaker revised or revoked his earlier thoughts? Are we to assume that his attitude in the first stanza was wise or naive? Is 'slumber' in this respect a species of romantic vision or an ordinary illusion? Is the word 'seemed' a matter of simple likeness or one of mistaken identity? Does the second stanza deny the spiritual significance claimed by the first, or does it complement it with a more informed and less naive view of 'nature'?

What reader-response criticism would claim is that the answers to such questions cannot be derived solely from the words of texts. The meaning of a text is never completely formulated, but rather 'activated' or 'realized' through the reader's involvement. Texts have gaps or blanks – such as the unclear relationship between the two stanzas in Wordsworth's poem – which the reader must endeavour to fill.

The obvious difficulty with reader-response criticism is in ascertaining the extent of the reader's freedom in realizing the potential meanings of the text. Is interpretation to be regarded as a matter of endlessly free variation, or is there a limit to the range of possible meanings that might be produced? Does the text itself govern the legitimate scope of interpretation, and – if so – through what means does it exert this power? Are some meanings more valid or more correct than others? Some reader-response critics carefully avoid the fraught and controversial issue of 'value' by suggesting that what they are advocating is a *descriptive* rather than *evaluative* theory of literature, but the issue doesn't simply disappear.

The complexity and persistence of such questions become apparent if we look at the theoretical precepts of a critic such as Stanley Fish, whose ideas about 'reader response' have been repeatedly modified since the 1960s. Literature, he maintains, is the activity that the reader performs: the place where meaning occurs is in the reader's mind and not in the space between the covers of a book. What governs the reader's developing responses is a set of 'interpretive strategies' – shared rules and conventions – which readers internalize and learn to apply in particular situations, just as all speakers must proceed according to certain rules and regulations. Fish's reader, then, is an *informed* reader – one who possesses both linguistic and literary *competence*.

The critical method Fish employs is a highly detailed exegesis of what words, phrases, sentences, paragraphs, chapters, novels, plays, poems *do,* in terms of affecting the reader. He describes this method of *affective stylistics* as 'an analysis of the developing responses of the reader in relation to the words as they succeed one another in time' ('Literature in the Reader: Affective Stylistics', 1970, in *Reader-Response Criticism: From Formalism to Post-Structuralism*, ed. Jane P. Tomkins, Baltimore and London: Johns Hopkins University Press, 1980, p.73). One of the examples he gives is a line from Book One of John Milton's *Paradise Lost*, alluding to Satan's fallen angels:

> Nor did they not perceive the evil plight.

The first word generates an expectation of what will follow: it constitutes a negative assertion which requires a subject and a verb (two vacant slots in the reader's mind waiting to be filled). Before the expected verb appears, however, there is a second negative which has an unexpected and intrusive effect. The reader's progress is halted by a syntactical uncertainty in the line. Fish claims that to invoke the rule of the double negative and assume that the line can be read as 'they *did* perceive the evil plight' is a mistake. The two negatives combine to produce a temporal suspension in the reading process; the resulting psychological unease is a critical part of the reader's encounter with the line, and consequently a critical part of the line's meaning. As Fish explains in his preface to *Surprised by Sin: The Reader in Paradise Lost* (London: Macmillan, 1967), Milton's readers undergo a process of humiliation and education in keeping with the Christian notion of 'the Fall': they discover their 'inability to respond adequately to spiritual conceptions' and are called upon to refine their perceptions (p.ix).

It might be argued, with some justification, that Fish privileges those texts which display syntactical hesitations and qualifications (the prose of Walter Pater is another favoured example) over those of a more obvious, declarative kind. It also seems doubtful that the majority of readers (even informed readers) respond to literature in the painstaking word-by-word fashion that Fish supposes. There are more important reservations to be made, however, and some of these have been pressed by the structuralist critic Jonathan Culler. It needs to be asked, for instance, why different readers produce different interpretations, even when they abide by similar rules and conventions. Culler adopts a much more enquiring approach to the idea of 'the competent reader' and insists that 'competence', far from being a neutral concern, is shaped and governed by those social institutions that teach us to read and, in doing so, establish what might be deemed an 'acceptable' or 'appropriate' interpretation.

Since the mid-1970s, Fish has revised his early views of the informed reader, gradually shifting his attention to the idea of *interpretive communities*, first introduced in 1976 in 'Interpreting the *Variorum*' (once again dealing with Milton). From this altered perspective, particular meanings are produced by particular *communities* of readers: the understanding of a text emerges from communally established and historically determined interests and beliefs. In this respect, Fish has become more obviously engaged in the politics of reading, raising questions that have a broad sociological and institutional application. Even so, he has been criticized by thinkers of a more radical political persuasion for not being explicit enough in describing the interests and beliefs of particular 'reading communities'. Edward Said was among those who took Fish to task in the 1980s:

> If, as we have recently been told by Stanley Fish, every act of interpretation is made possible and given force by an interpretive community, then we must go a great deal further in showing what situation, what historical and social configuration, what political interests are concretely entailed by the very existence of interpretive communities.
>
> (*The World, the Text, and the Critic*, Cambridge, Massachusetts: Harvard University Press, 1983, p.26)

Two other contemporaries of Stanley Fish – Norman Holland and David Bleich – have developed theories of reader reception which obviously owe more to psychoanalysis than to structuralism. Both critics view the dynamics of literary response according to the needs and demands of individual psychology, and are therefore concerned with the influence of personality and personal identity on literary interpretation. Individual readers are seen to re-create works of literature according to their personality traits or desire for self-knowledge.

German reception theory owes less to modern psychology than it does to aesthetic philosophy, especially to the enormous significance of phenomenology in the writings of Edmund Husserl, Martin Heidegger and Hans George Gadamer. The idea that the proper object of philosophical investigation is the contents of our consciousness rather than the physical world itself has been a central concern of reception theory. Wolfgang Iser, for instance, proposes what is essentially a phenomenology of reading, insisting that the study of literature should be concerned not only with the text but equally with the consciousness of the reader in responding to the text. Drawing on the influential work of the Polish phenomenologist Roman Ingarden, Iser advocates that the text be seen as a framework of *schematized aspects* or *schemata* that must be *actualized* or *concretized* by the cognitive activity of the reader. He refers to the literary work as a *virtual* work, in the sense of its unrealized potential for meaning. It is the gaps and blanks of the text that give rise to communication in the reading process; the indeterminacy of the text increases the variety of communication possible. The reader's viewpoint, however, cannot proceed arbitrarily. The blanks in the text both induce *and* guide the reader's constitutive activity, triggering off responses or 'projections' in the reader's mind *and* simultaneously regulating or controlling the range and sequence of possible responses. Meaning in literature arises from the convergence or interaction of text and reader.

Much of Iser's work is a highly detailed account of reading as a complex experiential and intellectual activity, and a worked example is needed to explain his dense array of critical terms. *Tom Jones* is the novel Iser chooses to discuss in his essay 'Interaction between Text and Reader' (in *The Reader in the Text: Essays on Audience and Interpretation,* ed. Susan R. Suleiman and Inge Crosman, Princeton: University of Princeton Press, 1980). Underlying Iser's theory is a conviction that literature 'tells us something about reality' by arranging its formal and structural devices in a way that will encourage readers to reflect upon prevailing social and cultural norms. This formal selection and presentation of thought systems is what Iser calls the *repertoire* of the text. In the case of *Tom Jones,* Fielding depicts human nature through a repertoire of the prevailing norms dictated by eighteenth-century philo-sophical, social and political systems. The repertoire is seen in the contrasting patterns of conduct represented by the principal characters: Allworthy (benevolence); Squire Western (ruling passion); Square (the eternal fitness of things); and Thwackum (the human mind as a sink of iniquity). Tom, as hero, is accordingly linked throughout the novel to a broad set of moral, theological and philosophical values. Whenever he violates these norms of conduct, his action either shows these norms in a critical light or reveals his own imperfection. Tom's perspective repeatedly shifts between foreground and background. The resulting contrasts and discrepancies provide blanks or missing links which stimulate the reader's powers of *ideation* or imaginative conception. These blanks might occur, for instance, in the plot (where the story-line breaks or changes direction) or in dialogue (where something is left unsaid). The reading process is one in which social and cultural norms are continually being challenged and renewed and redefined.

In *Tom Jones* and other conventional realist novels, Iser observes four vantage points:

- that of the narrator
- that of the characters
- that of the plot
- that of the implied reader.

These different perspectival arrangements constitute a field of vision for the reader's wandering viewpoint. In the 'time flow' of reading, only parts or *segments* of perspective are momentarily evident, and the shifting and switching of perspectives compels the reader to question the norms which the novel makes available. Iser claims that when we read a text, we are continuously evaluating events with regard to our expectations of the future and against the background of the past. Unexpected events in the text will cause us to reformulate our expectations and also reinterpret the significance of what has already happened. What Iser looks for ultimately is a transformation in the reader's consciousness. With *Tom Jones*, this amounts to a new awareness: the reader's attention is no longer focused on what the social norms of the novel represent but on what this representation excludes – the human experience that is suppressed or denied. What the novel provides, then, is a sense of the possibilities that have been devalued by the prevalent system, and a consequent extension of the reader's vision.

If Iser, like other reception theorists, avoids any obvious evaluative criticism (suggesting to what extent one work might be better or greater than another), he nevertheless locates some sense of value in the ability of literature to challenge and question the validity of social norms and conventions. There is, then, a concealed or undeclared politics in Iser's work, but this rarely proceeds beyond a vaguely defined liberalism. The text can prompt its readers to new levels of awareness, but in another way it also constrains its readers; it both allows the reader an active role in producing meanings and ultimately restricts the range of different interpretations.

Eighteenth-century fiction, with its palpable interest in matters of individual morality, lends itself well to Iser's theory, but the theory is perhaps less likely to produce results when applied to the literature of the Middle Ages, for instance, or to the prose style of James Joyce in *Finnegans Wake*. Perhaps the most important reservation to be made about Iser's theory, however, is that it fails to explore the widely differing responses of readers across literary history. Are we to assume that the response of a modern reader to an antique text is identical to that of previous readers? In this sense, Iser's 'reader' is a transcendental or idealized being, and to this extent his account of the reading process is necessarily an abstract, de-historicized performance.

In the work of Hans Robert Jauss, the relationship between literature and history provides the very core of a new understanding of how readers make sense of texts. Jauss's seminal essay, 'Literary History as a Challenge to Literary Theory' (first published in *New Literary History*, 2 (1967), 11–19), is widely regarded as one of the most important works of German literary theory in the past few decades, and has had enormous impact and influence in both Europe and the USA. Jauss notes a declining interest in literary history, one symptom of which is the increasing gap in criticism between historical and aesthetic considerations. This is typified for Jauss in the opposed theoretical interests of Marxism and Formalism. Marxism, he claims, seeks to understand the literary work in relation to some pattern of social process or artistic evolution, but has a limited sense of the aesthetic possibilities of form, with its emphasis being predominantly mimetic or representational. For Jauss, the historical essence of a work of art lies not merely in its representational or expressive function but also in the scope and power of its influence: 'The work lives to the extent that it has influence' (*Toward an Aesthetic of Reception,* Brighton: Harvester, 1982, p.15). Formalism, on the other hand, acknowledges the extent to which form is capable of shaping and altering perception, but neglects the relationship between formal issues and the general processes of history. Marxism and Formalism together provide an aesthetics of production and representation, but what is required in Jauss's estimation is an adequate aesthetics of literary reception and influence. The reader, the listener and the spectator must play a significant role in literary theory, since the historical life of a literary work is 'unthinkable' without the active participation of the public to whom it is addressed.

The central, defining statement of Jauss's essay provides a striking and dramatic contrast with those theoretical precepts (typified by the New Criticism) which would approach the text in terms of its autonomous existence and its timeless, universal appeal:

> A literary work is not an object that stands by itself and that offers the same view to each reader in each period. It is not a monument that monologically reveals its timeless essence.

Jauss, in this respect, is concerned with *reception history* as much as with *reception theory.* The key phrase in his methodology is *the horizon of expectations*, by which he means the range of vision associated with a particular vantage point in history. This horizon of expectations emerges from a reader's pre-understanding of the genre, form and themes of already familiar works, and from an awareness of the differences between poetic and pragmatic language-uses. A new text evokes for the reader or listener the horizon of expectations and rules familiar from earlier texts, which are then varied, corrected, altered or simply reproduced. *Don Quixote,* for instance, clearly draws on and appeals to a knowledge of old and familiar tales of knighthood, at the same time as it parodies and moves beyond them. What prevents 'reception' from being a highly variable and impressionistic set of responses is a sequence of signals and markers embedded in the text. Like Iser, Jauss believes in a process of directed perception, and in the possibilities of trans-subjective understanding so that certain meanings are shared among readers.

What lends Jauss's theory its distinctive character is its conviction that the artistic character and 'quality' of a work can be determined by the degree of its *influence* on a presupposed audience. Value or rank is attributed by Jauss to the aesthetic distance between a work and its horizon of expectations. Modern readers must therefore attempt to reconstruct the original context of reception for works that might initially have been regarded as shocking and subversive but that have since been comfortably accommodated as 'masterpieces'. The act of criticism, then, involves a fusion of horizons – a recognition of the successive unfolding of the potential for meaning that is embedded in a work and actualized in the various stages of its historical reception.

What also gives Jauss's approach its distinctive appeal among other reader-response theories is its insistence that literature can have a *socially formative* function: it can help to inform the idea of the society it presupposes, and not simply provide reflection or imitation of this. The illustration Jauss gives is the controversial trial that was instituted against Flaubert after the publication of *Madame Bovary* in 1857. Jauss maintains that it was the form as much as the content of *Madame Bovary* that created consternation in France of the mid-nineteenth century. The radically impersonal mode of narration compelled Flaubert's readers to perceive things differently by breaking with an older novelistic convention associated with unequivocal moral judgements. The resulting uncertainty of judgement caused the original occasion for the trial – alleged immorality – to recede into the background.

Jauss believes, then, that literature can have an emancipatory effect: the experience of reading can liberate the reader from existing prejudices and invite a new perception of 'lived praxis' – the way in which our actions can have decisive political effects. While this emphasis on the socially formative influence of literature is a positive contribution to modern theory, and while Jauss's work considerably enlarges the scope of reader-response criticism, a number of problems remain. There is, above all, the issue of how far we can objectify the horizon of expectations for any literary work. In some cases reception history is well documented: for a novel such as *Wuthering Heights* we have access to a large archive of nineteenth-century essays and reviews that provide some indication of the work's initial and subsequent reception; but in other cases we have only the surrounding or accompanying texts to suggest what standards and expectations were current. If Jauss accounts for readers in different historical positions, he nevertheless (like Iser) presupposes an informed reader (someone like himself, perhaps) and a homogeneous set of responses which we might suspect are compatible with those of a white, middle-class, male European. Whatever these reservations, it has to be said that reader-response criticism and reception theory have had enormous significance and effect in challenging author-centred and text-centred theories of literature. After encountering Iser and Jauss we are not likely to talk about the meaning of a text without some consideration of the role of the reader.

Questions and exercises

1   How important is the role of the reader in determining the meaning (or meanings) of a literary work? Is 'meaning' to some extent *created* by the reader? In answering these questions, refer to specific novels, poems or plays.

2   Discover what you can about the reception history of a specific text (preferably a controversial work such as *Wuthering Heights*), and then try to assess the importance and significance of this knowledge for the purposes of literary research. Where possible, compare some early reviews of a particular work with more recent critical assessments. The *Critical Heritage* and *Casebook* series are valuable sources for this kind of exercise.

3   How far would you agree with Jauss's opinion that 'A literary work is not an object that stands by itself and that offers the same view to each reader in each period'? How convincing do you find his argument that each historical period has its own 'horizon of expectations'? Refer, if possible, to a selection of literary works from different genres.

Selected reading

Andrew Bennett (ed.), *Readers and Reading* (London and New York: Longman, 1995). This is a very lively and stimulating collection of essays in the Longman Critical Readers series; the introduction gives an excellent account of the principal issues and debates in reader-response criticism.

Terry Eagleton, *Literary Theory: An Introduction*, 2nd edn (Oxford: Blackwell, 1996). This remains one of the most lively, engaging and provocative works of literary theory, and Chapter Two ('Phenomenology, Hermeneutics, Reception Theory') is an excellent guide to the history and development of reader-response criticism.

Umberto Eco, *The Role of the Reader; Explorations in the Semiotics of Texts* (Bloomington: Indiana University Press, 1979); an entertaining approach to the subject by the Italian novelist and critic, and one that provides an interesting contrast with the predominantly US and German approaches elsewhere.

Stanley Fish, *Surprised by Sin: The Reader in Paradise Lost* (London: Macmillan, 1967). In characteristic fashion, Fish has appended a lengthy Second Preface to the 1997 edition of this book, commenting on his own reading strategies.

Stanley Fish, 'Interpreting the *Variorum*' (1976), in *Is There a Text in This Class?* (Cambridge, Massachusetts: Harvard University, 1980). The essay is also reprinted in David Lodge (ed.), *Modern Criticism and Theory: A Reader.*

Stanley Fish, 'Literature in the Reader: Affective Stylistics', in *Reader-Response Criticism: From Formalism to Post-Structuralism*, ed. Jane P. Tomkins (Baltimore and London: Johns Hopkins University Press, 1980).

Elizabeth A. Flynn and Patrocino P. Schweickart (eds), *Gender and Reading: Essays on Readers, Texts, and Contexts* (Baltimore: Johns Hopkins University Press, 1986). Schweickart's essay, 'Reading Ourselves: Toward a Feminist Theory of Reading' is reprinted in Andrew Bennett (ed.), *Readers and Reading.*

Robert Holub, *Reception Theory: A Critical Introduction* (London: Methuen, 1984). This is the most comprehensive account to date of the various strands of reception theory in the German tradition.

Wolfgang Iser, *The Act of Reading: A Theory of Aesthetic Response* (Baltimore: Johns Hopkins University Press, 1978); the seminal work by Iser.

Wolfgang Iser, 'Interaction Between Text and Reader', in *The Reader in the Text: Essays on Audience and Interpretation,* ed. Susan R. Suleiman and Inge Crosman (Princeton: University of Princeton Press, 1980).

Hans Robert Jauss, *Toward an Aesthetic of Reception,* trans. T. Bahti (Brighton: Harvester, 1982). This is the best-known critical work by Jauss, and arguably his most important.

David Lodge (ed.), *Modern Criticism and Theory: A Reader* (London and New York: Longman, 1988). Lodge includes selections from the writings of Wolfgang Iser, E.D. Hirsch and Stanley Fish.

Philip Rice and Patricia Waugh (eds), *Modern Literary Theory: A Reader,* 3rd edn (London: Edward Arnold, 1996). This is an excellent 'reader'; Chapter Five gives prominence to the work of Iser and Jauss.

Raman Selden, *Practising Theory and Reading Literature: An Introduction* (Hemel Hempstead: Harvester Wheatsheaf, 1989). Selden's book offers valuable 'worked examples' of 'theory in practice', including illustrations of how the ideas of Iser and Jauss might be applied to plays by Beckett, Wesker and Pinter.

Raman Selden and Peter Widdowson (eds), *A Reader's Guide to Contemporary Literary Theory* (London: Harvester Wheatsheaf, 1993). Chapter Three ('Reader-Oriented Theories') offers a clear and detailed account of most of the major developments in both US and German variants of reader-response criticism.

Susan R. Suleiman and Inge Crosman (eds), *The Reader in the Text: Essays on Audience and Interpretation* (Princeton: University of Princeton Press, 1980). This is a very useful collection of essays, including some valuable work by Jonathan Culler, Wolfgang Iser, Gerald Prince and Norman Holland.

Jane Tompkins, *Reader-Response Criticism: From Formalism to Post-Structuralism* (Baltimore and London: Johns Hopkins University Press, 1980). This is another valuable collection of essays, with some seminal pieces from Gerald Prince, Michael Riffaterre, Wolfgang Iser, Stanley Fish, Jonathan Culler, Norman Holland and David Bleich. The introduction by Jane Tompkins is one of the best starting points for research in this theoretical field.

Dennis Walder (ed.), *Literature in the Modern World: Critical Essays and Documents* (Oxford: Oxford University Press, 1990). A judicious and substantial selection of theoretical statements makes this a deservedly popular book. Chapter II of Part One includes representative work by E.D. Hirsch, Stanley Fish, Robert Scholes and Hans Robert Jauss.

11 NEW HISTORICISM

by Graham Martin

In Chapter 7 we saw that Anglo-American New Criticism argued for 'the autonomy of the text' in order to rescue literature from the crushing embrace of the biographer, or the literary or cultural historian. We also saw that Matthew Arnold's influence provided a further means of rescue: while all texts might be 'historical', some were much more so than others. Evaluative criteria could sort out the too-historical 'goats' and – handing them over to the care of the literary historian – thus preserve for the literary critic the 'sheep', whose exceptional qualities enabled them to transcend their historical origins. From this process, there emerged a literary-critical 'canon' of writers whose formal study could claim to be the proper subject for university degrees in literature.

But what if the ability to transcend history were to be queried? And what if the argument *itself* – that the literature worth studying is strikingly a-historic – can be shown to be 'historical', the product of a particular cultural crisis now seen to belong to the past? Such questions have been pressed under the aegis of what has come to be known as 'New Historicism'. In what sense 'new'? In what sense an improvement on the earlier varieties? New Criticism's main objection to old-style literary history was its apparent indifference to the specificity of the literary works it surveyed, an indifference seemingly rooted in a refusal – or at least a failure – to *read* these works with a sufficient recognition of their intrinsic scope and complexity.

Critics of the mid-twentieth century who accepted the New Critical argument and wrote about particular texts with impressive insight into their distinctive structure nevertheless recognized that their historical aspect could not be ignored, the more especially in the case of novels which, as we have seen, are so clearly implicated in the culture and society of their original production. Thus Leavis went so far as to claim that Lawrence's *The Rainbow* (1915) recorded 'essential English history', as had the novels of his nineteenth-century predecessor George Eliot (*D.H. Lawrence, Novelist*, London: Chatto and Windus, 1955, p.107), while Arnold Kettle opened his account of Emily Brontë's novel with the claim that '*Wuthering Heights* is about England in 1847' (*An Introduction to the English Novel*, London: Hutchinson, 1951, p.139).

The difficulty with such claims is their underlying assumption that the novels give us unmediated access to the social conditions they refer to, that they 'reflect' those conditions or, to change the metaphor, that they act as windows through which we can confidently gaze upon the historical reality; and further, they assume that this ability to reveal the true history of their period constitutes a novel's greatness, its claim to privileged attention above and beyond the plethora of less insightful texts written and published in the same period. New Historicism rejects both the notion that literary texts can 'reflect' historical conditions, and also that there is any single essential historical narrative about which literature can itself directly speak. All texts, major and minor, whether great or trivial, are 'historical', which is to say they are events *in* the history of their time, as well as comments upon certain aspects of that history. Reading the texts therefore demands equal attention to both these dimensions.

Contextual reading

Jerome McGann's *The New Oxford Book of Romantic Period Verse* (1993) may serve as one example. The usual anthologist's procedure would be to concentrate on the acknowledged 'greats' – Blake, Coleridge, Wordsworth, Byron, Keats, Shelley – leaving space for only token representation for such as Burns, Southey, Moore, Clare, and entirely excluding all those writers normally described as 'of merely historical interest'. McGann aims instead to represent the characteristic writing of the whole period, 1785 to 1832, in some degree for its own sake but primarily to bring out the literary-historical context within which the more famous poets wrote and – equally important – were first read. His selection is organized, not author by author but chronologically according to the year of a poem's first publication. This scheme excludes any extract from Wordsworth's *The Prelude*, written during the period but not read (save by a few close friends) until it was published in 1850; and it locates Coleridge's 'Kubla Khan' – written in 1797 though not published till 1816 – cheek-by-jowl with poems by Byron, Scott, Hookham Frere, Leigh Hunt and Keats, also published in that year, and thus conveys some sense of the kind of poetry with which Coleridge's first readers would have been familiar.

'Contextual' reading of this kind is central to McGann's position: the publication of a poem, he insists, is as much a specific historical event as that of a declaration of war. Its author addresses it to a readership whose expectations, whether accommodated, challenged, or defied, necessarily enter into its contemporary meaning. In an essay about Tennyson's 'The Charge of the Light Brigade', McGann assembles information about the event itself, the military thinking that led to it, how it was reported in newspapers, contemporary social attitudes about English cavalry regiments, how cavalry charges in the Napoleonic Wars had come to be represented in French painting as the epitome of soldierly heroism, and moreover, how such heroism was held to be the special achievement of the French.

Modifying the celebrated remark of the French general who observed of the Light Brigade's charge, *C'est magnifique, mais ce n'est pas la guerre*, McGann proposes that here, precisely, lay the point of Tennyson's poem. What it claims for the English Light Brigade is *la gloire*, the heroic virtues of disciplined self-sacrifice most famously embodied in Napoleon's Imperial Guard, the post-war reputation of whose achievements had gained the French an ideological victory over the very nations and armies which had, militarily, defeated them. (See *The Beauty of Inflections*, Oxford: Clarendon, 1985, pp.191–203.) McGann's use of painting as a source of information relevant to the poem is also worth stressing: literary 'meaning' is sometimes a product of a text's interaction with non-verbal media.

In contrast with the New Critic – who, in post-Arnoldian spirit, seeks to reveal an a-historic complex of values shared in greater or lesser degree by some past literature, in the relative absence of which particular works become 'of merely historical interest' – McGann insists upon the historical particularity of each work, and therefore upon its difference from the world of the modern reader. Past literature presents us with a record of human experiences that are largely *alien*. They were formed by different historical conditions, and above all by different conceptions of 'the valuable'. By learning to read this record, to enter into its strangeness with 'critical sympathy', we gain a valuable perspective upon our own equally historical attitudes and assumptions.

Merely to read past literature for its 'contemporary relevance' is to slight its initial mode of existence – in effect, to deny the reality of the past. At the same time, that reality – no longer being ours – can be known only in part, and that part always 'critically'. Coleridge's recommendation that in reading *The Ancient Mariner* we need to practise a 'willing suspension of disbelief' applies to the reading of all past literature. We cannot share its structures of superannuated assumptions and attitudes – nor must we pretend to – but to reach some understanding of them we first need consciously to 'suspend our disbelief' in them, only later returning to measure their distance from our own beliefs.

This general argument raises at least three questions. Does its method work only for such poems as 'The Charge of the Light Brigade', prompted by and addressed to a public event? How would it bear upon more private poems, such as Wordsworth's 'A slumber did my spirit seal ...' (if you can stand yet another reference to it), or Donne's 'Sweetest love, I do not goe/For weariness of thee ...?' Would a historical interpretation of these poems differ significantly from that of today's uninstructed reader who happens upon them in *The New Oxford Book of English Verse* (ed. Helen Gardner, 1975)? More generally, while McGann's individual discussions of single poems are always perceptive, he says nothing about the difference between those which – so the implication runs – have the power to challenge the modern reader with their strangeness, the kind he chooses to discuss, and the enormously larger number of poems lacking that power, whose publication was just as much 'a particular historical event'.

It was, after all, precisely such 'difference' – perhaps 'set of differences' would be a better description – which the post-Arnoldian 'value' argument tried to account for. Furthermore, in what way do those 'strong' poems responsive to McGann's approach differ from the other historical documents – the letters, the essays, the newspaper articles – which he deems necessary to the establishment of their adequate historical reading? Or to put this another way, what argument is to be advanced for concentrating on the literary work, instead of the ancillary writings needed to interpret it?

While historians of the mid-Victorian period would benefit from McGann's essay, it would hardly persuade them to allot the poem any privileged position among the very many other pieces of written evidence for a survey of, say, 'contemporary attitudes to the Crimean War'. The literary scholar may well choose to concentrate on the poem, and why not? But then again, why? In eliciting a 'historical reading', how does the literary scholar's interest differ from that of the historian? And if the answer lies in the poem's ability to 'make strange' the values of its time, one continues to ask why the process of estrangement is not equally brought about by contemporary non-poetic writings. To make the point specifically: what distinguishes *Don Juan*, 'Ode to a Nightingale', 'Tintern Abbey' and *The Ancient Mariner* from Cobbett's *The Political Register*, Godwin's *Enquiry Concerning Political Justice*, Malthus's *An Essay on the Principle of Population* and *The Edinburgh Review* (*in toto*, not just its literary section)?

'Political' reading

A different style of New Historicist criticism is represented in the work of Stephen Greenblatt on Renaissance writing. While accepting the familiar sense of 'literature' as poems and plays (the novel as a literary genre in the modern sense had still to emerge), Greenblatt discusses work by Wyatt, Spenser, Marlowe and Shakespeare, not in the 'New Critical' manner as 'autonomous texts' but in terms of their social and political function, their relationships with the despotic power of the Tudor and Elizabethan monarchs, and with the gradual emergence during the sixteenth century of a society on the verge of 'modernity'.

This does not involve the tracing of specific themes, already formulated by the social historian from non-literary evidence and now shown by the literary critic to be variously 'reflected' in the poems and plays. Rather, Greenblatt's approach questions the familiar distinction between the *text* and the *context* – social, political, religious, intellectual, economic, and so forth – that has shaped it. The texts are conceived, not as mere reflectors of, but rather as active contributors to, the historical processes they illuminate. The implicit model for such discussion is cultural anthropology. What we call 'Elizabethan literature' is conceived as simply one of a number of cultural practices of the age. The texts are, we might say, their own evidence, but always along with other evidence – political writing, religious sermons as a medium for political control, the state's promulgations for the strict observance of its commands and prohibitions, accounts of formal Court entertainments, travellers' accounts of voyaging to the New World and of their aggressive encounters with its indigenous populations, handbooks for the instruction of would-be courtiers (how to defend one's reputation, how to dress, how to adapt one's speech for different occasions and listeners, and, above all, how to advance one's career).

Like McGann, Greenblatt concentrates on a historical reading of the texts, what their meaning and value were for their first readers and audiences, the ways in which they were actively made use of or, as we might say today, the ways in which they were consumed. While he inherits the New Critical insistence upon close reading, and practises it with skill, his interest lies less in the texts themselves than in what they can tell us about their time. To take them 'on their own', to abstract them from their initial socio-cultural materiality, is to indulge in anachronistic misreading. Yet, in contrast with the depersonalizing insistence of structuralist criticism, Greenblatt is perfectly happy with the notion of 'author', with the assumption that the poems and plays give expression, however indirect and secretive, to authorial feelings and ideas whose individual qualities are a proper object of study.

Thus, for example, in his analysis of Sir Thomas Wyatt's writings – the translations (literary and biblical), satires, sonnets and love poetry, and his correspondence as a skilled diplomat in the service of Henry VIII – Greenblatt concentrates on the kind of social identity that ambitious Tudor courtiers needed to create for themselves in relation to the King's absolute power as head of both state and church. The sturdily independent 'manliness' much praised by Wyatt's critics as the source of his literary inventiveness, plain diction and 'speaking' rhythms, Greenblatt considers to be a constructed 'fiction' – not a 'mask' in the self-dramatizing post-Romantic manner, but a necessary condition for psychic survival. The courtier's life demanded a resolute will to dominate over rivals, concealed within a daily practice of courteous dissimulation and treacherous manœuvre against their threats and contrivances, an art of adroit flattery of political superiors (subtle or gross according to the occasion), an ability to 'read' their exercises in duplicity and to tack and weave in response.

Power and its achievement were the reality and the ideal. To gain it required a ruthless individualism that recognized no loyalty beyond inner submission to an ultimate royal authority, both actual and ideological, for which the claims of moral virtue were as nothing. Or rather, they were no more than *forms*, publicly to be recognized, privately to be set aside as and when the situation demanded. The poems show a displacement of such tensions from political to sexual competition, and yet since poetic accomplishment greatly contributed to courtly reputation, the distinction of subject-matter was scarcely more than nominal. Poetry, in short, far from being an autonomous practice, was a means for advancing the courtier's career. Greenblatt's striking analyses of 'Whoso list to hunt, I know where is an hind' and 'They flee from me who sometime did me seek' should be consulted to bring out both his interpretive skill and the fresh light that his general argument sheds on these celebrated poems (*Renaissance Self-Fashioning: From More to Shakespeare*, Chicago: University of Chicago Press, 1980, pp.145–53).

Greenblatt's approach is more fully illustrated in his subsequent chapter about Edmund Spenser, civil servant rather than courtier, whose central ambition was the creation of poetry worthy of comparison with Virgil's or Homer's (op. cit., pp.157–92). Whereas Wyatt wrote love lyrics, Spenser's literary ambitions were formed by Renaissance Humanism and required the composition in English of works comparable in scope and weight to those of the Latin and Greek classics. This was most notably the case with his 'epic', *The Faerie Queene*. Traditional accounts of the poem have tended to hive off its literary achievement from the elaborate political and religious allegory conveying a mystic devotion to Queen Elizabeth, to her defence of the Protestant Church of England against the ever-present threat of militant Catholicism striving to recapture a heretical state for the True Faith, and referring in certain Books to the Elizabethan military campaigns for the subjugation of Ireland and its transformation into England's first colony. Greenblatt, on the other hand, puts these matters at the very centre of his analysis.

As 'civil servant', Spenser was also a colonizer. In his capacity as secretary to Lord Grey, appointed by the Queen to oversee the Irish campaigns, Spenser's attitude to the indigenous population resembled that of the European colonizers of the Americas. He held himself to be the loyal instrument of an Elizabethan 'civilization' struggling to put down Irish 'savagery' by all necessary means. Yet this savage condition had its insidious attraction, only to be guarded against by an austere moral authoritarianism. The poem's declared ambition to teach the virtues necessary for a Renaissance English gentleman is represented in the endless struggles of its various knightly heroes with tempters, magicians, monsters of all kinds. The conquest of Ireland required of its agents a strenuous moral self-conquest, and this inner turmoil is at the poem's centre. Greenblatt's account thus directly engages the politics of the Elizabethan state, exploring both the way its ideological demands entered into the psychic constitution of its servants, and also an English version of the way they advanced those European imperialist ambitions which, increasingly since the time of Columbus and Magellan, had led to the conquest of the New World and the reduction of its native population to slavery. In these ways, *The Faerie Queene* actively contributed to the maintenance of Elizabethan state power, and to the furthering of its colonial aggressions.

It will be seen from even these brief summaries of Greenblatt's wide-ranging analyses that he conceives the literary scholar's task as that of a cultural historian. Or as he puts it himself:

> We must ... incorporate the work of art into the texture of a
> particular pattern of life, a collective experience that transcends it
> and completes its meaning. (p.179)

How far this approach can engage with later periods when 'literature' had achieved a relatively autonomous condition remains, of course, a question. And it will be noted that Greenblatt discusses very substantial works – Marlowe's and Shakespeare's plays as well as Spenser's epic. To raise again the 'value' question that McGann seems to set aside, one is left wondering about the many lesser productions of the Elizabethan period, and the way in which the different 'patterns of life' to which they belong would relate to the one most relevant to that of *The Faerie Queene*. The logic seems to imply a 'value' contrast, less between particular literary productions than between the different life-patterns which 'transcend and complete their meaning'; and, in the absence of other evidence for these life-patterns, the critical potential of literary texts seems wholly discounted. But perhaps Greenblatt would think it anachronistic to assume any such potential.

One further point may be noted. That it is 'the great works of literature' which direct us to the most important truths about the societies that produce them is a notion central to those earlier accounts of the novel by such as Leavis and Kettle which New Historicism found faulty. Yet just such an assumption appears to underpin Greenblatt's choice of these particular Renaissance poems and plays. Thus he does not concentrate on the poems of Wyatt's contemporary, the Earl of Surrey, nor on the contributions of Sir Thomas Sackville to *A Mirror for Magistrates* (1559) and (together with Thomas Norton) to the tragedy of *Gorboduc, or Ferrex and Porrex* (1561), nor on Thomas Kyd's *The Spanish Tragedy* (1592), nor on Robert Green's *The Honourable History of Frier Bacon and Bungay* (1594). Yet these are all works of ability entirely characteristic of the period – even if less highly regarded than the productions of Wyatt, Spenser, Marlowe and Shakespeare.

Is there, in other words, an *unargued connection* between the texts Greenblatt has selected for discussion and the centrality of the cultural-historical themes he disengages? On the other hand, to any such assumption he introduces a crucial modification: no literary text, whatever its range and complexity, can claim to be a privileged source of cultural insight. Literature provides only one 'discourse of knowledge' about the society, and what it tells us can only emerge from its detailed interrelationships with those other 'discourses' represented in the various writings Greenblatt draws into his analyses.

Greenblatt's approach, applied to eighteenth-century novels, would thus lead the researcher to connect Defoe's insistence that his tales of Moll Flanders, Robinson Crusoe and others were 'true', with the socio-cultural assumptions of his original readership, and of its growing political significance. Similarly, Richardson's work would be considered in relation to the many conduct books of the period, which offered detailed moral and social advice, and which he studiously consulted in drafting his novels. One issue, for example, could be his characterization of Sir Charles Grandison's refusal to engage in duelling without incurring the charge of cowardice, and how this could be reconciled with the conviction that an eighteenth-century gentleman's honour, if affronted, could only be defended in a duel. The stress of such investigation would fall less directly upon Richardson's novels than upon the life-patterns of their readers.

In contrast with the traditional literary-historical account of 'the origins of the Novel', the Greenblatt approach would conceive Richardson's work as one powerful agent in the formation of entirely specific eighteenth-century socio-cultural structures and processes. In Fielding's case, the novels could be seen as articulating issues which Richardson's either failed, or more probably refused, to acknowledge. Fielding, it should be here remembered, was a Justice of the Peace in the City of Westminster, and wrote many pamphlets as part of his campaign against corruption in the judiciary and the power of London's criminal gangs. The theoretical issue here would require attention to such non-literary writings, not as an informative 'context' (bearing one way or another on aspects of a 'text') but as having equal status with the various novels in an investigation of the 'pattern of life' of their eighteenth-century readers.

Questions and exercises

1   How far does McGann's argument that we should focus on the historicity of poems of the Victorian period apply to those that, unlike 'The Charge of the Light Brigade', deal with non-public issues?

2   What kinds of writing other than 'literary' would you need to look into if you were to apply to such works as *Moll Flanders* or *Caleb Williams* or *In Memoriam* or *Amours de Voyage* Greenblatt's conviction that these texts should not be abstracted as 'literature' from the complex of social, political and cultural conditions of their first publications?

3   New Historicism appears to erode the distinct category of 'Literature' by treating literary texts as if they were no more than a particularly tricky kind of historical document. Would you want to argue against this view? And if so, what points would you make?

4   Sarah Fielding, sister of the better-known Henry, also published several novels, though none that came to be so highly regarded as *Tom Jones*. A New Historicist approach to her *œuvre* seems likely to set aside this 'canonical' evaluation on the grounds that, just as with her brother's novels, the publication of hers constituted historical events, equally deserving detailed investigation. How might the critic, concerned nevertheless to insist upon the 'value' case for *Tom Jones*, deal with the New Historicist position?

Selected reading

Stephen Greenblatt, *Renaissance Self-Fashioning: from More to Shakespeare* (Chicago: University of Chicago Press, 1980).

Stephen Greenblatt, *Representing the English Renaissance* (London and Berkeley: University of California Press, 1988).

Stephen Greenblatt, *Shakespearean Negotiations: The Circulation of Social Energy in Renaissance England* (Oxford: Clarendon, 1988).

Jean E. Howard and Marion F. O'Connor (eds), *Shakespeare Reproduced: The Text in History and Ideology* (London: Methuen, 1987).

Jerome J. McGann, *The Beauty of Inflections: Literary Investigations in Historical Method and Theory* (Oxford: Clarendon, 1985).

Kiernan Ryan, *New Historicism and Cultural Materialism: A Reader* (London: Arnold, 1996).

Raman Selden and Peter Widdowson, *A Reader's Guide to Contemporary Literary Theory,* 3rd edn (London: Harvester Wheatsheaf, 1993). See, especially, pages 161–9.

H. Aram Veeser (ed.), *The New Historicism* (New York and London: Routledge, 1989).

Don E. Wayne, 'New Historicism' in *Encyclopaedia of Literature and Criticism,* ed. Martin Coyle, Peter Garside, Malcolm Kelsall and John Peck (London: Routledge, 1990).

12 POST-COLONIAL THEORY

by Dennis Walder

Introduction

> You taught me language; and my profit on't
> Is, I know how to curse.
>
> (Caliban to Prospero, *The Tempest*, 1611, I.2.365–6)

Post-colonial theory is an area of literary criticism and cultural studies that has come into being in response to (a) the post-war upsurge in literary creativity in countries formerly under colonial rule, (b) the persistence of colonial, 'neo-colonial' or imperialist influence in the modern world, and (c) by analogy, the use of terms such as 'post-structuralist' and 'postmodern' to generate a challenge to monolithic or universalist claims. The theoretical writings that fall into the category of 'post-colonial' are engaged in the discovery or rediscovery of neglected texts, while analysing the forces which may be said to have marginalized them. They entered the intellectual agenda as part of the 'metropolitan' left-wing response to the 'Third World' struggles of the 1950s onwards.

'Neglected' may seem an exaggeration when one considers how many writers in English from outside the US and UK have made a name for themselves by winning major literary awards such as the Nobel Prize in Literature – awarded to Wole Soyinka of Nigeria, Nadine Gordimer of South Africa and Derek Walcott from the Caribbean. But this is a recent phenomenon, and there remain vast areas of outstanding literary endeavour which, if they have been heard of, have yet to be considered worthy of inclusion in the standard English literary histories. Andrew Sanders's *Short Oxford History of English Literature* (1994) is apparently too short to mention Soyinka, Gordimer or Walcott, although a one-sentence gesture is made towards the 'destabilizing' and 'decentralizing' effect upon 'the canon' of the 'distinctive English-language literatures of Canada, Australia, New Zealand, Africa, India and the Caribbean' (p.13); and a small clutch of ex-colonial writers who have settled in Britain, such as Salman Rushdie from India and Timothy Mo from Hong Kong, are said to represent the impact of 'writers and subjects from the old colonial Empire' (p.636).

Post-colonial theory has a subversive posture towards the canon. It brings with it a particular politics, history and geography. It is anti-imperial; it may look back as far as the first moment of colonization by the West; and it reaches all those parts of the world touched by Empire. This means it may also take the classics of the literary canon from Shakespeare onwards as grist to its mill. It is not confined to written literature: oral and performance media, art and film are also considered fit areas for study. But since we are mainly concerned with literature here, I will confine my account to the writings that have attended literary production. And I will confine myself to writings in English, although of course Britain was not the only country to exercise formal control over large areas of the world, imposing a language that its subjects then used as a means of literary and cultural expression.

Commonwealth Literature

First there was Commonwealth Literature. Sometime during the 1950s, what was called English literature ceased to be a unitary subject. Before then, most writers who lived outside the UK but who wrote in English – such as the South African Olive Schreiner (1855–1920) or the Indian Rabindranath Tagore (1861–1941) – were either ignored or assimilated. Literature from the USA was not normally studied outside North America. Then things changed. Courses in American, Commonwealth, Irish and African literature began to emerge in a few US and UK universities. The newly independent nations, such as Ghana and Kenya, and the older dominions of settlement, such as Canada and Australia, were producing literary works that seemed important outside their countries of origin.

It was probably no coincidence that this happened as British power and influence in the world went into decline. The effect of the Second World War had been to weaken British prestige, while stimulating local economies and the demand for independence. The granting of independence to India, the largest country of the Empire, in 1947, was an important moment; another was the Suez crisis of 1956, which marked the permanent demotion of the former imperial power, in the face of nationalist strivings. The literary and cultural expression of these strivings during the (often lengthy) process of decolonization produced some of the first writings in English to have a major impact abroad – from the novels of Mulk Raj Anand and Raja Rao in India during the thirties, to the fiction and drama of the Kenyan Ngugi wa Thiong'o and the Nigerian Wole Soyinka in the fifties. Summing up what these writers were trying to do, while speaking to its own Nigerian audience, was Chinua Achebe's *Things Fall Apart* (London: Heinemann, 1958), a hugely successful novel (sales over three million world-wide by 1988) which set out to tell his people's story from his own, as opposed to the colonizers', point of view.

The first school of Commonwealth Literature was founded at Leeds University in 1964. By then, works such as Anand's and Achebe's, and many others from around the English-speaking former empire, had come to be recognized by wide readerships at home and abroad, and had found their way onto the Leeds syllabus. The first Commonwealth Literature conference was simultaneously organized by the Leeds enthusiasts, with the resulting papers published the following year as *Commonwealth Literature: Unity and Diversity in a Common Culture*, ed. John Press and published by Heinemann Educational in 1965: Heinemann took an initiative in the field from then on.

The speed with which this new category of literary study emerged and become institutionalized was striking. By 1970, William Walsh, Professor of

Education and Commonwealth Literature Fellow at Leeds, had produced *A Manifold Voice: Studies in Commonwealth Literature* (London: Chatto), in which he showed which of the 'authors writing in English outside Britain and the United States' had made a significant and creative contribution to 'the canon of Literature in English' (preface). The book included lucid and persuasive studies of such well-known writers as V.S. Naipaul, Patrick White, R.K. Narayan and Katherine Mansfield, as well as the less familiar Nirad Chaudhuri, A.D. Hope and Chinua Achebe.

In the following year, the first volume of a new series of Penguin Companions to Literature appeared, ed. David Daiches of Sussex University, covering *British & Commonwealth Literature*. And by 1973 Walsh, now the first full Professor of Commonwealth Literature, produced his

> personal chart of writing in the English language outside the traditions of Britain and the United States – essentially writing within those areas of the world loosely gathered together into the British Commonwealth. Not that I have any structural theory of the nature of this institution. I take it to mean what most people do, and while I recognize that the writers I speak of see themselves as Africans or Canadians, and not as contributors to some nebulous international organization, the term is at least a useful category of denotation grounded in history and making a point of substance about those it is applied to.
>
> (*Commonwealth Literature*, London: Macmillan, 1973, preface)

The study that followed identified 'six major divisions' of writing – Indian, African, West Indian, Canadian, New Zealand and Australian. The arbitrary mix of countries and continents reflected the difficulties into which the Commonwealth label was leading Walsh.

His emphasis upon the importance of national identity, or how the writers saw themselves, was important – as was his insistence that the term carried a certain history for the writers he applied it to. But he thereby implied a wider reach than the book was able to deliver, which arguably undermined the whole enterprise of defining from within the UK the worthwhile writers to add to the canon of what was now routinely called 'Literature in English'. Yet it was still another ten years before the whole project was seriously challenged. This was in part a result of the general debate within English studies centring on 'the canon', with its tendency to set up a small cast of writers as *the* central tradition, harking back to the 'standards' of the mainstream. It was also the result of a growing concern to include the wider range of what was coming to be called 'Literatures of the World in English'.

New writings in English

Literatures of the World in English (London: Routledge, 1974) was in fact the title of a book edited by Bruce King, a US Professor of English with experience of teaching in Africa, who pulled together a multinational group of critics to introduce the important authors, themes and works. Ironically, William Walsh was given the job of surveying the literature of England, and another Leeds enthusiast, A.N. Jeffares, wrote about Ireland – which had some justification because the former was English and the latter Irish. (Nobody wrote about Scotland or Wales.) For the first time, it seemed important to attend to those who could claim more than outside knowledge of a given field. Thus King himself covered the USA, Brian Elliott from Adelaide introduced Australian writing, and the Trinidadian Kenneth Ramchand discussed the literature of the West Indies.

This was in line also with King's emphasis upon the importance of cultural differences, as well as similarities. Moving outside the Commonwealth frame – which, according to a contradiction inherent in the way it was used, often did not include the writings of its leading member, the UK – this meant acknowledging the range and variety, not only of subject and genre but also of methods of evaluation. Nor did King ignore history. As he pointed out

> Colonialism is as responsible in North America and Australia as in Africa and Asia for the development of national English literatures around the world. Colonialism, whether as indirect rule or the exploration and settlement of continents, brought with it the English language, English literary forms, and English cultural assumptions. Colonization also brought the possibility of a new literature emerging once English becomes a vehicle for the expression of local culture. A new English literature may express a culture which has grown up with the settler communities, it may be a continuation of indigenous cultural traditions, or it may be some mixture of the effects of colonization, including the bringing together of various races into one nation. (Introduction, p.2)

This emphasis upon the newness of the literatures emerging outside the UK and the USA, which in effect meant concentrating upon the writings of the post-war period of decolonization, was more fully developed in King's *The New English Literatures – Cultural Nationalism in a Changing World*, published by Macmillan in 1980 as part of a series on the 'major "new" literatures', ed. A.N. Jeffares. In this useful and wide-ranging 'handbook', King paid particular attention to six so-called new literatures – those of Nigeria, India, Australia, Canada, New Zealand and the West Indies – and the work of a number of so-called major writers such as Achebe, Soyinka, Patrick White, V.S. Naipaul, R.K. Narayan, Wilson Harris and Derek Walcott.

The formation of a Commonwealth or 'new literatures' canon in its own right was implicit in the way in which certain authors, and countries or areas, were being introduced or surveyed again and again. By the time of the appearance of *The New English Literatures*, critical and scholarly periodicals were taking up the job of asserting the importance of the field, from the rather staid *Journal of Commonwealth Literature* (started at Leeds by South African Arthur Ravenscroft, and with important annual bibliographies), to the livelier *Wasafiri* and *Kunapipi* (also founded by ex-colonials). *Ariel: A Review of International English Literature*, edited and produced at the University of Calgary, and WLWE (*World Literature Written in English*), first published in the USA and now edited in Singapore, represented the new literatures outside the UK.

Commonwealth, originating in Dijon, reflects the sharp growth of interest in continental Europe – especially in the large English departments of French and German universities. The editors, Jean-Pierre and Carole Durix of the University of Burgundy, have gone on to produce *An Introduction to the New Literatures in English* (Paris: Longman France, 1993), a title offering 'a valid alternative for a body of writing which has emerged mostly in the last hundred years and which now stands on a par with the older British, Irish and American literatures' (p.5).

Meanwhile, the terrain had long come to be more intensively covered by monographs on individual authors, such as G.D. Killam's *The Novels of Chinua Achebe* (London: Heinemann, 1960), group studies such as Gerald Moore's influential *Seven African Writers* (London: Hutchinson, 1962; revised to *Twelve* in 1980), or Louis James's *The Islands in Between: Essays in West Indian Literature* (Oxford: Oxford University Press, 1968) and Kenneth Ramchand's *The West Indian Novel and Its Background* (London: Faber, 1970). Area series such as Heinemann's Studies in African Literature had begun to appear, as had descriptive bibliographies such as *A Reader's Guide to African Literature*, ed. Hans Zell (London: Heinemann, 1971; rev. edn, 1983).

The African and Caribbean writers in English were as much (if not more) written about by Western expatriates as by indigenous critics, causing some resentment at 'metropolitan bias'. On the other hand, Australasian writers tended to find themselves scrutinized by home-based critics – in now-classic works such as K.R. Srinivasa Iyengar's *Indian Writing in English* (Bombay: Asia Publishing House, 1962; rev. edn, 1973), Wystan Curnow's *Essays on New Zealand Literature* (Heinemann: Auckland, 1973), C. Nair's *Singapore Writing* (Singapore: Woodrose, for the Society of Singapore Writers, 1977), or Tom Moore's *Social Patterns in Australian Literature* (Sydney: Angus and Robertson, 1971).

The arrival of post-colonial theory

The tension between the former imperial centre or 'metropolis', and the former colonies or 'periphery', became the central metaphor for the first book claiming to offer post-colonial literary theory as such – *The Empire Writes Back: Theory and Practice in Post-Colonial Literatures* (London: Routledge, 1989). This was written by three Australian academics, Bill Ashcroft, Gareth Griffiths and Helen Tiffin, all of whom had already published 'Commonwealth' or 'New Writings' literary criticism and scholarship. It represents the new generation, as its appearance in 1989 in Routledge's New Accents series – under the general editorship of Terence

Hawkes – implies. Structuralism, deconstruction, reception theory, cultural politics, postmodernism, narrative poetics, semiotics: all the trends that had come to affect traditional notions of English studies since the 1960s were represented, and so it was inevitable that the 'post-colonial' should join them – if a little late.

A major difficulty for the authors of this new attempt to register the developing debates about the writings of India, Australia, the West Indies and so on, was that they took it upon themselves to reflect also the impact of developments in English studies since the 1960s – no mean task, since most writing about Commonwealth or New Literatures remained blissfully unaware of these developments. This was partly because the main academic players (such as Walsh, Jeffares and King) preferred on the whole to keep to the established methods and judgements, merely extending them to include (not always with conviction) writings from outside the UK or the USA.

It was also because much of the best criticism and commentary came from the producers of those writings themselves, who did not know or did not care to know about what was going on in what they thought of as the increasingly rarefied atmosphere of the academy. Novelists, poets and dramatists such as Raja Rao, Chinua Achebe, Ngugi wa Thiong'o, Wole Soyinka, Derek Walcott, Edward Kamau Brathwaite, Edwin Thumboo, Margaret Atwood and Stephen Gray had all published introductions, essays and even books, upon the literature of their countries – documents that were of prime importance, and still are.

The main point of *The Empire Writes Back* was that there is no escape from global power-structures, because there is no escape from language. This is true historically, too: the colonized have been part of the processes of subjugation accompanying European advance around the world, from the moment of its inception. So for Ashcroft *et al.* the term 'post-colonial' is used 'to cover all the culture affected by the imperial process from the moment of colonization to the present day'. What each and every national literature has in common 'beyond their special and distinctive regional characteristics' is their emergence out of this process, and their assertion of differences from 'the assumptions of the imperial centre' (p.2). In practice, the book conflates distinct but related kinds of colonial as well as post-colonial writings or 'sets of discourses', while demonstrating from a wide range of literary texts how they offer a 'radical critique' of 'Eurocentric' assumptions about race, nationality, language and literature. Its concern with 'textuality' tends to function at the expense of specific histories and power-relations in different parts of the world. This has been well demonstrated by two articles – Vijay Mishra and Bob Hodge, 'What is Post(-)colonialism?' (*Textual Practice*, 5 (1991), 399–414), and Anne McClintock, 'The Angel of Progress: Pitfalls of the Term "Post-colonialism"' (*Social Text*, 10 (1992), 1–15). Both are included in *Colonial Discourse and Post-Colonial Theory: A Reader* (London: Harvester Wheatsheaf, 1993), edited by Patrick Williams and Laura Chrisman and the first of its kind.

The publication of *The Empire Writes Back* in 1989 coincided with the twenty-fifth anniversary conference of the Association for Commonwealth Literature and Language Studies (ACLALS) at the University of Kent. The keynote speaker was Edward Said, a Palestinian based at Columbia University in New York (and a disciple of Michel Foucault), who proposed in his book *Orientalism* (1978) that the Western image of the Orient has been constructed by generations of writers and scholars, who thereby legitimated imperial penetration and control. If, as Said argued, the languages of communication are subject to prevailing power structures, they inevitably reinforce control. However, they may also generate resistance, as one can tell from the many 'oppositional' writings of the colonized.

Said's overriding aim, however, as expressed at the Kent conference, was to continue to undermine the 'humanist' overtones of Commonwealth literary study, by arguing that the literatures it took as its subject should be reinterpreted in terms of the 'revolutionary realities' of the world today, in which post-colonial societies were embattled and marginalized. Criticism should, according to Said, 'situate' literature in terms of emerging connections across national boundaries and other 'coercive', global power-structures ('Figures, Configurations, Transfigurations', in Anna Rutherford (ed.), *From Commonwealth to Post-Colonial*, Coventry: Dangaroo Press, 1992, pp.3–17). In this international context, 'Commonwealth' was not much more than a temporary label of convenience, carrying unfortunate overtones of neo-imperial control. How might such situating criticism operate in practice? Far from granting much attention to the literary products of the colonized, as one might have expected from his stance, Said looked for support from the familiar monuments of the literary canon, especially the nineteenth-century realist novel and its modernist successors. Thus, in his *Culture and Imperialism* (London: Vintage, 1993), it is in the 'great canonical texts' – by Defoe, Jane Austen, Dickens and Conrad – that he goes on to find 'what is silent or marginally present', reading them afresh in the context of the imperial history (London: Vintage edn, 1994, p.78).

Said's influence in the field can hardly be overestimated. Yet, more recently, while acknowledging his importance in critically illuminating the ways in which the processes of imperialism and colonization are represented, critics have come to see him as fatally resembling what he wants to undermine – the globalizing, humanist and (by virtue of his position if not his language) Western intellectual. This is what his most forceful critic, Aijaz Ahmad, claims in '*Orientalism* and After' (*In Theory: Classes, Nations, Literatures*, London: Verso, 1992, pp.159–220). Ahmad, who shares Said's basic anti-colonial stance while differing with him on almost every other point, is a post-colonial critic who avoids the label because of its globalizing reach. An academic in New Delhi, he argues that what we now need to recognize is that Western 'Third Worldism' and 'post-structuralism' have succeeded each other in misrepresenting the many different literatures and cultures flourishing in Africa and Asia.

Disparaging the whole discourse-oriented, Foucauldian trend of post-colonial theory as a Western imposition, Ahmad wishes to remind us of the distinct and varied traditions of resistance to colonial ways of thought developed by the colonized themselves. In particular, as Benita Parry pointed out in a cogent and forceful account of 'Problems in Current Theories of Colonial Discourse' (*Oxford Literary Review,* 9 (1987), 27–58), the ideas of Frantz Fanon should not be overlooked. Fanon (1925–61), a French-educated Martinican psychiatrist based in Algeria during the independence struggle of the 1950s, linked psychoanalytic notions of the sense of alienation in the colonized, with Marxist notions of the economic, material forces which have brought about that alienation, most notably in his visionary work, *The Wretched of the Earth* (*Les damnés de la terre,* Paris, 1961, trans. Constance Farrington, London: McGibbon, 1965). Here it was argued that the dispossessed poor of the title were the only likely source of retribution and reclamation for countries still held in the grip of imperialist power. Least of all were the post-independence ruling class, including intellectuals, likely to bring real dignity and freedom to the people.

Fanon's corrosive insights into the condition of the colonized (pre- and post-independence) involved a cultural, and specifically literary, dimension. According to this, 'native' writers go through three phases in their relationship with the occupying power – assimilating the foreign culture and its values to begin with, then 'remembering' their own culture, and finally fighting to 'become the mouthpiece of a new reality in action' (Penguin edn, Harmondsworth, 1967, pp.177–8).

These, and other ideas derived from Fanon, remain influential, particularly for the materialist, political wing of post-colonial theory. His deep interest in French psychoanalytic notions, especially as interpreted by Lacan, has also had its effect – for instance upon Homi Bhabha. Formerly of Bombay and Sussex, Bhabha is now based – like most Western post-colonial theorists – in the USA, where critics such as Henry Louis Gates, Jnr have begun to develop a powerful new theory of African American writing as subversively imitative of European American models. Like Bhabha, Gates aims in his writing to unsettle, to break the grip of 'universalist' or 'essentialist' ways of thinking. But Bhabha's (and others') characteristic use of the tricky rhetorical strategies beloved of post-structuralist and deconstructionist critics, while exciting to fellow academics, puts off many interested parties, who see it as a way of denying their experience, and it has led to a reaction against theory as an elitist, 'Eurocentric' activity – whatever its radical claims.

This is unfortunate, since the purpose of post-colonial theory, whatever its origins, is to aid, not hinder, critical thought about a proliferating area of new literary creativity in the world, as well as to reinterpret the texts of the past from a newly aware position. Further, theorists have begun to address two constituencies neglected by the major early participants – women and migrants. The 'double colonization' experienced by women in formerly colonized societies has been explored by an increasing number of writers and thinkers around the English-speaking world, such as Trinh T. Minh-Ha, Anne McClintock and Gayatri Spivak in the USA, Margaret Daymond and Dorothy Driver in South Africa, Vrinda Nabar in India, Elaine Fido in the Caribbean and Jane Miller and Susheila Nasta in the UK – to name only a few of those concerned to develop feminist critiques of gender, as well as of race or ethnicity. And the growing sense of the world as a network of patterns of migration, largely from the former imperial areas of influence towards the metropolitan 'centres', registered by such writers as V.S. Naipaul (the Trinidadian grandson of indentured labourers from the Indian subcontinent, who has now settled in England), has produced a growing body of writing emphasizing 'hybridity' as the characteristic feature of post-colonial histories, cultures, literatures.

It may be that ideas of cross-fertilization, of the richness of traffic between and across boundaries – racial, national, or international – will return post-colonial theory to a more celebratory mode, as a way of continuing to resist the oppressions of the past. If so, then perhaps it will become possible to replace Caliban's retort to Prospero in *The Tempest*, with Grace Nichols's

> I have crossed an ocean
> I have lost my tongue
> from the root of the old one
> a new one has sprung

('Epilogue', *The Fat Black Woman's Poems*,
London: Virago, 1984; by permission of Little, Brown & Co.)

Questions and exercises

1   How far does Defoe's *Robinson Crusoe* benefit from being read in the light of recent thought about the post-colonial dimension to literature? Are there any other familiar eighteenth-century novels which would also find new bearings in this way, or do you have to go outside the usual texts – for example, to consider Goldsmith's *Citizen of the World* (1762)?

2   In *England and Englishness* (1991), John Lucas argues that Victorian poetry constructed 'a myth of Englishness which became increasingly troubling as the century progressed because it was increasingly xeno-phobic and eventually racist' (p.173). How far do you agree? See, for example, Wordsworth's 'To Toussaint L'Ouverture' (written 1802); Tennyson's 'O Mother Britain Lift Thou Up' (1833–4), and 'The Defence of Lucknow' (1878); Arthur Hugh Clough's 'Columbus' (1852) and Christina Rossetti's 'In the Round Tower at Jhansi, 8 June 1857'; Kipling's 'The Story of Uriah' (1886) and 'Recessional' (1897).

3   How do you think the familiar canon seems to people who read literature in English in former British colonies? Which literary works

you have studied might be thought to bear on their histories, and the question of colonialism?

4   Why has the term 'Commonwealth' been overtaken by 'post-colonial' in literary studies, and does this development appear justified?

5   How much does 'post-colonial' theory have in common with feminist theorizing about literature? What are the important differences?

Selected reading

I have asterisked those with especially useful bibliographies.

Chinua Achebe, 'Colonialist Criticism', in *Morning Yet on Creation Day: Essays* (London: Heinemann Educational, 1975).

Aijaz Ahmad, *In Theory: Classes, Nations, Literatures* (London: Verso, 1992).

*Bill Ashcroft, Gareth Griffiths, Helen Tiffin, *The Empire Writes Back: Theory and Practice in Post-Colonial Literatures* (London: Routledge, 1989).

Homi Bhabha, 'Representation and the Colonial Text: A Critical Exploration of Some Forms of Mimeticism', in *The Theory of Reading,* ed. Frank Gloversmith (Brighton: Harvester, 1984), pp.93–122.

Homi Bhabha, *The Location of Culture* (London: Routledge, 1994).

*Elleke Boehmer, *Colonial and Postcolonial Literature: Migrant Metaphors* (Oxford: Oxford University Press, 1995).

Frantz Fanon, *Black Skin, White Masks* (1952), trans. C.L. Markmann, foreword by Homi Bhabha (London and Sydney: Pluto Press, 1986).

Frantz Fanon, *The Wretched of the Earth* (1961), trans. C. Farrington, introduction by Jean-Paul Sartre (Harmondsworth: Penguin, 1967).

Henry Louis Gates, Jnr (ed.), *Black Literature and Literary Theory* (London: Methuen, 1984).

Paul Gilroy, *Ain't No Black in the Union Jack* (London: Hutchinson, 1987).

*Padmini Mongia, *Contemporary Postcolonial Theory: A Reader* (London: Arnold, 1996).

Susheila Nasta (ed.), *Motherlands: Black Women's Writing from Africa, the Caribbean and South Asia* (London: Women's Press, 1991).

Ngugi wa Thiong'o, *Decolonising the Mind: The Politics of Language in African Literature* (London: James Currey, 1986).

Anna Rutherford (ed.), *From Commonwealth to Post-Colonial* (Coventry: Dangaroo, 1992).

Edward Said, *Orientalism,* first published 1978 (Harmondsworth: Penguin, 1995), with afterword.

Edward Said, *Culture and Imperialism* (London: Vintage, 1993).

Gayatri Chakravorty Spivak, *In Other Worlds: Essays in Cultural Politics* (New York and London: Methuen, 1987).

Gayatri Chakravorty Spivak, *The Post-Colonial Critic: Interviews, Strategies, Dialogues,* ed. S. Harasym (New York and London: Routledge, 1990).

Dennis Walder, *Post-Colonial Literatures in English: History, Language, Theory* (Oxford: Blackwell, 1998).

Jonathan White (ed.), *Recasting the World: Writing After Colonialism* (Baltimore and London: Johns Hopkins University Press, 1993).

*Patrick Williams and Laura Chrisman (eds), *Colonial Discourse and Post-Colonial Theory: A Reader* (Hemel Hempstead: Harvester Wheatsheaf, 1993); contains the articles by McClintock, Mishra and Hodge, and Parry referred to above.

13 PLANNING, WRITING AND PRESENTING A DISSERTATION

by W.R. Owens

To gain an MA degree in literature, you will almost certainly have to write a dissertation. This is usually the last piece of work to be completed, and is designed to round off your MA studies. Usually the topic will be one you have devised for yourself, and the length will be set somewhere between 10,000 and 20,000 words. The purpose of a dissertation is to enable you to demonstrate (a) that you know how to use libraries effectively to locate relevant materials, (b) that you can prepare and write up a sustained and logically structured academic argument in clear prose, and (c) that you can present your work well, using appropriate scholarly conventions. In short, your dissertation gives you the opportunity to show that you are capable of undertaking independent (perhaps even original) work at postgraduate level.

Deciding on a topic

One of the points to stress at the outset is that the range of possible dissertation topics in literature is very wide indeed. Whatever your interest, you should find that you can follow it up – providing only that the materials you need are available to you. Some students want to explore the work of a particular author, whether well known or not. Others are interested in a theme or issue, or may want to address some historical or literary-historical problem, tracing it through the writings of selected authors. Others, again, want to test how a given theoretical approach may be applied to a particular text or group of texts.

In order to turn any one of these approaches into a viable dissertation topic, it must be focused on a particular, manageable body of material. Nothing is more fatal than to attempt a blanket coverage of a large field – let's say a topic such as 'Narrative Technique in the Eighteenth-Century Novel', or 'The Representation of Women in Nineteenth-Century Poetry'. The objection to such a topic is not merely that you could not hope to cover it effectively in the time and space at your disposal, but also that it would be difficult to achieve much that would be of interest (either in terms of ideas or of factual discovery) in such a broad field.

A good general tip is: *choose a relatively narrow and sharply defined topic which nevertheless opens out into large and important issues.* Thus, for example, 'The Use of Parallel Narrations as a Narrative Technique in Richardson's Novels', or 'Tennyson and the Education of Women', would be more suitable topics than the larger ones just cited. Remember, too, that there are many lesser-known authors whose works would repay study. Indeed an out-of-the-way topic, provided it offers serious interest and the materials are available to carry it through, has certain advantages over a well-worn or middle-of-the-road one. To give you a sense of the wide variety of possible research topics, here is a selection of titles of successful MA dissertations produced by students on The Open University's MA in Literature programme. (Students were restricted to topics within 'The Eighteenth-Century Novel' or 'Poetry and Criticism, 1830–90'.)

'The Role of the Servant in Selected Eighteenth-Century Novels'

'Poetry and its Readers in 1850'

'Sarah Fielding and "The Stations of Life allotted to the Female Character"'

'The Significance of the Country House in the Novels of Richardson, Fielding and Sterne'

'"Congestion of the Brain is what we suffer from": The Significance of Disorder in Selected mid-Victorian Poetry'

'Towards a Critical Edition of *The History of Miss Betsy Thoughtless* by Eliza Haywood'

'Frances Burney and the Ideology of Womanhood'

'The Contribution of William Whewell and Sir John Herschel to the Hexameter Debate of the 1840s'

'William Allingham (1824–89): English Poetry and Irish Politics'

'Laurence Sterne: A Review of the Critical Literature since 1950, with an Annotated Bibliography (1966–92)'

Checking on availability of materials

A crucial part of deciding on a topic is making sure that you can get hold of the materials you need. Indeed, if you discover that you can't obtain easy access to the necessary materials, you may need to switch to another topic. Thus, for example, it is no use deciding to work on a little-known writer unless you are certain that you can borrow or buy copies of the key primary texts, or live close enough to a non-lending research library to be able to do intensive reading and note-taking there.

When it comes to secondary materials, critical articles and the like, it will be essential to plan well ahead and make sure that important material will have arrived via inter-library loan by the time you need it. Remember that, just as with everything else, Sod's Law applies to literary research – and you are certain to find that some books or articles become unavailable just when you need them most!

Turning a topic into an argument

Having limited the scope of your topic, the next step is to *give it a direction*. Virtually every good dissertation will take the form of an *argument*, of an attempt to prove or establish something by means of analysis and presentation of *evidence*. There are many possible ways of achieving this. To give some examples, your dissertation might be one of the following:

- an argument for or against an existing critic (or critical position) in relation to the author or group of works you are studying
- an argument about the importance of a particular influence on a writer, or influence exerted by him or her
- an argument for the importance of some hitherto little-regarded piece of evidence to the discussion of the work of some author or group of authors
- an argument about the value of a new theoretical approach to a text or set of texts
- an argument turning upon the nature of the genre of a work or group of works
- an argument about the significance of a little-known or undervalued author or work
- an argument about some historical or literary-historical aspect of literature
- an argument about the adequacy of existing scholarly texts of a particular work
- an argument showing how a particular theme or concept may be related to a group of texts
- an argument bringing together some aspect of a well-known literary text with a lesser-known text or texts.

If you can frame your topic in some way such as this, you will find that it helps you work out a suitable structure, a matter we will come on to now.

Working out a structure

In writing your dissertation, you will usually have between 10,000 and 20,000 words (usually excluding the abstract and bibliography, but including footnotes and any quotations). It may sound a lot, but it isn't. Of one thing you can be certain: any topic you choose will be subject to a version of Parkinson's Law whereby it will expand to fill, and more than fill, your word-allowance.

So, the first principle is the one we have already been discussing: choose a topic which is capable of being dealt with adequately within the allocated word-limit. This may seem like a counsel of perfection, because of course any worthwhile research topic is liable to develop once work gets under way. One way of thinking through this problem is to look for areas where you might be flexible, areas which might be cut back or even omitted altogether if other, more relevant, material needed to be included.

Thinking carefully at the outset about the question of length should also influence the way in which you structure your dissertation. Any dissertation will have, at least, an introduction, a middle and a conclusion. Obviously an introduction is important: you need to tell your reader what you are intending to do, and why. A conclusion is equally important: it should briefly summarize what you have done, explain its significance and, if appropriate, suggest how the subject might be extended.

In between the introduction and the conclusion comes the body of the work in which you *assemble* the evidence, *analyse* it, and put forward your *argument* based on that analysis. This middle section of your dissertation would need to be divided into chapters, each of which would represent a major step in the development of the argument. It is difficult to produce a chapter that can accommodate the amount of evidence and the detailed analysis required, and at the level expected, in under 3,000–4,000 words. Let us say that your introduction and conclusion take up no more than 1,500 words each: you can see that if you are aiming to produce, say, a 15,000-word dissertation, you would have no more than three, or at the most four, main chapters available to you.

It is important to recognize these limitations of space right from the beginning, and to plan accordingly. It is pointless to plan a structure that includes six or seven chapters, and then find that you need to cut, or significantly restructure, during the final stages of writing.

Preparing a research proposal

Assuming that you have an idea for a possible dissertation project that is sufficiently tightly defined so that it is do-able in the time and space available, and further assuming that you have checked that you can get hold of the necessary materials, you will usually need to write a research proposal for approval by your tutor or supervisor. This should probably be not more than about 1,000 words in length, and should be presented in continuous prose.

The purpose of the proposal is to show that you have a promising line of research and to indicate how you hope it will develop. The following list of headings will give you an idea of what is required.

Title	Do not feel bound by this (it can be altered in the finished product).
Thesis	State as quickly and clearly as possible what your argument will be, and what primary text(s) you intend to use.
Materials and chapter structure	Go into more detail about your materials, giving some indication as to their aptness for your project, and how you think your discussion of them may be organized, chapter by chapter, in the final product. A provisional chapter structure is important, so make sure it is clear to the reader how many chapters there are going to be, what

is going to go into each, and how they will connect with each other. If possible give provisional chapter titles.

Think of this as an exercise in persuasion: you are trying to convince your tutor or supervisor that you have evidence (although as yet unexploited) for your thesis. You should allude throughout this section to the secondary literature on the subject (historical, critical, theoretical, etc.) and indicate how you might use it. You may choose to argue in support of some commentator's work, or alternatively take issue with it; but you must at the very least demonstrate an awareness of some of the major secondary literature.

Conclusion Clearly this will be provisional. You have not yet argued your case, merely outlined the materials and likely directions of your argument. You might also like to indicate at this stage what problems you think you might encounter along the way: your tutor or supervisor is at least as interested in these as in your thesis.

Bibliography A list of the primary and secondary texts you intend using should be appended to the proposal – though, again, this list will be provisional and will certainly expand once you begin serious work on your dissertation.

Writing your dissertation

Once your research proposal has been approved, you are ready to begin work on the dissertation. All your previous MA study has been leading up to this moment, and it is worth remembering that although writing a dissertation of 15,000 words may not in theory be *more* difficult than writing a 2,000-word essay (it is just a different *kind* of difficulty) – it will almost certainly feel as if it is. You need stamina to keep going; you need to be organized about such practical matters as note-taking and developing a filing system; most of all, you need to start writing early, and keep writing all the way through.

What follows is a brief list of 'Do's and Don'ts' – mainly 'Do's' – to help you with the business of writing your dissertation.

1 *Do* make sure that you have a clear timetable of contacts with your tutor or supervisor.

2 *Do* plan well ahead. Organize library-visits and things like inter-library loans in advance. It is an infallible rule that everything (research, writing-up, typing and correcting) will take longer than you expect, so *do* plan in some spare time.

3 *Do* start compiling a bibliography as soon as you start work. *Don't* put it on scraps of paper: put it in a ring binder. Better still, use 6x4 index

cards and keep them in a secure box. Make sure that you record all the bibliographical information you will need: include the place, publisher and date and, in the case of articles in journals, page references. Include a note of where the source is available to you, in case you need to return to it. Record only one book or article on each sheet of paper or card, so that later you can shuffle entries around.

Alternatively store the information on your PC. However, if you do this, make sure that you have a back-up disk that is kept up to date: never store important electronic information in only one place. To be safe from disaster such as theft, have a copy of your bibliography and draft dissertation both on the hard disk in your machine and on a floppy disk that you store away from your PC.

4   *Do* keep a weather-eye open for new publications in your own field, checking current abstracts, indexes and specialist bibliographies. It's often easier to do this electronically via a PC and the Internet.

5   *Do* make notes and *do* record page references at the same time. *Don't* write reams and reams of notes; you'll never have the time to sort them out, and so they will prove useless. Writing notes on 6x4 cards can be a useful discipline: a lack of space concentrates the mind wonderfully.

6   *Do* write as you go along. *Don't* get so carried away by research that you only write notes (or even nothing at all) for weeks on end. Writing drafts is scarcely ever a distraction from research. When writing, make sure that from the very beginning you use the proper scholarly conventions: getting it right from the start will save you an awful lot of time later on.

7   *Do* write clearly and crisply and avoid jargon wherever possible. Short sentences are more easily controlled than long ones.

8   *Do* keep in mind that a dissertation should be a form of argument in which the writer must attempt to convince the reader of his or her case. Be honest with yourself, and make sure that you understand your own argument – and that it *is* an argument and not just an unsubstantiated speculation.

9   *Do* remember also that an argument is not the same as an assertion. You must make sure that you prove, or justify, or offer evidence for whatever you say – by including properly referenced citations from primary sources (texts contemporary with those you are discussing) and/or from secondary sources (critical books, articles, historical studies, etc.). Remember, too, that your argument will be greatly strengthened if you recognize the force of points that might be made against – or that qualify – the case you are advancing. Try to suggest ways in which these objections or qualifications might be answered.

10 *Do* aim to have the first rough draft of your dissertation complete so that you have plenty of time to refine and revise it. Unless you've been very restrained, your first draft is likely to be over-length and you will

need to slim it down. You will also need some time to add any introduction and/or conclusion necessary. As a general rule, you should
always leave both the introduction and the conclusion until the bulk of
the research has been written up.

Presenting your dissertation

Format of text

Each university will have its own regulations governing the format and
submission arrangements for MA dissertations, and you will need to check
carefully whether there are any special requirements about the style of
references, layout of bibliography etc. to which you will have to conform.
What follows is some *general* guidance on the presentation of a dissertation
in literature.

Your dissertation will have to be either typewritten or, if you use a word-
processor, printed in letter-quality (or near letter-quality) print, on white
paper of good quality. Some institutions allow you to use both sides of the
paper, but it is better to use one side only. (This is partly because you can
then take out single pages for correction more easily, but also because it is
usually more convenient for an examiner to work with text printed on only
one side.) The main text should be typed in double spacing throughout. The
only exceptions to this are that inset quotations and footnotes may be in
single spacing, and items listed in a bibliography may be in single spacing,
with double spacing between items.

It is important to leave good margins. The *minimum* widths should be
40mm at the inside margin (to allow for binding), 15mm for the top and
outside margins, and 20mm for the bottom.

If you are using a word-processor, you should choose a font size of about 12
point. Italic font should be used for titles of books, foreign words and
phrases, etc., but underlining is also acceptable. As regards the layout of
paragraphs, the first line of the opening paragraph of a chapter or section
should always begin 'flush left'. For subsequent paragraphs you may *either*
indent the first line by four spaces, *or* begin it 'flush left'. Whichever style
you choose, you should apply it consistently throughout. There is no need
to insert extra space between paragraphs: the usual double spacing is
sufficient.

The pages of the dissertation should be numbered consecutively throughout, and each chapter should begin on a new page. The titles of chapters
should be in capital letters, and be centred on the page. Section headings (if
any) within chapters should be in italics, and aligned with the left-hand
margin. A table of contents should be provided, listing all the parts of the
dissertation, with page references. Check that the wording of the chapter
titles is identical with that in the body of the dissertation.

You should make sure that you leave time to proof-read your dissertation thoroughly before submission. Punctuation and grammar, as well as spelling, should be checked carefully, and particular attention should be paid to quotations to ensure that you have transcribed them accurately. These are all matters to which examiners will pay close attention.

Notes and bibliography

MHRA or Author–Date system?

The most widely used system of referencing in literary studies is the MHRA system – so called because it is recommended by the Modern Humanities Research Association. In this system, a superscript number is placed in the text itself at the relevant point, and its note (single-spaced) is placed at the foot of that page. (Sometimes all the notes are grouped as endnotes – at the end of a chapter or at the end of the main text.)

If you have a choice as to whether to have footnotes or endnotes, it is worth opting for the former. This is primarily for the convenience of your most important readers, your examiners, who will be interested to see what sources you are using, and who may want to check some of your references. It is distracting for them to have to keep flicking to the end of a chapter to look at notes. But *any* reader of your work will benefit from having ready access to the sources and routes of the evidence, argument and discoveries you are presenting.

The main rival to the MHRA system is the 'Author–Date' system. In this system, superscript numbers and footnotes/endnotes are not used. Instead of superscript numbers, the surname, year of publication and (if relevant) page number are placed inside parentheses at the appropriate point in the text; for instance:

Others have argued (for example, Stern, 1973, p.24) that ...

Depending on the sentence, there may be no need to repeat the surname:

Stern argues (1973, p.24) that ...

Instead of footnotes/endnotes, all the references are placed, alphabetically by author's or editor's surname, in one list at the end of the work. The Author–Date system has its supporters, and is widely used in the social sciences, but '(Stern, 1973, p.24)' does interrupt the flow of the text more than a small, superscript number. Because the Author–Date system is not common in academic studies of literature, in what follows I will concentrate on the MHRA system. But whichever system you adopt, the most important thing is to be consistent and accurate in your use of it.

The MHRA system

The importance of learning how to present footnotes (or endnotes) properly cannot be over-emphasized. A dissertation submitted for an MA degree should show that the author knows what scholarly apparatus is for, and is able to use it in a clear and consistent way. The primary function of foot-notes is to indicate as concisely as possible the sources of all quotations used and all works referred to in your dissertation. Footnotes should not nor-mally be used to amplify points made in the main text: if amplification is needed, it should be worked into the text or, exceptionally, added as an appendix.

In the MHRA system, the basic information required in a full reference to a book is as follows: author, title, place of publication, publisher and date. Often, however, more detail is needed. The list below gives examples of how to present references to a variety of books, including edited works, multi-volume works, translated works, and works in series. You should note carefully the order in which information is presented and the punc-tuation used.

The following would be footnotes or endnotes:

[1] Michael Dobson, *The Making of the National Poet: Shakespeare, Adaptation and Authorship, 1660–1769* (Oxford: Oxford University Press, 1992), p.95.

[2] *The Letters of Robert Louis Stevenson*, ed. Bradford A. Booth and Ernest Mehew, 8 vols (New Haven and London: Yale University Press, 1994–5), II, 189–90.

[3] Alethea Hayter, *Elizabeth Barrett Browning*, Writers and their Work Series, 182 (London: Longman, 1965), p.18.

[4] F.A. Wolf, *Prolegomena to Homer (1795)*, trans. and ed. Anthony Grafton, Glenn W. Most, and James E.G. Zetzel (Princeton: Princeton University Press, 1985), pp.45–67.

[5] Seán Burke (ed.), *Authorship: From Plato to the Postmodern. A Reader* (Edinburgh: Edinburgh University Press, 1995), p.xiv.

[6] James Joyce, *Ulysses*, ed. Jeri Johnson (Oxford: Oxford University Press, 1993), p.247.

[7] Livia Veneziani Svevo, *Memoir of Italo Svevo*, trans. Isabel Quigley (London: Libris, 1989), pp.100–110.

[8] William Shakespeare, *Hamlet: a New Varorium Edition*, ed. Horace Howard Furness, 2 vols (1877; rep. New York: Dover, 1963), I, 146–50.

[9] Aphra Behn, 'The Disappointment', in *The Works of Aphra Behn*, ed. Janet Todd, 7 vols (London: Pickering and Chatto, 1992–6), I: *Poetry* (1992), pp.65–9.

(As you see from 2 and 8 above, it is not necessary to insert 'p.' or 'pp.' immediately after a volume number.)

References to articles in books should be given as follows (the second example indicates that an article has been previously published elsewhere):

[10] Penelope Wilson, 'Classical Poetry and the Eighteenth-Century Reader', in *Books and their Readers in Eighteenth-Century England*, ed. Isabel Rivers (Leicester: Leicester University Press, 1982), pp.97–126.

[11] G. Thomas Tanselle, 'Textual Study and Literary Judgment', in his *Textual Criticism and Scholarly Editing* (Charlottesville and London: University Press of

Virginia, 1990), pp.325–37 (first publ. in *Papers of the Bibliographical Society of America*, 65 (1971), 109–22).

References to articles in journals should be given as follows:

[12] Alice Walker, 'Principles of Annotation: Some Suggestions for Editors of Shakespeare', *Studies in Bibliography*, 9 (1957), 95–105.

[13] Margreta De Grazia, 'The Essential Shakespeare and the Material Book', *Textual Practice*, 2 (1988), 69–86.

[14] Anne McDermott, 'The Defining Language: Johnson's *Dictionary* and *Macbeth*', *RES*, n.s. 44 (1993), 521–38.

[15] Grace Ioppolo, '"Old" and "New" Revisionists: Shakespeare's Eighteenth-Century Editors', *Huntington Library Quarterly*, 52 (1989), 347–61.

Note that it is not necessary to precede the page span of articles in journals by 'pp.', nor to precede the volume number by 'vol.'. The inclusion of 'n.s.' (i.e. 'new series') in footnote 14 indicates that the journal has begun a new sequence of numbering. When abbreviating a journal title to initials, full stops are not used: see footnote 14 above, where *RES* is short for *Review of English Studies*.

So far, I have been giving examples of how to cite printed materials. With the increase in electronic publication, whether on cd-rom or on the Internet, it will become necessary to devise a generally accepted style for referring to such material. A book on this subject is listed under 'Selected reading'. For details of how to refer to other kinds of material, such as manuscripts or unpublished theses, you should consult more specialized works listed in 'Selected reading'.

All the examples given in 1–15 above are for the *first* reference to a book or article: at that point, details need to be presented in full. It is not necessary to keep repeating all the bibliographical information in later references, and these can be shortened to the author's surname, or surname and brief title, or brief title, depending on which will be more intelligible to readers.

So, in relation to our first example, if no other work by Michael Dobson was being referred to, subsequent references could be shortened to:

[16] Dobson, p.72.

But if this was one of several works by Dobson, second and subsequent references would be:

[16] Dobson, *Making of the National Poet*, p.72.

Second and subsequent references to articles in books and journals can be shortened in a similar way:

[17] Walker, 'Principles of Annotation', p.100.

It is also possible to limit the number of footnotes by incorporating a very brief reference in parentheses in the main text. For example, if you were writing a chapter which included frequent quotations from Virginia Woolf's novel *The Voyage Out*, your first reference could be given in full as a footnote, but explaining that all future page references would be to this edition and would be included in the text:

[1] Virginia Woolf, *The Voyage Out*, ed. Lorna Sage (Oxford: Oxford University Press, 1992), pp.128–9. Future page references are to this edition, and are included in parentheses in the text.

Thereafter, you would simply include '(p.75)' after quotations, without any need for footnote reference numbers.

Another way of limiting the number of separate footnotes is by putting a single reference number at the end of a paragraph and grouping, in one footnote, all the references for that paragraph. Care should be taken that there is no ambiguity, however, and a footnote should not cover more than a single paragraph.

Your dissertation will need to conclude with a bibliography. This should contain details of *all* the books and articles you have consulted in the preparation of your dissertation, not just the ones from which you have actually quoted. It is usually helpful to subdivide it in some way. For example, if your dissertation is on a particular author or group of authors, a list of the editions of their works which you have used should come first. This section might be followed by a list of other *primary* sources used (i.e. other works from the period of the subject or author(s)), and then by a list of all the *secondary* books and articles consulted.

Works in each section of the bibliography should be listed alphabetically under the surname of the author or editor (which is therefore placed first), with the full reference following. Note that where there is more than one author or editor, only the first has the surname preceding the forename(s), as in the example of the book edited by Booth and Mehew below:

Booth, Bradford A. and Ernest Mehew (eds), *The Letters of Robert Louis Stevenson*, 8 vols (New Haven and London: Yale University Press, 1994–5).

Other parts of the dissertation

There are three other important parts of your dissertation that will require attention. First of all, you will almost certainly be required to supply an abstract, or synopsis, of the contents. This is usually no more than about 400 words in length, and a copy should be placed at the front of the dissertation, immediately following the cover and before the contents page. The purpose of the abstract is to provide the reader with a brief but accurate summary of the content and structure of the dissertation – a bit like the 'blurb' provided on the flap or backcover of the dust-jacket of a book. You should try to describe clearly and concisely what your dissertation is about, giving an indication of the main divisions or chapters, how your argument is developed, and the conclusions reached.

Secondly, you must of course provide a title page. On both the title page *and* the cover, you should give the following information:

- the full title of the dissertation

- your full name and first degree

- the degree for which it is submitted (for example, MA in Literature)

- the date (month and year) of submission

Finally, you should include a statement making clear whether any part of the dissertation has previously been submitted for a degree or other qualification of any university or other institution. Where this is not the case, you should say so explicitly.

You should also include a sentence making clear that the entire work has been prepared by you alone or, if this is not the case, what part of it is your independent contribution.

Selected reading

MHRA *Style Book: Notes for Authors, Editors and Writers of Theses*, 5th edn (London: Modern Humanities Research Association, 1996). This is perhaps the single most useful work of its kind; it is certainly the cheapest, and is highly recommended. It provides guidance on the MHRA system and the Author–Date system.

Walter S. Achest and Joseph Gibaldi, *The MLA Style Manual* (New York: Modern Language Association of America, 1985). Describes a system widely used in the USA. See also, by the same authors and publishers, the *MLA Handbook for Writers of Research Papers*, 4th edn (1995).

Zia Li and Nancy B. Crane, *The Official Internet World Guide to Electronic Styles: A Handbook to Citing Electronic Information* (Westport, WA: Meckler, 1996).

George Watson, *Writing a Thesis: A Guide to Long Essays and Dissertations* (London and New York: Longman, 1987). Contains much useful advice.

Part 5

REFERENCE

glossary

library exercises – model answers

checklist of libraries, reference books and other sources

14 GLOSSARY

by Simon Eliot and W.R. Owens

This is a brief and highly selective list of words and abbreviations that you are likely to come across when doing research in literature. For more detailed and/or more comprehensive coverage, see the reference books at the end of this Glossary (p.198).

A

accidentals, term in textual editing, meaning the factors that determine a word's appearance on the page (for example, spelling, capitalization, word-division and punctuation). The words themselves are commonly refered to as 'substantives'.

alexandrine, *see* **metre**.

allegory, figurative description or narrative with hidden meaning – for instance, Bunyan's *The Pilgrim's Progress*, in which the vicissitudes of a Christian's experience are represented under the guise of the adventures and mishaps of a pilgrim.

anapaest, *see* **metre**.

Aslib, The Association for Information Management (formerly The Association of Special Libraries and Information Bureaux); provides a forum (through conferences, publications and research support facilities) for discussion and exchange of information on the management and use of information, and related problems.

Augustan, term applied to late seventeenth- and early eighteenth-century English literature, implying its similarity to the great age of Latin literature under the Emperor Augustus (from 27 BCE to 14 CE); this period – the epoch of Virgil, Horace and Ovid – showed a concern for decorum, urbanity and 'correctness'.

B

bibliographical ghost, book that has never really existed – often the result of an error in transcription, in editing or in printing during the production of a catalogue or bibliography; should not be confused with either a book that was cancelled in the press and was therefore never published, or a book that *was* published but of which no copies now exist.

bibliography (analytical), 'technical investigation of the printing of specific books, or of general printing practice, based exclusively on the physical evidence of the books themselves' (Fredson Bowers, *Principles of Bibliographical Description*, Winchester: St Paul's Bibliographies, 1986).

bibliography (descriptive), use of the techniques of analytical bibliography to describe the **format** and printing history of a specific book or books.

bibliography (enumerative), the recording and enumeration of all known editions (and sometimes impressions) printed during a defined period or in a specific region or country; the entries are usually listed alphabetically by author or title and frequently contain information on the location of copies.

bibliography (historical), the study of the book as a product of material resources and technical processes which are themselves changing over time; as the materials change and processes evolve, so do the nature and form of the book.

bibliography (textual), application of analytical bibliography to the editing of texts, particularly where a question of meaning is involved.

BL, British Library.

BLAISE, British Library Automated Information Service.

blank verse, unrhymed verse, in iambic pentameters (*see* **metre**); peculiar to English verse, it was first used by the Earl of Surrey in his translation of Books 2 and 4 of Virgil's *Aeneid, c.*1540.

BLC, British Library General Catalogue of Printed Books (in electronic form, either as an online database or on cd-rom). This is now also available as an OPAC on the **Web.**

BM, British Museum.

BUCOP, British Union Catalogue of Periodicals.

C

c., abbreviation of the Latin *circa* ('around [date]').

caesura, from the Latin ('a cutting'); a heavy pause in, or near, the middle of a verse line.

canon, on the analogy of the biblical 'canon' (i.e. the books of the Bible regarded as Scripture, as opposed to the Apocrypha), the term 'the literary canon' means those works of literature regarded as possessing especial authority or literary merit.

catchword, first word of the next page printed at the foot of the preceding page; catchwords were a common feature of books until the nineteenth century, and were used by printers as a means of telling which page followed which during imposition.

catharsis (literally 'purgation'), term applied by Aristotle in his *Poetics* to the function of tragedy in purifying the emotions of pity and terror by vicarious experience of them in the theatre.

CBEL, The Cambridge Bibliography of English Literature; superseded by the *NCBEL*, which in turn will be replaced by *CBEL* 3 which is currently (1998) in production.

cd-rom, compact disc with read-only memory; a compact disc that carries various types of data rather than just sound data, and that can be read by a computer. Many cd-roms are used to deliver multimedia – a system which offers an integrated information package combining text, graphics, audio and video.

CHEL, *The Cambridge History of English Literature.*

collate, to compare (usually) a copy-text with other available versions of a text in order to detect variants in the text; this is usually done to establish the best or most likely reading of a given word or line, and to plot the bibliographic history of a text as it underwent revisions by the author and reprintings by the publisher(s). This necessary but laborious process is now made somewhat easier by such machines as the Hinman Collating Machine, which optically superimposes two texts so that they can be compared.

copy-text, copy of a manuscript or printed version of a text that is chosen by an editor as the basis for a critical edition. The choice and nature of a copy-text are highly contentious issues.

CQ, *Critical Quarterly* (journal).

D

dactyl, *see* **metre**.

deconstruction, name given to one aspect of the work of the French critic and philosopher, Jacques Derrida. A 'deconstructive' reading of a text tries to bring out the logic of the text's language as opposed to the logic of the author's claims or intentions, and it is governed by the theory (a) that concepts tend to involve their opposites, and (b) that language is a labyrinth from which there is no escape, there being no 'real world' that serves as its boundary or external point of reference.

diachronic, occurring in succession, as opposed to **synchronic**.

dialogic structure, 'dialogic' has been given currency by the Russian scholar Mikhail Bakhtin, according to whom language is always social in that by its nature it presupposes dialogue with others. He sees the novel as the most dialogical of literary forms in its capacity to subvert the single (monological) voice of the author.

DNB, *Dictionary of National Biography*, to be replaced by the *New Dictionary of National Biography* (*New DNB*).

duodecimo (or twelvemo), book **format** produced when the original **sheet** has been folded so as to produce twelve leaves (24 pages). Because the sheet has been folded a number of times, this format tends to be very small; commonly abbreviated to *12mo*.

E

edition, 'all the copies of a book printed at any time (or times) from *substantially the same setting of type*, and includes all the various impressions, issues, and states which may have been derived from that setting' (Philip Gaskell, *A New Introduction to Bibliography*, Oxford: Oxford University Press, 1972).

edition (critical), authoritative edition of a given work, whose aim is to present a text as close as possible to the author's original or ultimate intentions (so far as they are ascertainable); the edition is based on a **copy-text**, lists textual **variants** and is often extensively annotated.

edition (variorum), has two meanings:

(a) an edition that lists all the **variants** in the author's manuscript and in editions other than the **copy-text**;

(b) an edition that includes some of the annotations and commentaries of previous editors.

Some variorum editions do both, for example *The New Variorum Shakespeare*.

E in C, *Essays in Criticism* (journal).

elegy, although originally a much broader term, since the sixteenth century this has come to mean a poem lamenting the death of (usually) a specific person.

ELH, *A Journal of English Literary History*.

ELN, *English Language Notes* (journal).

enjambement, when the end of a line of verse does not correspond to any natural speech-pause, there is said to be *enjambement* (French, 'bestriding'). A line of which this is true is called a run-on line; for example: 'Instead of sweets, his ample palate took/Savour of poisonous brass and metal sick' (Keats, *Hyperion*).

epic, long narrative poem written in an elevated style about a great or heroic subject; the term is also sometimes applied to large-scale novels that tackle many subjects and deal with a multitude of characters (for example, Tolstoy's *War and Peace*).

ESTC, the *Eighteenth Century Short Title Catalogue*; also now stands for the *English Short Title Catalogue* – which aims to integrate the short-title catalogues covering the period 1473–1800.

et al., abbreviation of the Latin *et alia* ('and others').

et seq., abbreviation of the Latin *et sequens* ('and the following').

exegesis, originally a commentary on a particular biblical text; now used to mean a rigorous analysis and explication of any text. *See also* **hermeneutics**.

external evidence, any evidence – not derived from the text itself – for the authorship, intended meaning, circumstances of production, or date, of a particular work; it includes biographical information, as well as evidence from analytical and other bibliographical studies, and from publishing history. *See also* **internal evidence**.

F

fl., abbreviation of the Latin *floruit* ('he [or she] flourished'); used of a writer whose birth and/or death dates are not known, but who was alive and active around the time specified.

folio, large book **format** produced when the printed **sheet** is folded only once; commonly abbreviated to *fol.*

format, size and shape of a book. Standard formats are **folio, quarto, octavo, duodecimo**; these are relative sizes, as the exact dimensions of a book depend on the size of the original **sheets** on which it is printed. Some of the most common traditional (imperial dimensions) sheet sizes were: Foolscap (17 x 13 in.), Post (19 x 15 in.), Crown (20 x 15 in.), Demy (22 x 17 in.), Royal (25 x 20 in.).

fourteener, *see* **metre**.

G

gathering, 'pamphlet-like' section of a book produced when the printer folds and cuts the original printed **sheet**. A gathering is usually of two, four, eight, twelve or sixteen leaves, depending on the number of folds made; the number of folds determines the **format** of the book. In the case of **folios** and **quartos**, the gatherings are sometimes made up of more than one sheet (often one and a half sheets). A number of gatherings are sewn together to make the final book. Approximate synonyms for gathering are **quire** and **signature**.

Gothic, in its literal sense, pertaining to the Goths who invaded the Roman Empire. Retrospectively, it was used to describe a set of building styles prevalent in Europe between the late twelfth and early sixteenth centuries. The so-called 'Gothic' (or *Gothique*) novel of the eighteenth century specialized in medieval horrors and the macabre; it coincided with a Gothic-revival style in architecture.

H

hermeneutics, originally the study of biblical interpretation, but now used more generally to mean the study of the nature and theory of interpretation. From the Greek *hermeneus* ('an interpreter'). *See also* **exegesis**.

heroic couplets, rhymed iambic pentameters (*see* **metre**)**,** a form much used by Dryden and Pope.

hexameter, *see* **metre**.

I

iamb, *see* **metre**.

ibid., abbreviation of the Latin *ibidem* ('in the same place'); used when making a second or subsequent reference to the same work where there is no intervening reference to another work.

idyll, lyrical poem usually depicting an idealized version of rural or pastoral life; sometimes indicates non-rural subjects that are nevertheless being idealized (for example, Tennyson's *Idylls of the King*).

imposition, creation of a composed area of type large enough to print a whole **sheet** of paper at one time. This was done by taking the required number of pages of movable type and locking them firmly, in the correct order for printing, in a rectangular iron frame (or 'chase') by means of wooden blocks and wedges ('furniture'). The result of this process was a 'forme'.

impression, all those copies of an edition printed at one time.

infra, Latin for 'below', as in *vide infra* ('see below').

internal evidence, any evidence for the authorship, intended meaning, circumstances of production, or date, of a particular work derived from the text itself (for example, stylistic features and references to events contemporary with the writing). *See also* **external evidence**.

ISBN, International Standard Book Number.

J

JHI, *Journal of the History of Ideas*.

L

LC, The Library of Congress, the most comprehensive library in the USA.

leaf, single piece of paper, being two pages back to back.

letterpress, has two meanings:

(a) the text of a book (including any line illustrations) but not its plates (if any);

(b) printing from raised type or blocks (as opposed to printing from lithographic plates).

loc. cit., abbreviation of the Latin *loco citato* ('in the place cited').

logocentrism, term used by Jacques Derrida (*see* **deconstruction**) to refer to the priority given to the spoken, as opposed to the written, word in Western philosophy – with the further implication that a text will be governed by a *centre* which is not itself part of the text's structure.

M

metaphor, naming or describing something in terms of something else, as for instance speaking of the 'neck' of a bottle or of 'swallowing' an insult. In a broad sense it includes **metonymy, synecdoche** and **simile**.

metonymy, rhetorical figure by which the name of an attribute is substituted for the thing itself, as for instance the use of the word 'throne' to signify monarchy.

metre, the commonest metres in English are the *iambic*, the *trochaic*, the *anapaestic* and the *dactylic* – that is to say, metres composed of the type of feet known respectively as iambs, trochees, anapaests and dactyls.

iamb (or *iambus*), foot consisting of an unstressed syllable followed by a stressed syllable (for example, 'pretend');

trochee, foot consisting of a stressed syllable followed by an unstressed (for example, 'gaily');

anapaest, foot consisting of two unstressed syllables followed by a stressed (for example, 'disinclined');

dactyl, foot consisting of a stressed syllable followed by two unstressed syllables (for example, 'gloomily');

(*Note* By tradition, the metres of English verse have been given names taken from Greek and Latin prosody. This is unfortunate, because Greek and Latin verse works on a different principle from English verse: Greek and Latin verse is 'quantitative', i.e. a matter of the alternation of 'long' and 'short' syllables, whereas English metre is a matter of the alternation of stressed and unstressed syllables.)

A line of three feet is known as a *trimeter*, of four feet a *tetrameter*, of five feet a *pentameter*, of six feet a *hexameter* or *alexandrine*, and of seven feet a *fourteener* (on the assumption that each foot would be of two rather than three syllables).

In practice, a metrical label gives only a very rough description of the rhythmical effect of a particular poem; appreciation of rhythm springs from perceiving simultaneously both a regular pattern and variations of that pattern. Sometimes the variations are slight; at other times they are strong enough to induce a strong sense of tension between them and the regular pattern.

MHRA, Modern Humanities Research Association.

microform (or microtext), generic terms meaning manuscripts and books that have been photographically reproduced on a very small scale – for reading on special machines. The two most common forms are:

microfiche: sheet of film (normally about 13 x 8 cm) that allows 'random access' (i.e. you can get to any part of the sheet equally quickly, just as you can lower the stylus to any part of a record). Many library catalogues are now in microfiche form.

microfilm: usually a roll of 35mm film with one or two pages reproduced per frame. Because the information is organized in 'linear' form (i.e. like an audiocassette rather than a long-playing record), it can take quite a lot of fast-forward winding, or rewinding, to find what you want.

MLA, Modern Language Association of America.

MLQ, *Modern Language Quarterly* (journal).

MLR, *Modern Language Review* (journal).

MP, *Modern Philology* (journal).

MS, MSS, manuscript, manuscripts.

N

narratology, theoretical study of the various forms of narrative.

NCBEL, *New Cambridge Bibliography of English Literature.*

n.d., no known date (or 'not dated'). Any date in brackets that follows this can be assumed to be the product of an educated guess. If the date is known but not printed in the book, then it should appear in square brackets thus: [1970].

n.p., no known place of publication. Any place in brackets that follows this can be assumed to be the product of an educated guess.

N & Q, *Notes and Queries* (journal).

NUC, *National Union Catalog* (USA). *See also* **union catalogue.**

O

octavo, book **format** produced when the original **sheet** is folded three times to produce a gathering of eight leaves; commonly abbreviated to '8vo' or '8°'. The majority of modern books are octavo in format.

ode, long lyric poem, dignified in style and serious in subject-matter, often a formal address to a person or personified subject; characterized by an elaborate stanzaic structure.

OED, *The Oxford English Dictionary*, now in a revised edition (1989).

OHEL, *The Oxford History of English Literature.*

OPAC, Open Public Access Catalogue; this system allows a user to access and search an electronic library catalogue via the Internet and the Web.

op. cit., abbreviation of the Latin *opere citato* ('in the work [already] cited').

P

page, has two meanings:

(a) one side of a leaf;

(b) type arranged for the printing of one side of a leaf.

passim, Latin for 'everywhere' (or 'throughout'). In other words, 'references to this subject are found throughout the work'.

pastoral, the representing of urban or civilized existence under the disguise of an idealized rural one.

PBSA, *Papers of the Bibliographical Society of America* (journal)

pentameter, *see* **metre**.

periodical, serial normally issued at regular intervals; *see also* **serial**.

PMLA, *Publications of the Modern Language Association of America* (journal).

PQ, *Philological Quarterly* (journal).

press-mark, numbers and/or letters indicating the location of a given book in a library that has fixed locations (i.e. the book is always to be found in a set range of shelves, and is not moved around to accommodate additional or new books). In practice, such libraries tend to have controlled access (for example, the British Library Reference Division) rather than being open-access libraries (for example, public libraries). Sometimes called 'shelf-mark' or 'call-number' (USA).

PRO, Public Record Office.

Q

quantitative verse, poetry written on the Greek and Latin principle of the alternation of long and short syllables, rather than of stressed and unstressed syllables. As English tends to be an accentual language (i.e. one that is prone to use stress rather than length of sounds to convey meaning), the writing of English quantitative verse has proved neither very easy nor very rewarding. *See also* **metre**.

quarto, book **format** produced when the original **sheet** is folded twice to produce a gathering of four leaves. Commonly abbreviated to '4to' or '4°'.

quire, 'pamphlet' produced when the printer folds and cuts his original **sheet**. *See also* **gathering** and **signature**.

q.v., q.v.v., abbreviation of the Latin *quod vide* and *quae vide*, meaning (respectively) 'which see' and 'all of which see'; in other words: 'refer to this other entry [or entries]'. Commonly used in dictionaries and encyclopaedias.

R

recto, front of a leaf (i.e. the right-hand page); opposite of **verso**.

RES, *Review of English Studies* (journal).

S

SB, *Studies in Bibliography* (journal).

semiology, science of signs. It studies signs as a form of language and, like **structuralism**, is influenced by the linguistic theories of Ferdinand de Saussure, who defined a linguistic sign as the combination of a 'signifier' and a 'signified'.

serial, any work issued at intervals in successive parts, sometimes irregularly and frequently with no expected limit on the number of parts; *see also* **periodical**.

sheet, large piece of paper which, when printed and folded, goes to make up a **gathering, quire** or **signature**. Every book is composed of a series of such gatherings sewn or stuck together. The number of pages printed is determined by the number of times the sheet is to be folded. If folded once (thus producing two leaves or four pages), two pages are printed on one side of the sheet and two pages on the other (once this is complete, the sheet is said to have been 'perfected'). If folded twice (thus producing four leaves or eight pages), four pages are printed on each side of the sheet. Sheets vary in size, so **format** names (for example, **folio**) are only an approximate indication of size.

signature, has two meanings:

(a) printed **sheet** folded and cut; there are two synonyms for this – **gathering** and **quire**;

(b) printer's mark (usually a letter or a number, or a combination of the two) that appears at the foot of the **recto** of the first **leaf** of a **gathering** (and sometimes on the second leaf as well); these marks are used by the binder to make sure that the gatherings are assembled in the correct order. **Catchwords** were used for the same purpose.

simile, metaphorical comparison introduced by 'as', 'like', etc.

sonnet, verse-form consisting, in English, of fourteen iambic pentameter lines; 'Miltonic' sonnets rhyme abbaabbacdecde, or have a very similar arrangement, whereas most Shakespearian sonnets rhyme ababcdcdefefgg. The first eight lines of a sonnet are frequently called the 'octave', and the last six lines the 'sestet'.

SP, *Studies in Philology* (journal).

STC, short-title catalogue.

structuralism, theory that human activities are structured like a language. (Thus, for instance, the structuralist critic Roland Barthes analysed the 'grammar' and 'syntax' of women's fashions.) The movement was inspired by the theories put forward by the linguist Ferdinand de Saussure in his *Cours de linguistique générale* (1916), according to which language is a system of differences, its terms conveying meaning only in relation to other terms. The structural anthropologist Claude Levi-Strauss represents the culture of primitive societies as organized around binary differences or oppositions, such as raw versus cooked. *See also* **semiology**.

substantives, *see* **accidentals.**

supra, Latin for 'above', as in *vide supra* ('see above').

synchronic, occurring simultaneously, as opposed to **diachronic**.

synecdoche, figure of speech in which a part is used for a whole (for example, 'all *hands* were on deck'), or a whole for a part (for example, '*Pakistan* won the test').

T

tetrameter, *see* **metre**.

TLS, *The Times Literary Supplement*.

trimeter, *see* **metre**.

trochee, *see* **metre**.

U

ULS, *Union List of Serials*.

union catalogue, catalogue that lists the holdings of two or more libraries; for example, *The British Union Catalogue of Periodicals* lists the serial holdings of around 400 British libraries.

V

variant, alternative reading of a given word or passage in a text; for example, in the line from *Hamlet*:

'O that this too, too solid flesh would melt'

the variants for 'solid' found in other editions include 'sallied' and 'sullied'.

variorum, *see* **edition (variorum).**

verso, back of a leaf (i.e. the left-hand page); opposite of **recto**.

vide, Latin for 'see'.

viz., abbreviation of the Latin *videlicet* ('namely').

W

Web, the World Wide Web or WWW; that part of the Internet which allows the easy transmission, not just of text but also of graphics, audio and video. It is also characterized by the use of hypertext, which allows a user to jump from one piece of information to a related piece by means of 'hot' links between words or phrases in different documents, or in different parts of the same document.

Y

YWCCT, The Year's Work in Critical and Cultural Theory.

YWES, The Year's Work in English Studies.

Selected reading

The following specialist reference works will help you refine and enlarge the Glossary:

A Glossary of Literary Terms, ed. M.H. Abrams, 6th edn (New York: Harcourt Brace, 1992).

The Fontana Dictionary of Modern Thought, ed. Alan Bullock and Oliver Stallybrass (London: Fontana, 1987).

John Carter, *ABC for Book Collectors,* 6th edn (London: Granada, 1980).

A Dictionary of Modern Critical Terms: Revised and Enlarged Edition, ed. Roger Fowler (London: Routledge, 1987).

G.A. Glaister, *Glaister's Glossary of the Book*, 2nd edition (Delaware and London: Oak Knoll Press and The British Library, 1996).

David Kirby, *Dictionary of Contemporary Thought* (Basingstoke: Macmillan, 1984).

MLA International Bibliography (New York: Modern Language Association of America, 1922–). Each annual volume prints a very comprehensive list of scholarly periodicals and their abbreviations.

The Oxford Dictionary for Writers and Editors (Oxford: Oxford University Press, 1981).

Dictionary of World Literary Terms, ed. J.T. Shipley, 2nd rev. edn (London: Allen and Unwin, 1970).

Raymond Williams, *Keywords*, rev. edn (Oxford: Oxford University Press, 1985).

15 LIBRARY EXERCISES – MODEL ANSWERS

by W.R. Owens

The solutions below relate to the practical exercises in Chapter 2. They are not necessarily the only routes to the same goal. Different combinations of tools and techniques can be just as rewarding: the important skill to develop is the knack of working out a combination that fits the resources and time available to you. (Some of the material was located using computer catalogues or annually updated cd-roms; these references were correct at the time of going to press but may have been updated since.)

Question 1

A very simple query; the most obvious solution is to consult the *Dictionary of National Biography* (DNB) or, of course, one of the standard biographies of Tennyson.

Question 2

This is solved simply by consulting the *British Union Catalogue of Periodicals* (*BUCOP*) (see Checklist, p.213), which gives locations for runs of periodicals. This exercise is complicated by the fact that *BUCOP* only mentions volume numbers, not dates. Some libraries near Preston do not have full sets of *Blackwood's*, but from *BUCOP* it is not possible to match volume numbers with dates.

Question 3

The *NCBEL*, in conjunction with the *British Library General Catalogue of Printed Books* (see Checklist, p.211), ought to provide an answer to the first half of this question, though you would be wise also to consult the bibliography at the end of the 'Fielding' entry in the *DNB*. The second half of the question ('Which is the most recent book-length critical study of Fielding?') requires consultation of the 'National bibliographies' listed on pp.209ff. of the Checklist; and, since it won't always be obvious from the bare title of a book that it is a critical study, it may be necessary to consult the description of a given book in the publisher's catalogue (most large libraries stock publishers' current catalogues), or in annual bibliographies and surveys (see Checklist, p.217) of the appropriate year.

The chronological format of the *NCBEL* makes it very useful in answering the first half of the question. Computers are useful for finding the most recent critical study of Fielding. Using the BL Online Catalogue, *Humanities and Social Sciences Books and Periodicals (1975–)*, a title search with the key phrase 'henry fielding' will give post-1975 books. The search can then be refined to give publications from, say, 1994 to 1998. If you really want to be up to date, you could refer to the online version of *Whitaker's Books in Print* (used in libraries and larger bookshops), which will also tell you about forthcoming books on the subject.

Question 4

The answer to this should be obtainable from the 'National bibliographies' listed on pp.209ff. of the Checklist, care being taken to distinguish critical studies from straightforward biographies. *British Books in Print* is probably the most convenient source.

Question 5

To answer this from printed sources alone calls for careful consultation of subject-guides, bibliographies and indexes listed in the Checklist. Additionally, there is a useful list of books in volume II of the NCBEL on 'Book Production and Distribution'. A check through *British National Bibliography* and other national bibliographies (Checklist, p.209) provides a slightly longer route.

For a computing approach, a search of the BL Online Catalogue, *Humanities and Social Sciences Books and Periodicals (to 1975)*, with the title keywords 'history' and 'publishing', produces 44 items, among them Frank Arthur Mumby, *Publishing and Bookselling: A History from the Earliest Times to the Present Day* (London: Cape, 1949). The same search of the Online Catalogue, *Humanities and Social Sciences Books and Periodicals (1975–)*, will produce 102 items, including John Feather's *A History of British Publishing* (London: Routledge, 1988). Of course, keyword searches like this are by no means comprehensive, but a book such as Feather's will point the way to further reading. A similar title keyword search could be done using 'book' and 'trade' and 'English', which will turn up, among others, Marjorie Plant, *The English Book Trade,* 3rd edn (London: Allen and Unwin, 1974).

Question 6

Consult *Annals of English Literature* (see p.218 of the Checklist).

Question 7

Consult the works listed under 'Chronology and dates' in the Checklist (p.223).

Question 8

Consult Halkett and Laing, *A Dictionary of Anonymous and Pseudonymous Publications in the English Language, 1475–1640,* rev. John Horden (London: Longman, 1980); Checklist, p.217. (You could also answer this from the BL *General Catalogue of Printed Books to 1975* and some of the other national bibliographies.)

Question 9

Consult the various dictionaries of literary terms on p.228 of the Checklist (remembering that the definitions found there may not necessarily altogether agree).

Question 10

This calls for careful exploration in the subject-guides, bibliographies and indexes given in the Checklist, and for hit-or-miss consultation of other general works, such as the *Encyclopaedia Britannica*, the NCBEL, *British Books in Print*, etc. Remember that the actual word 'chivalric' may not appear in the title of relevant books, and you may need to try synonyms, such as 'Arthurian'. Alternatively, a search of the MLA cd-rom will turn up a number of titles.

Question 11

Consult pp.209–210 of the Checklist, which will put you on the right track. Particularly useful are *The Bookseller, Whitaker's Books of the Month and Books to Come*, publishers' catalogues and the US *Forthcoming Books*. Under the CIP (Cataloguing in Publication) programme, the *British National Bibliography* notes some books in advance of publication.

Question 12

Check NCBEL (vol. II, column 468) for first date of appearance. As the item is an essay, not a book, the printed library catalogues will probably not be of much use. The title's earlier form was 'On the Study of Poetry: General Introduction', as the essay was a preface to the anthology *The English Poets*, ed. T.H. Ward. The title changes to 'The Study of Poetry' when reprinted in *Essays in Criticism*, 2nd series, 1888. The DNB entry (Supplement, p.71) makes the context a bit clearer. If more biographical and bibliographical details are required, check some of the references identified in NCBEL and DNB.

Question 13

Check either the BL *General Catalogue of Printed Books to 1975*, vol. 152, p.263, or the Online Catalogue, *Humanities and Social Sciences Books and Periodicals (to 1975)*, or, if this isn't available, NCBEL (vol. III, column 581). If further details of particular poems in the collection are required, follow up bibliographical references or editions noted in NCBEL.

Question 14

Check the dictionaries (Checklist, 226), in particular the *Oxford English Dictionary* which has dated examples of use of words at different periods. This is an extremely useful way of charting shifts in meaning. Volume 6, p.702 provides a wide range of meanings and examples of 'Gothic', including Horace Walpole's *The Castle of Otranto, a Gothic Story* (1765 [for 1764]). General encyclopaedias and literary handbooks provide brief articles on the Gothic novel (for example, *Oxford Companion*). For more detailed information and comment on the origins and application of the term to the novel, it will be necessary to look at some studies. NCBEL (vol. II, columns 870–71) details studies of the Gothic novel, as does Howard-Hill, *Index to British Literary Bibliography*, vol. 1 (Checklist, p.216). Both lead to Montague Summers, *A Gothic Bibliography* (London: Fortune Press, 1941). An online search of decent-sized library catalogues would reveal the existence of three book-length bibliographies listing studies of the Gothic novel, published in 1975, 1984 and 1995. A search of the cd-rom of *ESTC* under the word 'gothic' would produce 92 occurrences of the word on title-pages of works published in the eighteenth century.

Question 15

The article and opinions of Johnson may not take the form of separate publications or even discrete statements and so cannot be identified through *NCBEL* references. Close attention to standard biographies (*DNB* will point to Boswell and other biographers as well as editions of letters) and scholarly editions of Johnson's writings (*NCBEL,* vol. II, columns 1125ff.) will indicate the Yale edition and others. The notes and indexes contained in these will pinpoint the statements concerned. An alternative route is to check criticism of Fielding's work, through bibliographical guides to the novel (Checklist, p.219), works cited in *NCBEL* or even BL *General Catalogue* and *British National Bibliography.* This procedure can be slow and lengthy but it may lead to *The Rambler,* No. 4, 31 March 1750, which is reprinted in *Henry Fielding: The Critical Heritage,* ed. Ronald Paulson and T. Lockwood (London: Routledge and Kegan Paul, 1969). As Johnson does not mention Fielding by name, the reader has to rely on the editor for identification, and Boswell and the letters for the less formal comments.

Question 16

In the BL Online Catalogue, *Humanities and Social Sciences Books and Period- icals (to 1975),* a computer search under the keywords 'circulating' and 'library' produces 86 items. Most of these are circulating library catalogues, but we also find Guinevere Lindley Griest, *Mudie's Circulating Library and the Victorian Novel* (Newton Abbot: David and Charles, 1970). A similar search of the post-1975 Online Catalogue produces 55 items, among them several studies of particular libraries. A search through the MLA cd-rom will produce six recent items on the subject. Again, 'Book Production and Distribution' in volume II of the *NCBEL* contains some useful material including Alan D. McKillop, 'English Circulating Libraries, 1725–50', *Library,* 4th ser., 14 (1934), 447–85.

Question 17

Check *Annals* (Checklist, p.218) for details of principal publications of the years around 1830 and who died. *DNB* and the biographical dictionaries (Checklist, 223–5), together with *NCBEL,* will give an idea of the productivity and productions of the surviving Romantic poets. For closer evaluation, check some of the detailed early Victorian studies identified in *NCBEL,* updated by references from *MLA* and annual bibliographies (Checklist, p.217). The 'fresh poetic talent' of which the extract speaks is presumably a reference to Tennyson, whose *Poems, Chiefly Lyrical* appeared in 1830 (*Annals of English Literature*).

Question 18

Check *Annals* for the years 1740–55 to note important works published in this period. Bibliographies of the novel in the eighteenth century (Checklist, p.219) will provide useful references to studies of the novel of this period, together with NCBEL, updated by the MLA and other annual bibliographies (Checklist, p.217). This should produce references to key studies including the following:

Lennard Davis, *Factual Fictions* (New York: Columbia University Press, 1983).

J. Paul Hunter, *Before Novels* (New York: Norton, 1990).

Michael McKeon, *The Origins of the English Novel* (Baltimore and London: Johns Hopkins University Press, 1987).

Ian Watt, *The Rise of the Novel* (London: Chatto and Windus, 1957).

A valuable approach to this question would be to use the ESTC to see how many books termed themselves novels before 1740. The command for this is:

kwt=novel and py<1740

This search produces 82 hits. Significantly, however, many works which we now describe as novels (for example, *Robinson Crusoe* and *Moll Flanders*) are absent because they did not present themselves as fiction.

16 CHECKLIST OF LIBRARIES, REFERENCE BOOKS AND OTHER SOURCES

by Anthony Coulson

HOW TO USE THE CHECKLIST

This Checklist has been designed to help with fundamental aspects of research:

(a) identifying and locating appropriate studies and documents, and

(b) checking and elucidating facts and points of detail.

Part 1, 'Finding libraries and collections', identifies directories that will provide details of collections that may be useful/available for research.

Part 2, 'Finding documents and references', introduces a wide range of bibliographies, indexes, directories, surveys and guides that help to locate specific published and (some) unpublished work from the vast field of literary and related studies. There are many subdivisions in this Part, as the job of tracking down works in different forms (books, articles, pamphlets, papers, theses) frequently involves the use of a very wide range of quite specialized reference works.

Part 3, 'Sources of information for facts and details', presents reference tools that can be used to check points of fact (such as chronology, biographical and general data, meanings of words) and details (such as allusions and quotations).

Selectivity not exhaustion

The Checklist is long and detailed, and refers to sources that will take time and practice to find, use and digest. Don't be put off by this or the range of its references: it has been planned to help with an infinite variety of enquiries/types of research – far more than any individual project will need. It was also planned for dipping into over a long period.

Perhaps the best advice is to skim the whole document fairly quickly to get an idea of its range and structure. By doing this you will discover at an early stage which sort of books exist to help with particular problems. There is no point in trying to master the details of all the works mentioned, but do try to decide at an early stage which works you are likely to need most, and where they are located in the libraries.

Accuracy

Though the Checklist tries to include only the most authoritative and reliable reference works, it is important to realize that most books contain inaccuracies. These may be misprints, educated guesses or mistakes from faulty sources/evidence. It is sensible to be circumspect *at all times*. If there is any doubt or uncertainty, it is always a good idea to check two or more unrelated sources of information.

For any work you consult, read the preface/introduction to find out how the work is organized. Most of the publications in the Checklist have their own quirks and distinctive structures. Before plunging into any work of reference that is unfamiliar, it is *always* sensible to spend a little time reading the preface and/or introduction, as well as looking at the contents page and index to be clear about the key features of the work. Find out, in particular:

- how the information is set out and organized

- why the information is presented in this particular way

- the rationale for including certain types of information and excluding others (most works *are* selective).

Being clear in advance about these points, and so being aware of the potential limitations of individual works, can save a lot of worry and frustration. It also makes it easier to use complex reference works selectively but effectively. This all helps save time and effort.

Electronic sources

Sources that are also available electronically (on cd-rom or online via the Internet) are noted in individual references. For guidance on locating some of the many potential sources available on the Internet, please see Simon Eliot's advice in Chapter 3, 'Using the Internet for literary research'.

PART 1
FINDING LIBRARIES AND COLLECTIONS

The annual

> *World of Learning* (London: Europa)

provides a concise and up-to-date **world-wide** guide. There are entries for academies, societies, research institutes, libraries, archives, museums, universities and colleges, with details of address, scope, telephone and fax numbers as well as key publications. The index is of names of institutions only.

The most useful and detailed directory of **British libraries** is

> *The Libraries Directory 1995–7*, ed. Naomi Davis (Cambridge: James Clarke, 1996)

which lists public libraries, special libraries (academic, commercial, industrial and learned-society) and many museums and galleries (including some stately homes) by place in separate alphabetical sequences. Entries include a note of the range of the library, special collections, details of addresses and service points, telephone numbers, names of officers, opening hours, conditions and special features.

Briefer current details of libraries, particularly public libraries, are to be found in the annual

> *Libraries in the United Kingdom and the Republic of Ireland*, ed. Ann Harrold (London: Library Association)

and there are fuller details of academic libraries in

> *Academic Libraries in The United Kingdom and The Republic of Ireland*, ed. Ann Harrold (London: Library Association).

Details of many more specialist libraries, including many not easily available to the public, are contained in

> *Aslib Directory of Information Sources in the United Kingdom*, ed. Keith Reynard, 10th edn (London: Aslib, 1996). This work is also available on cd-rom.

Collections of more specific relevance to literary and historical studies are described in greater detail in

> *Aslib Directory of Literary and Historical Collections in The United Kingdom*, ed. Keith Reynard (London: Aslib, 1993)

> *A Directory of Rare Book and Special Collections in The United Kingdom and The Republic of Ireland*, ed. B.C. Bloomfield, 2nd edn (London: Library Association, 1997)

> *Directory of Literary Societies and Author Collections*, ed. Roger Sheppard (London: Library Association, 1994).

PART 2
FINDING DOCUMENTS AND REFERENCES

Bibliographies and indexes to published work

National bibliographies

By becoming familiar with these reference works, you can

- check that the details of a particular book reference are correct
- find out what else an author has written
- discover other books that have been published on a topic.

The following are the most widely available in libraries of all sizes:

> *British Books in Print* (London: Whitaker). There is one alphabetical sequence of authors, titles and some subject headings. The printed copies are updated and published annually; it is also available in a monthly microfiche edition and on cd-rom. It contains details of some books three months in advance of publication.

> *British National Bibliography* (Wetherby: British Library, National Bibliographic Service, 1950–). Under the terms of the Copyright Acts, every publisher in the UK is required to deposit one copy of every new book at the Copyright Receipt Office of the British Library. From these works the entries for the *British National Bibliography* (BNB) are compiled. The first issues of new journals are also recorded with a note of their planned frequency. Many books are noted in advance of publication.

A particularly valuable feature of BNB is that its weekly parts cumulate monthly and annually with some longer cumulations. There are cumulated indexes covering the period 1950–85, and a microfiche cumulation 1950–84 (published in 1986). Entries are in classified order according to the Dewey Decimal Classification system used in different forms by many libraries. There is a subject index and an author and title index. BNB is also available on cd-rom.

Other current general lists of books published regularly, which may be available in libraries, are

> *Whitaker's Booklist* (previously titled *Whitaker's Cumulative Book List*) (London: J. Whitaker, 1924–). Books printed and reprinted in the UK are listed under author, title and broad subject. It is published annually with larger cumulated volumes for the period to 1975. This is particularly useful for tracing full details of books of which only the title is known initially

and these works from the USA:

> *Cumulative Book Index: World List of Books in the English language* (New York: H.W. Wilson, 1898–). An author-, title- and subject-listing in one alphabetical sequence, this world list of books is published in the English language but has a clear bias towards US publications and editions. There are eleven issues per year, with annual and larger cumulations.

Books in Print (New York: Bowker); separate author and title indexes to books published in the USA and still in print. This is an annual publication with monthly microfiche editions. It also exists in cd-rom form as *Global Books in Print* and online.

Subject Guide to Books in Print (New York: Bowker); annual alphabetical subject-listing of books in print.

To help identify books in English published outside the UK and USA, there is

International Books in Print: English Language titles published outside The United States and The United Kingdom (Munich: K.G. Saur); a subject-guide is published in a separate volume.

For more up-to-date information about books only just published or soon to be published, libraries may also be able to provide the weekly

Bookseller (London: J. Whitaker); with large and informative spring and autumn export number cumulations

or a file of publishers' catalogues.

There are a number of older printed national bibliographies that may be particularly useful for tracing works published in the eighteenth and nineteenth centuries and not recorded in the better-known bibliographies detailed above. The oldest is

Robert Watt, *Biblioteca Britannica; or, a General Index to British and Foreign Literature* (Edinburgh: Constable, 1824), 4 volumes.

A much fuller and more accurate compilation is provided by the later

William Thomas Lowndes, *The Bibliographer's Manual of English Literature, Containing an Account of Rare, Curious and Useful Books, Published in or Relating to Great Britain and Ireland, from The Invention Of Printing* (London, Bohn, 1857–64; repr. Detroit: Gale, 1968), 7 volumes.

There is also the more extensive

English Catalogue of Books (London: Sampson Low). 1801–36 is covered in a single volume, ed. R.A. Peddie and Q. Waddington, published in 1914. Vol. 1 covers 1835–62. For the years 1837–1900 it was an annual with larger cumulations. The information was based on *The Publishers' Circular* (1837–1959), *British Books* (1959–60) and *The Publisher* (1967–70).

The Publishers' Circular is also a useful source of data on publishing policies and marketing.

Both *English Catalogue of Books* and *The Publishers' Circular* 1837–1900 have been published on microfiche by Chadwyck-Healey of Cambridge.

Printed library catalogues

National libraries and some major public libraries publish catalogues. Some are printed, but many more are available only on microfiche. These works are often the best source for details of earlier out-of-print materials, rare books, pamphlets and other items that have not been widely circulated or collected. Perhaps the most valuable are

> *The British Library General Catalogue of Printed Books to 1975* (London: Bingley/K.G. Saur, 1979–1988)

and

> *The British Library General Catalogue of Printed Books: 1976–1985* (London: K.G. Saur/British Library, 1986); microfiche together with its supplements

and their predecessor

> *British Museum General Catalogue of Printed Books* (various editions).

The catalogue is also available online through the BLAISE system and through its own OPAC (open public access catalogue).

In addition to the author catalogue, the earlier publication has a number of useful subject indexes:

> *Subject Index of the Modern Works added to the Library of the British Museum in the Years 1881–1900,* ed. G.K. Fortescue (London, British Museum, 1902–3; reprinted 1966), with supplements until 1970. The titles of the supplements vary.

The period before 1880 is covered by

> Robert A. Peddie, *Subject Index of Books Published before 1880* (London: Grafton, 1933–48; repr. London: Pordes, 1962)

and later by

> *British Library General Subject Catalogue 1975 to 1985* (London: K.G. Saur); also available on microfiche

and

> *British Library Subject Index of Modern Books Acquired 1961–75, 1982–6* (London: British Library).

There is a useful guide to the published catalogues, checklists and directories of the resources of many kinds of library, in the form of

> Robert B. Downs, *British and Irish Library Resources: A Bibliographical Guide* (London: Mansell, 1981).

Of particular interest to students of eighteenth-century literature is the ambitious project to create the fullest listing based on the national collections:

> *Eighteenth-Century British Books: An Author Union Catalogue, Extracted from The British Museum General Catalogue of Printed Books and The Catalogues of Bodleian Library and of The University Library, Cambridge,* compiled by F.J.G. Robinson and others (London: Dawson, 1981), 5 vols.

> *Eighteenth-Century British Books: A Subject Catalogue, Extracted from The British Museum General Catalogue of Printed Books,* compiled by G. Averley and others (London: Dawson, 1979), 4 vols.

> *The Eighteenth Century Short Title Catalogue: Catalogue of the British Library Collections,* ed. R.C. Alston (London: British Library, 1983); microfiche.

and, covering an even broader range of libraries, there is available both on microfiche and cd-rom

> *The Eighteenth Century Short Title Catalogue* (London: British Library, 1990).

There is a similar project aimed to extend this type of coverage to nineteenth-century literature:

> *The Nineteenth Century Short Title Catalogue, Series I, 1801–15, Series II, 1816–70, Series III, 1871–1919* (Newcastle upon Tyne, Avero Publications, 1984–in progress).

The listing is based on the holdings of the British Library, Bodleian, University Library Cambridge, National Library of Scotland, Trinity College Library (Dublin) and the University Library of Newcastle upon Tyne. From 1816 onwards it also includes the holdings of Harvard University and the Library of Congress. It also offers a subject index.

Some larger libraries may also have the larger American Library of Congress catalogues:

> *National Union Catalogs, 1956–82* (Washington: Library of Congress and various publishers)

> *National Union Catalog, pre-1956 imprints* (London: Mansell). The microfiche supplement has been available since 1983, as have other subject and date sequences. The Library of Congress catalogue is also available online.

Since 1971

> *Books in English* (London: British Library Bibliographical Services); six issues per year, annual cumulations and larger cumulations 1971–80, 1981–5

has provided a major microfiche bibliography of English-language titles published throughout the world based on records created by the British Library and the Library of Congress.

Another printed catalogue of a library rich in books for the literary researcher is

> *Catalogue of the London Library*, ed. C.T. Hagberg Wright and C.J. Purnell (1913), with supplements *1913–20* (1920), *1920–28* (1929), *1928–50* (London: London Library, 1953) and *Subject indexes* (1909–55), repr. by Nedeln: Kraus, 1968).

Directories of periodicals

To help identify periodicals published to serve particular subjects and interests, the most comprehensive current listing is

> *Ulrich's International Periodicals Directory, including Irregular Serials And Annuals* (New Providence, New Jersey: Bowker). Basically this is an annual classified guide to current periodicals world-wide, with regular supplements; it has title and subject indexes.

A more selective but annotated guide is

> Current British Journals (London: British Library, 1986); a classified guide with a brief description of the scope of each periodical.

Location guides

A number of publications list the collected journal holdings of different groups of libraries. They are often styled 'union' lists or catalogues. One used very extensively by libraries for locating older files of periodicals is:

> British Union Catalogue of Periodicals (London, BUCOP, 1955–8, with supplements to 1960).

Additional lists of periodical titles appearing later were published under the title *British Union Catalogue of Periodicals, incorporating 'World list of Periodicals': New Periodicals 1960–68, 1969–73*, then annually 1974–1980.

To bring the record up to date, this has been largely replaced by the publications concentrating on the holdings of the British Library Document Supply Centre:

> Keyword Index to Serial Titles (quarterly publication on microfiche); an alphabetical listing by keyword of the serials holdings of larger UK libraries
>
> Serials in the British Library (quarterly with cumulations)
>
> Current Serials Received (annual); a list of all serials currently received by the Document Supply Centre and the Science Reference and Information Service as at January of each year.

Many county libraries and local groups of libraries also publish union lists of journals held by constituent libraries.

Indexes to periodicals

Published indexes can save a lot of the time and physical effort needed to search files of periodicals. Perhaps the most readily available general index is

> British Humanities Index (East Grinstead: Bowker-Saur, 1962–)

From 1915 to 1961 it existed in a more limited form as *Subject Index to Periodicals*. The current publication is quarterly with annual cumulations and author and subject indexes. It indexes over 380 general periodicals broadly relevant to the arts, including some of the main literary journals as well as such weeklies as *The Economist*. It also includes substantial articles from *The Guardian* and *The Times*. More recent entries are available on cd-rom.

Some larger libraries may also have the US publication and cd-rom

> Humanities Index (New York: H.W. Wilson, 1974–).

From 1907 to 1955 it was titled *International Periodicals Index*, changing its name to *Social Sciences and Humanities Index* for the period 1956–74. It is quarterly with annual cumulations and has a single index giving authors and subjects. Since 1974 the number of periodicals indexed has grown from 170 to (at the time of writing) 260.

Details of the contents of some thirty major literary journals (authors, titles and pagination) appear regularly in the 'summary of periodical literature' contained in every issue of the following quarterly:

> *Review of English Studies* (Oxford: Clarendon Press, 1925–).

It is difficult to keep in touch with all journal contents as they appear, but there is a US publication that may be useful:

> *Current Contents: Arts and Humanities* (Philadelphia: ISI, 1979–); a weekly publication reproducing the contents pages of over 1000 journals with an index.

Often it may be helpful to trace the development of particular interests, related writing and even controversies through the links provided by references and footnotes. This can be laborious, but there is a very useful tool to help with more recent work:

> *Arts and Humanities Citation Index* (Philadelphia: ISI, 1977–).

The index is based on the analysis of footnotes and references contained in articles and papers published in over 6,400 journals and some books. It is a complex work consisting of four main sequences that can be used independently:

(a) Source Index (an author index of every item analysed)

(b) Permuterm Subject Index (an alphabetical index of every significant term or keyword contained in the titles of the articles and books indexed)

(c) Corporate Index (alphabetical listing of authors under particular organizations and geographical locations)

(d) Citation Index (an alphabetical listing by the names of the cited authors and artists).

The whole index is available online.

Victorian periodicals

A lot of valuable work has been done creating indexes and directories of the large body of nineteenth-century journals. The key directory is being created in Canada:

> *The Waterloo Directory of Victorian Periodicals 1824–1900*, ed. Michael Wolff, John S. North and Dorothy Deering (Waterloo, Ontario: North Waterloo Academic Press, 1977).

Phase 1 of the project lists all newspapers and journals accurately, and later phases have subject indexes and fuller bibliographical information.

The most accessible earlier index is

> Poole's Index of Periodical Literature (Chicago: Poole, repr. by Peter Smith, Gloucester, Mass., 1963): vol. 1, 1802–81; vol. 2, 1882–7; vol. 3, 1887–92; vol. 4, 1892–6; vol. 5, 1897–1902; vol. 6, 1902–6; with supplements.

The major literary journals are indexed in detail in

> The Wellesley Index to Victorian Periodicals 1824–1900, ed. Walter E. Houghton et al. (Toronto: University of Toronto Press, 1966–90).

Developments in the whole area are surveyed in

> Nineteenth-Century Periodical Press in Britain: a Bibliography of Modern Studies 1972–87, ed. Larry K. Uffelman, Lionel Madden and Diana Dixon (Niwot, Colorado: University of Colorado Press for Victorian Periodicals Review, 1992)

and in this collection of essays:

> Victorian Periodicals and Victorian Society, ed. J. Don Vann and Rosemary T. Van Arsdel (London: Scolar Press, 1993).

Current research on Victorian journals is discussed/reviewed in

> Victorian Periodicals Review (1968–quarterly), Niwot, Colorada: University of Colorado Press for Edwardsville, Research Society for Victorian Periodicals).

Guides to subject-areas

For more detailed work it may be necessary to check some more specialized bibliographies, indexes and guides that have evolved to serve the needs of more limited subject-areas.

Some of these are introduced in the following pages, but there are many more. Finding the appropriate work can be quite a problem, and so it might help to start by looking at some of the general tools that have been constructed to guide librarians and researchers through this wealth of material. The most valuable introduction is provided by

> Walford's Guide to Reference Material, vol. 2, Social and Historical Sciences, Philosophy and Religion, 7th edn (1997); vol. 3, Generalia, Language and Literature, the Arts, 6th edn (1995) (London: Library Association). Each entry is carefully annotated and indexed, providing important details of the scope and limitations of key reference works.

In larger libraries it may help to look for a similar US publication which offers a slightly different viewpoint and some additional suggestions:

> Guide to Reference Books, ed. Robert Balay, 11th rev. edn (Chicago: American Library Association, 1996).

Handbooks and guides to English literature

When looking at these and other specialist works, it is always wise to check two features:

(a) Is the work an attempt to include everything, or is the listing very selective? It is always sensible to look carefully at the preface and/or introduction to get a clear idea of the sort of approach and selection criteria that the compiler has used; these will explain how and why the entries are organized in a particular way.

(b) It may help to know a bit about the credentials of the compiler(s). A selective bibliography can constitute a most useful source in that the user may assume with some confidence that items listed have been sifted from the mass of available literature by someone who knows the subject-area thoroughly.

A few useful general guides are:

A Reference Guide to English Literature, ed. Daniel Kirkpatrick, 2nd edn, (London: St James Press, 1991), 3 vols

Paul A. Doyle, *Guide to Basic Information Resources in English Literature* (Chichester: John Wiley, 1976)

Frederick W. Bateson and Harrison T. Meserole, *A Guide to English and American Literature*, 3rd edn (London: Longman, 1976).

Retrospective bibliographies

Brief introductions are provided by

Selective Bibliography for the Study of English and American Literature, ed. Richard D. Altick and Andrew Wright, 6th edn (New York: Collier Macmillan, 1979)

Arthur G. Kennedy and Donald B. Sands, *A Concise Bibliography for Students of English, revised by William E. Colburn*, 5th edn (Stanford: Stanford University Press, 1972).

Perhaps the most important retrospective work is

The New Cambridge Bibliography of English Literature, ed. George Watson (Cambridge: Cambridge University Press, 1969–77), 5 vols with supplements (vol. 2, *1660–1800*, vol. 3, *1800–1900*). A new edition of this (*CBEL* 3) was in preparation when we went to press.

More limited in scope, but useful, are:

T.H. Howard-Hill, *Index to British Literary Bibliography* (Oxford, Clarendon Press):

Vol. 1: Bibliography of British Literary Bibliographies, 2nd edn (1987)

Vol. 3: British Bibliography to 1890 (not yet published)

Vol. 4: British Bibliography and Textual Criticism: a Bibliography (1979)

Vol. 5: British Bibliography and Textual Criticism: a Bibliography (authors) (1979)

Vol. 6: British Literary Bibliography and Textual Criticism, 1890–1969: an Index, 2nd edn (1985)

Vol. 7: British Literary Bibliography, 1970–79 (1992).

Anonymous and pseudonymous works

Many early works written either anonymously or under pseudonyms can be very difficult to trace or identify. However, there is a valuable guide in the form of

> Samuel Halkett and John Laing, *A Dictionary of Anonymous and Pseudonymous English Literature*, 2nd edn (Edinburgh: Oliver and Boyd, 1926–62) (1st edn 1882–8), 9 volumes and supplements.

This is being revised with fuller details, and issued according to historical period as

> Samuel Halkett and John Laing, *A Dictionary of Anonymous and Pseudonymous Publications in the English Language, 1475–1640*, rev. John Horden (London: Longman, 1980).

Further volumes covering 1641–1700 and 1701–1800 are in preparation. An even wider guide to pseudonyms is provided by

> *Pseudonyms and Nicknames Dictionary: A Guide to 80,000 Aliases, Assumed Names, Code Names, Cognomens, Cover Names, Epithets, Initialisms, Nicknames, Noms de Guerre, Noms de Plume, Pen Names, Pseudonyms, Sobriquets and Stage Names of 55,000 Contemporary and Historical Persons, including the Subjects' Real Names, Basic Biographical Information and Citations from which the Entries were Compiled*, ed. J. Mossman, 3rd edn (Detroit: Gale, 1987).

Annual bibliographies and surveys

There are three basic survey works:

> *The Year's Work in English Studies* (London: English Association, 1919–); a critical survey of scholarly periodicals, essays and monographs published during the year. The work is arranged by period, and indexes authors, authors written about, and subjects.

> *The Year's Work in Critical and Cultural Theory* (London: English Association, 1994–). As its title indicates, this companion volume concentrates on literary theory.

> *Review of English Studies* (Oxford: Oxford University Press, 1925–), 4 issues a year with cumulations; contains detailed reviews, notes, articles and a summary of periodical literature.

Much larger collections of references are provided by

> MLA *International Bibliography of Books and Articles on the Modern Languages and Literatures* (New York: Modern Language Association of America, 1969–); 6 issues a year with cumulations. From 1922 to 1969 (covering 1921–68), MLA *International Bibliography* was published as part of *Publications of the Modern Language Association of America*, volumes 37–82. Entries from 1981 to the present are also available on cd-rom.

and

> *Annual Bibliography of English Language and Literature* (London: Modern Humanities Research Association, 1967–).

Reviews

Perhaps the most accessible sources of detailed reviews of recent work are provided by

The London Review of Books (1979–); fortnightly

and

The Times Literary Supplement (1902–); weekly.

The latter has an annual index of authors and titles, correspondence and articles. There are three larger cumulated indexes:

The Times Literary Supplement Index, 1902–39 (Reading: Research Publications 1978), 2 vols

The Times Literary Supplement Index, 1940–80 (Reading: Research Publications, 1982), 3 vols

The Times Literary Supplement Index, 1981–5 (Reading: Research Publications, 1987), 1 vol.

Later annual indexes are available, and material from 1990 to the present can be traced on the cd-rom *British Newspaper Index*.

There are innumerable reviews elsewhere, and tracing them can be a problem. As well as the general periodical indexes mentioned already – *British Humanities Index, Humanities Index, Arts and Humanities Citation Index* – there are a number of specialized US periodical services that may help:

Book Review Index (Detroit: Gale, 1965–); bimonthly with annual cumulations

Book Review Digest (New York: H.W. Wilson, 1905–); 10 per year with quarterly and annual cumulations and also available on cd-rom and online.

Abstracts

Abstracts of English Studies (Calgary: University of Calgary, 1958–91); ceased publication, quarterly.

MLA *Abstracts of Articles in Scholarly Journals* (New York: Modern Language Association of America, 1970–75); ceased publication, 3 per year with annual cumulations.

This latter work is much more effective if used in conjunction with the relevant MLA *International Bibliography,* which should be consulted first. Entries in the printed *Bibliography* included in the *Abstracts* carry an asterisk. *Abstracts* volumes have neither cross-references nor author indexes.

Annals

To identify books that people were likely to be reading, or books published in any particular year, it may be helpful to check

Annals of English Literature, 1475–1950: The Principal Publications of Each Year Together with an Alphabetical Index of Authors and Their Works, 2nd edn (Oxford: Clarendon Press, 1961).

A lot of this information is also available in more basic chronological listings:

> M. Gray, *A Chronology of English Literature* (London: Longman, 1989)
>
> S.J. Rogal, *Chronological Outline of British Literature* (Westport: Greenwood, 1980).

Bibliographies of specific literary forms

These are extremely numerous, but the following might be worth looking for:

Novels

> A.E. Dyson, *The English Novel: Select Bibliographical Guides* (Oxford: Oxford University Press, 1974)
>
> Helmut Bonheim *et al.*, *The English Novel before Richardson: a Checklist of Texts and Criticism to 1970* (Metuchen: Scarecrow, 1971)
>
> Andrew Block, *The English Novel, 1740–1850: A Catalogue including Prose Romances, Short Stories and Translations of Foreign Fiction* (London: Greenwood, 1982; 1st edn, 1939)
>
> H. George Hahn and Carl Behm III, *The Eighteenth-Century British Novel and its Background: An Annotated Bibliography and Guide to Topics* (Metuchen: Scarecrow, 1985)
>
> Robert Letellier, *The English Novel 1660–1700: An Annotated Bibliography* (London: Greenwood, 1997)
>
> Helen H. Palmer and Anne J. Dyson, *English Novel Explication: Criticisms to 1972* (North Haven, Connecticut: Shoestring, 1973); with supplements
>
> Inglis F. Bell and Donald Baird, *The English Novel, 1578–1956: A Checklist of Twentieth-Century Criticisms* (London: Bingley, 1974).

Poetry

> *English Poetry: Select Bibliographical Guides,* ed. A.E. Dyson (Oxford: Oxford University Press, 1971)
>
> Gloria S. Cline and Jeffery A. Baker, *An Index to Criticism of British and American Poetry* (Metuchen: Scarecrow, 1974)
>
> Joseph M. Kuntz, *Poetry Explication: A Checklist of Interpretation since 1925 of British and American Poems Past and Present* (Boston: G.K. Hall, 1980).

Indexes to poetry

> *Columbia Granger's Index to Poetry,* ed. Edith P. Hazen (New York: Columbia University Press, 10th edn, 1990); consists of a title and first-line index, author index, subject index.

Collections of texts

A large corpus of English poetry texts is available on cd-rom as:

> *English Poetry Plus* (Cambridge: Chadwyck-Healey, 1995)

or, with even greater numbers of literary texts, through the same publisher's library of databases:

> *Literature Online* (available on the Web).

Bibliographies of bibliographies

The bibliographies and guides detailed so far are only a selection covering major interests and fields of study. There are many more, and for more particular and specialized research it may be necessary to hunt down some of the listings and bibliographies devised for these specific subjects. Information about existing works is available in:

> Theodore Besterman, *A World Bibliography of Bibliographies and Bibliographical Catalogues, Calendars, Abstracts, Digests, Indexes and the Like* (Lausanne: Societas Bibliographica, 4th edn, 1965–6), 5 vols.

Entries are arranged alphabetically by subject with brief scope notes, and the whole work has been updated by

> A.F. Toomey, *A World Bibliography of Bibliographies, 1964–1974* (New York: Rowmann and Littlefield, 1977).

An invaluable tool for keeping track of bibliographies as they appear, particularly in series, is

> *Bibliographic Index* (New York: H.W. Wilson, 1937–); 2 issues a year, and annual cumulation; a subject-list of bibliographies published separately or appearing as parts of books, pamphlets and periodicals. Selection is made from bibliographies that have fifty or more citations. It is also available online.

There is also a useful but elderly survey of the range of bibliographies world-wide in

> Robert L. Collison, *Bibliographies: Subject and National* (London: Crosby Lockwood, 1962).

Indexes to theses, research documents and manuscripts

A lot of research first appears in theses before formal publication in books or periodicals.

Theses

More recent theses and dissertations submitted for higher degrees can often be made available for reference and research on library premises through interlibrary loan. Earlier works, if available, may have to be bought in the form of a microfilm or photocopy if they are not available for loan: at the major library that you use for research, ask for advice from a librarian – who will also give you details of formalities and conditions when you need to study particular theses.

Guides to theses

Index to Theses with Abstracts Accepted for Higher Degrees by The Universities of Great Britain and Ireland and the Council for National Academic Awards (London: Aslib, 1950–); this covers British theses under fairly general subject headings but with detailed indexes; also available on cd-rom.

Dissertation Abstracts International (Ann Arbor: University Microfilms International, 1938–); monthly with larger cumulations; formerly titled *Dissertation Abstracts*. This covers mainly US universities, but since 1970 has included more British and European universities. Section A covers the humanities and social sciences. It is also available as an online database.

There is a much fuller compilation by the same publisher:

Comprehensive Dissertation Index 1861–1972 (Ann Arbor: Xerox University Microfilms), with later supplements; and:

Retrospective Index to Theses of Great Britain and Ireland 1716–1950, vol. 1: *Social Sciences and Humanities*, ed. Roger Bilboul (Oxford: Clio Press, 1975).

There are a number of subject-listings that might be useful, for example:

Richard D. Altick and W.R. Matthews, *Guide to Doctoral Dissertations in Victorian Literature 1886–1958* (Urbana: University of Illinois Press, 1960, reissued by Greenwood Press, London, 1973)

Patsy C. Howard, *Theses in English Literature 1894–1970* (Metuchen: Scarecrow, 1975)

L.F. McNamee, *Dissertations in English and American Literature: Theses accepted by American, British and German Universities 1865–1964* (New York: Bowker, 1968); with supplements *1964–8* (1969), *1969–73* (1974)

G.U. Gabel and G.R. Gabel, *Dissertations in English and American Literature: a Bibliography of Theses accepted by Austrian, French and Swiss Universities 1875-1970* (Basel: Editions Gemini/Saur, 1977); with supplement *1971–5*, 1981

Historical Research for University Degrees in the United Kingdom (London: University of London, Institute of Historical Research, 1971–); annual.

Many universities publish more detailed lists of their own theses.

Non-thesis research and registers of research in progress

It is very difficult to trace research that is not registered for formal academic qualifications. An overview of research in institutions of education is provided by the annual

Current Research in Britain: the Humanities (London: Cartermill Publishing in association with the British Library).

For more up-to-the-minute information, it may be worth checking the British Library Document Supply Centre monthly list (with annual cumulations):

> *British Reports, Translations and Theses* (Wetherby: British Library, 1975–) (before 1980 titled *BLLD announcement bulletin*). Reports are usually identified by numbers, and so the numbers appearing in any reference to a report should be carefully noted to avoid confusion and loss of time.

Manuscripts

There is an ambitious project to publish a census of major English literary manuscripts:

> Barbara Rosenbaum and Pamela White, *Index of English Literary Manuscripts*, (London: Mansell, 1980–).

There is a comprehensive index to the largest collection of UK manuscripts in the form of

> *Index to Manuscripts in the British Library* (Cambridge: Chadwyck-Healey, 1984–5), 10 vols; it codifies the many older catalogues and offers an alphabetical sequence of holdings with an index of persons and places.

Conference proceedings

This heading is used to cover conferences, symposia, congresses, meetings, and refers to the reports of the meetings. Many are not published but, when they are, they are valuable as an up-to-date source of information. They can often be very difficult to trace: a useful starting point is the collection built up by the British Library:

> *Index of Conference Proceedings Received* (Wetherby: British Library Document Supply Centre 1973–); monthly with annual cumulations and microfiche cumulation *Index of Conference Proceedings Received, 1964–1988* and also available online.

There are also two predominantly US indexes that may be some help with British material:

> *Directory of Published Proceedings* (Harrison: Interdok Corporation, 1968–)
>
> *Series SSH, Social Sciences and Humanities* is published quarterly with a cumulative index in the fourth issue.

Papers at conferences are sometimes republished in appropriate journals or collections, but often there may be a considerable delay. It may be useful to try to locate very recent conferences through the lists of forthcoming meetings (which often cover both the present and the immediate past):

> *World Meetings: outside United States and Canada* (New York: Macmillan, 1968–)
>
> *World Meetings: United States and Canada* (New York: Macmillan, 1963–).

These are companion publications, revised and updated quarterly, providing a two-year register of conferences and meetings with details of their publication plans.

PART 3
SOURCES OF INFORMATION FOR FACTS AND DETAILS

Chronology and dates

These are useful if you want to check particular dates:

> *Handbook of British Chronology*, ed. F.M. Powicke and E.B. Fryde, rev. edn (Woodbridge: Boydell and Brewer, 1996)
>
> *Handbook of Dates for Students of English History*, ed. C.R. Cheney, rev. edn (Woodbridge: Boydell and Brewer, 1995)
>
> *Dent Dictionary of Dates*, ed. Audrey Butler, 8th edn (London: Weidenfeld and Nicolson, 1986)
>
> Cyril L. Beeching, *Dictionary of Dates* (Oxford: Oxford University Press, 1993).

Basic historical details are usefully collected in

> *British Historical Facts, 1688–1760*, ed. Chris Cook and John Stevenson (London: Macmillan, 1988)
>
> *British Historical Facts, 1760–1830*, ed. Chris Cook and John Stevenson (London: Macmillan, 1980)
>
> *British Historical Facts, 1830–1900*, ed. Chris Cook and Brendan Keith (London: Macmillan, 1984).

For fuller information it may be useful to check the appropriate year's volume of

> *Annual register [year]* (London: Longman, 1758–)

or the more detailed chronologies in

> Neville Williams, *Chronology of the Modern World, 1763–1992*, rev. edn (New York: Simon and Schuster, 1995)
>
> Neville Williams and P.J. Williams, *Chronology of the Expanding World, 1492–1762*, 8th edn (New York: Simon and Schuster, 1995).

With practice, detailed indexes to long-lived journals can be used to pinpoint events, publications, etc. Perhaps the most important of these is the official index to *The Times*, 1907 to the present, which was previously

> *Palmer's Index to The Times Newspaper* (London: Samuel Palmer, 1868–1906, Kraus Reprint); covers 1790–1906, and is also available on microfiche and cd-rom (Cambridge: Chadwyck-Healey).

Biographical information

Searching for information on people is often much easier than trying to follow up ideas and concepts, because it is simpler to index and search for names.

Although most general encyclopaedias contain a lot of information on major figures, it may be more useful to check dictionaries and encyclopaedias solely of biographies. The most accessible is probably

> *Dictionary of National Biography: From Earliest Times to 1900* (Oxford: Oxford University Press, 1885–1901); 22 vols. This exists in many editions (including a compact form) and has important updating supplements. There is also a concise version in two volumes; it also exists on cd-rom.

It is usefully supplemented (with much more information on less important nineteenth-century figures) by

> Frederic Boase, *Modern English Biography, Containing Many Thousand Memoirs of Persons who have Died Since The Year 1850* (London: Bohn, 1892–1921)

and two microfiche publications

> *British and Irish Biographies, 1840–1940*, ed. David Lewis Jones (Cambridge: Chadwyck-Healey, 1984–6); 272 biographical dictionaries are reproduced on microfiche with a computerized index of names

> *British Biographical Archive* (London: British Library, 1984–); an alphabetical assembly on microfiche of entries from 310 biographical reference works published between 1601 and 1929.

A concise single-volume collection of information on people dead and alive is provided by

> *Chambers Biographical Dictionary*, ed. Melanie Parry, rev. edn (Edinburgh: Chambers, 1997).

Biographies of authors

A concise collection:

> David C. Browning, *Everyman's Dictionary of Literary Biography, English and American* (London: Dent, 1972).

The US compilation is much more ambitious:

> *Dictionary of Literary Biography* (Detroit: Gale, 1978–91).

Much older is the very large, erratic but very useful compilation covering over 46,000 authors, provided by

> Samuel Austin Allibone, *A Critical Dictionary of English Literature and British and American Authors Living and Deceased, from the Earliest Accounts to The Latter Half of the Nineteenth Century* (London: Trubner, 1872); 3 vols with a later supplement (1891), compiled by John F. Kirk.

Two more reliable, but smaller, works are

> Stanley J. Kunitz and Howard Haycraft, *British Authors Before 1800: A Biographical Dictionary* (New York: H.W. Wilson, 1952); 650 authors

> Stanley J. Kunitz and Howard Haycraft, *British Authors of the Nineteenth Century* (New York: H.W. Wilson, 1936); 1000 authors.

There are many other selective biographical dictionaries and lists, such as

> *A Dictionary of British and American Women Writers, 1660–1800*, ed. Janet Todd (Lanham: Rowmann and Littlefield, 1985).

These specialist/selective listings can be identified by checking the general bibliographies described earlier, or inspecting the valuable US compilations:

> *Biography Index* (New York: H.W. Wilson, 1946–); quarterly with cumulations, it is also available online
>
> *Biographical Books, 1876–1949* (New York: Bowker, 1983)
>
> *Biographical Books, 1950–1980* (New York: Bowker, 1980)
>
> *Biographical Dictionaries and Related Works*, ed. R.B. Slocum, 2nd edn (Detroit: Gale, 1986)

Diaries and autobiographies

There are two elderly but useful indexes in the form of

> *British Diaries: An Annotated Bibliography of British Diaries Written between 1442 and 1942*, compiled by William Matthews (Cambridge: Cambridge University Press, 1950)
>
> *British Autobiographies: An Annotated Bibliography of British Autobiographies Published or Written before 1951*, compiled by William Matthews (Berkeley: University of California Press, 1968).

The first of these has been enlarged for the nineteenth century by

> *British Manuscript Diaries of the Nineteenth Century*, compiled J.S. Batts (Totowa, New Jersey: Rowman and Littlefield, 1976).

Encyclopaedias

In practice, encyclopaedias, companions and dictionaries are often synonymous. In this section, I will concentrate on works that attempt to satisfy an encyclopaedic need (i.e. as general collections of facts and analysis). Dictionaries that concentrate primarily on terms and their meanings will be found in the next section.

General encyclopaedias

The easiest and most convenient way to acquire a large body of information rapidly is probably to check the articles, references and, above all, indexes of the major encyclopaedias. Perhaps the most accessible in print or cd-rom form is

> *Encyclopaedia Britannica* (Chicago: Encyclopaedia Britannica International).

Earlier editions are still very useful, particularly if they are also checked with the updating annual *Britannica Book of the Year*. The nineteenth-century editions (from fourth edition of 1810 to tenth edition of 1902) are valuable reference sources for accepted contemporary viewpoints and attitudes.

Other widely accessible encyclopaedias that have gone through many editions are

> *Chambers Encyclopaedia*, 4th rev. edn (London: International Learning Systems, 1973); 15 vols (with yearbooks)
>
> *Everyman's Encyclopaedia*, 6th edn (London: Dent, 1978); 12 vols.

For a useful European perspective there is

> *Encyclopaedia Universalis* (Chicago: Encyclopaedia Britannica Educational Corporation, 1990); 30 vols.

Specialist or subject encyclopaedias

While the general encyclopaedias can provide a useful start, the researcher will soon have to resort to the much larger range of specialist encyclopaedias, dictionaries and companions for more detailed information.

For general information on English literature:

> *The Oxford Companion to English Literature*, ed. Margaret Drabble, 6th edn (Oxford: Oxford University Press, 1995)
>
> *Bloomsbury Guide to English Literature,* ed. Marion Wynne-Davies, 2nd edn (London: Bloomsbury, 1995)
>
> *Dictionary of Literature in the English Language: from Chaucer to 1940*, compiled by Robin Myers (Harmondsworth: Penguin, 1978); 2 vols
>
> *The Cambridge Guide to Literature in English,* ed. Ian Ousby, 2nd edn (Cambridge: Cambridge University Press, 1994)
>
> *Cassell's Encyclopaedia of World Literature*, ed. S.H. Steinberg, 2nd rev. edn (London: Cassell, 1973)
>
> *Encyclopaedia of Literature and Criticism,* ed. Martin Coyle, Peter Garside, Malcolm Kelsall and John Peck (London: Routledge, 1990).

Poetry

> Alan Bold, *Longman Dictionary of Poets: the Lives and Works of 1001 Poets in the English Language* (London, Longman, 1985)
>
> *The New Princeton Encyclopedia of Poetry and Poetics*, ed. Alex Preminger and T.V. Brogan (Princeton: Princeton University Press, 1993)
>
> William J. Courthope, *History of English Poetry* (London: Macmillan, 1895–1910); 6 vols.

Dictionaries

General

Terminology can give rise to many problems, and so it might be helpful to use some of the larger dictionaries of usage (as distinct from translation) when working through unknown or difficult concepts and expressions. The most familiar are the general language dictionaries providing definitions. The biggest is

> *The Oxford English Dictionary* (Oxford: Oxford University Press, 1989), rev. edn; 20 vols. It also provides examples of different meanings at various stages in the history of each word. There is a photographically reduced 'compact edition', and the whole work is available on cd-rom.

Its smaller relatives are

> *The Shorter Oxford Dictionary* (which also provides examples), and *The Concise Oxford English Dictionary*

but it may also be worth checking some of its rivals:

> *Chambers Dictionary* (Edinburgh: Chambers, 1993)
>
> *The Penguin English Dictionary,* rev. edn (Harmondsworth: Penguin, 1992)
>
> *Longman Dictionary of the English Language and Culture* (London: Longman, 1994)
>
> *Collins English Dictionary* (London: HarperCollins, 1997).

There are a number of dictionaries designed to help trace changes in meaning in culture and the arts:

> Raymond Williams, *Keywords: a Vocabulary of Culture and Society,* rev. edn (London: Fontana, 1988).

While the general language dictionaries are extremely useful guides to current usage, meaning and implication, they often cannot provide the detail and explanation to be found in more specialized dictionaries devoted to a single subject. It may therefore be helpful to consult other types of general dictionary that can serve a useful reference function:

Etymological

The larger dictionaries provide details of the date of the appearance of particular words, but sometimes it can be useful to know more about the origins of particular words. This is where the following type of dictionary may help:

> Eric Partridge, *Origins: A Short Etymological Dictionary of Modern English,* 4th edn (London: Random House, 1966)
>
> C.T. Onions, *The Oxford Dictionary of English Etymology* (Oxford: Oxford University Press, 1967).

Antonyms and synonyms

The following deal with antonyms (words opposite in meaning) and synonyms (words with the same meaning). Perhaps the most accessible, because it exists in many forms and editions, is:

> Peter Mark Roget, *Roget's International Thesaurus of English Words and Phrases* (London: HarperCollins, 1994).

Also useful:

> *Macmillan Dictionary of Synonyms and Antonyms,* ed. Lawrence Urdang and Martin Manser (London: Macmillan, 1995)
>
> *Longman Synonym Dictionary* (London: Longman, 1986).

Literary terms

There are many glossaries or dictionaries of literary terms, but they are often erratic and incomplete. One that is fairly reliable and has survived five editions is

> *A Glossary of Literary Terms,* ed. Michael H. Abrams, 7th edn (New York: Harcourt Brace, 1998).

Other collections to be found widely are:

> Sylvan Barnet, *A Dictionary of Literary, Dramatic and Cinematic Terms,* rev. edn (London: HarperCollins, 1987)
>
> Arthur Ganz, *Literary Terms: A Dictionary,* rev. edn (London: Deutsch, 1990)
>
> J.A. Cuddon, *Dictionary of Literary Terms and Literary Theory* (Oxford: Blackwell, 1991)
>
> *Concise Oxford Dictionary of Literary Terms,* ed. Chris Baldick (Oxford: Oxford University Press, 1990)
>
> Martin Gray, *Dictionary of Literary Terms* (London: Longman, 1992).

Some lay more stress on technical and critical vocabulary:

> *Dictionary of World Literary Terms: Forms, Techniques and Criticism,* ed. Joseph T. Shipley, 2nd rev. edn (London: Allen and Unwin, 1970)
>
> Patrick Murray, *Literary Criticism: A Glossary of Literary Terms* (London: Longman, 1978)
>
> *A Dictionary of Modern Critical Terms,* ed. Roger Fowler, rev. edn (London: Routledge, 1987)
>
> Jeremy Hawthorne, *Contemporary Literary Theory: A Glossary* (London: Routledge, 1992)
>
> Miller Williams, *Patterns of Poetry: An Encyclopedia of Forms* (Lanham: Louisiana State University Press, 1986)
>
> *The Princeton Handbook of Poetic Terms,* ed. T.V.F. Brogan (Princeton University Press, 1994).

Abbreviations

> *Abbreviations Dictionary,* ed. Ralph De Sola *et al.,* 9th edn (London: CRC Press, 1993)
>
> *Dent Dictionary of Abbreviations,* ed. John Paxton, rev. edn (London: Dent, 1995).

Allusions and quotations

As well as the encyclopaedias and dictionaries already mentioned, there are a number of more specialized reference works that may help in the identification of allusions, references and quotations:

Proverbs and phrases

Probably the most widely available treasury of literary bric-à-brac is

> *Brewer's Dictionary of Phrase and Fable*, rev. A. Room (London: HarperCollins, 1995); many earlier editions.

Other useful details may be culled from

> A.M. Hyamson, *Dictionary of English Phrases, Phraseological Allusions, Catchwords, Stereotyped Speech and Metaphors, Nicknames, Soubriquets, Derivations from Personal Names* (London: Routledge, 1922; repr. by Gale, Detroit, 1969).

Classical background

Two surveys:

> James A.K. Thomson, *The Classical Background of English Literature* (London: Allen and Unwin, 1948)

> Gilbert Highet, *The Classical Tradition: Greek and Roman Influences on Western Literature* (Oxford: Oxford University Press, 1949; repr. 1985).

Two dictionaries/encyclopaedias:

> *Oxford Classical Dictionary*, ed. Simon Hornblower and Anthony Spawforth, 3rd edn (Oxford: Oxford University Press, 1996)

> *The Oxford Companion to Classical Literature*, rev. M.C. Howatson (Oxford: Oxford University Press, 1989).

Other literatures

> Sir Paul Harvey and Janet E. Heseltine, *The Oxford Companion to French Literature* (Oxford: Oxford University Press, 1959)

> *The Oxford Companion to German Literature*, ed. Henry and Mary Garland, 3rd rev. edn (Oxford: Oxford University Press, 1997).

Biblical allusions and details

> W.B. Fulghum, *A Dictionary of Biblical Allusions in English Literature* (New York: Holt, Rinehart and Winston, 1965)

> Abraham H. Lass, *Dictionary of Classical, Biblical and Literary Allusions* (New York: Ballantine, 1988)

> *A Dictionary of the Bible, dealing with its Language, Literature and Contents, including Biblical Theology,* ed. James Hastings (Edinburgh: T. and T. Clark, 1898–1904); 5 vols

Complete Who's Who in the Bible, ed. Paul Gardner (London: Marshall Pickering, 1995)

R. Browrigg, *Who's Who in the New Testament*, 2nd edn (London: Weidenfeld and Nicolson, 1994)

John Comay, *Who's Who in the Old Testament*, 2nd edn (London: Weidenfeld and Nicolson, 1994)

Allusions: Cultural, Literary, Biblical and Historical – A Thematic Dictionary, ed. Laurence Urdang, 2nd edn (Detroit: Gale Research, 1986).

Philosophy and contemporary ideas

Paul Edwards, *The Encyclopedia of Philosophy* (New York: Macmillan, 1967); 8 vols (shorter edition 1972)

Dictionary of Philosophy and Psychology, Including Many of The Principal Concepts of Ethics, Logic, Aesthetics, Philosophy of Religion, Mental Pathology, Anthropology, Political and Social Philosophy, Philology, Physical Science and Education, and Giving a Terminology in English, French, German and Italian, ed. J.M. Baldwin (London: Macmillan, 1901–5) (later edition 1925, repr. 1977, Peter Smith)

Dictionary of the History of Ideas: Studies of Selected Pivotal Ideas, ed. P.P. Wiener (New York: McGraw-Hill, 1968–73); 4 vols and index

Fontana Dictionary of Modern Thought, ed. Alan Bullock and Oliver Stallybrass (London: Fontana, 1987)

Fontana Dictionary of Modern Thinkers, ed. Alan Bullock and R.B. Woodings (London: Fontana, 1989).

Quotations

Oxford Dictionary of Quotations, rev. Angela Partington, 4th edn (Oxford: Oxford University Press, 1992)

Robert Collison and Mary Collison, *Dictionary of Foreign Quotations* (London: Macmillan, 1980)

Penguin Dictionary of Foreign Terms and Phrases, ed. Eugene Ehrlich (Harmondsworth: Penguin, 1993)

John Bartlett, *Familiar Quotations: A Collection of Passages, Phrases and Proverbs Traced to their Sources in Ancient and Modern Literature*, rev. edn (New York: Little Brown, 1992); 1st edn, 1855

R.E. Stevenson, *The Home Book of Quotations, Classical and Modern*, 10th edn (London: Cassell, 1967)

Richard Branyon, *Dictionary of Latin Phrases and Quotations* (New York: Hippocrene, 1994)

M.J. Cohen, *The New Penguin Dictionary of Quotations* (Harmondsworth: Viking Penguin, 1994).

INDEX